MARXISM AND EDUCATION

MARXISM AND EDUCATION

This series assumes the ongoing relevance of Marx's contributions to critical social analysis and aims to encourage continuation of the development of the legacy of Marxist traditions in and for education. The remit for the substantive focus of scholarship and analysis appearing in the series extends from the global to the local in relation to dynamics of capitalism and encompasses historical and contemporary developments in political economy of education as well as forms of critique and resistances to capitalist social relations. The series announces a new beginning and proceeds in a spirit of openness and dialogue within and between Marxism and education, and between Marxism and its various critics. The essential feature of the work of the series is that Marxism and Marxist frameworks are to be taken seriously, not as formulaic knowledge and unassailable methodology but critically as inspirational resources for renewal of research and understanding, and as support for action in and upon structures and processes of education and their relations to society. The series is dedicated to the realization of positive human potentialities as education and thus, with Marx, to our education as educators.

Series Editor:
Anthony Green

Renewing Dialogues in Marxism and Education: Openings
Edited by Anthony Green, Glenn Rikowski, and Helen Raduntz

Critical Race Theory and Education: A Marxist Response
Mike Cole

Revolutionizing Pedagogy: Education for Social Justice within and beyond Global Neo-Liberalism
Edited by Sheila Macrine, Peter McLaren, and Dave Hill

Marxism and Education beyond Identity: Sexuality and Schooling
Faith Agostinone-Wilson

Blair's Educational Legacy: Thirteen Years of New Labour
Edited by Anthony Green

Racism and Education in the U.K. and the U.S.: Towards a Socialist Alternative
Mike Cole

Marxism and Education: Renewing the Dialogue, Pedagogy, and Culture
Edited by Peter E. Jones

Marxism and Education

Renewing the
Dialogue, Pedagogy, and Culture

Edited by
Peter E. Jones

MARXISM AND EDUCATION
Copyright © Peter E. Jones, 2011.

All rights reserved.

First published in 2011 by
PALGRAVE MACMILLAN®
in the United States—a division of St. Martin's Press LLC,
175 Fifth Avenue, New York, NY 10010.

Where this book is distributed in the UK, Europe and the rest of the world,
this is by Palgrave Macmillan, a division of Macmillan Publishers Limited,
registered in England, company number 785998, of Houndmills,
Basingstoke, Hampshire RG21 6XS.

Palgrave Macmillan is the global academic imprint of the above companies
and has companies and representatives throughout the world.

Palgrave® and Macmillan® are registered trademarks in the United States,
the United Kingdom, Europe and other countries.

ISBN: 978–0–230–11169–1

Library of Congress Cataloging-in-Publication Data

Jones, Peter E., 1954–
    Marxism and education : renewing the dialogue, pedagogy, and culture /
Peter E. Jones.
        p. cm.
    ISBN-13: 978–0–230–11169–1 (hardback)
    ISBN-10: 0–230–11169–6 ()
        1. Education—Philosophy. 2. Socialism and education. 3. Critical
pedagogy. 4. Marx, Karl, 1818–1883. I. Title.

LB1025.2.J664 2011
370.1—dc22   2011005263

A catalogue record of the book is available from the British Library.

Design by Newgen Imaging Systems (P) Ltd., Chennai, India.

First edition: August 2011

10 9 8 7 6 5 4 3 2 1

Printed in the United States of America.

Contents

Part III   Marxism and Education:
Advancing Theory

Series Editor's Foreword

This volume is a most welcome addition to the Marxism and Education Series. It constitutes a collection of analyses reflecting the ongoing significance of Marxist historical materialist praxis of critical analysis while articulating the socialist pedagogic project of social and economic transformation. As the third volume in the Series to directly emerge from our ongoing seminar activities under the banner *Marxism and Education Renewing Dialogues* (MERD) and standing alongside other current and forthcoming books in the Series emergent from beyond MERD, it attests to the energy and significance of Marxist antihegemonic dialectical analysis in and around culture and education most widely conceived. The aim has been to work on and for transformative classed identity formation mindful of and articulating with all manner of social segmentation, collective memory, renewal, and affirmation in transformation. The work in this volume also attests to the capacity of capitalism to constantly demonstrate both its own deep contradictions and the ways it throws up opportunities for critical analysis, mobilization, and recognition of the ongoing need to conduct struggle in and through cultural dimensions of the social. Most significantly, Peter Jones and each of the contributors demonstrate, sometimes in dialogue and debate with one another, the powers of taking Marx and Marxism seriously across all dimensions of social methodology, theory, and social practices in order to address the huge problems and issues crowding in, onto, and directly inhibiting human possibilities. These operate at the global, national, regional, and local levels, and not least the personal, too, as commodification and class forms reach all dimensions of collectivity and individuality in our living and productive working. Overall, this approach within Marxism recognizes the emergent nature of social relational forms, their ontological depth, and the ever-present need to be wary of the foreshortening effects of undialectical abstraction and reifying practices.

The time is always right for critical activity and engagement in the breaking wave of the present, the situations always already structured by circumstances we cannot choose, for taking up what amount to complex challenges for socialist renewal. The ongoing question concerns the mechanisms structuring the circumstances of struggles and transformations. This book provides a richness of disciplined intellectual production, inspiring description, analysis, and observations in support of positive energy required for progressive transformation by demonstrating that critique of political economy, ideology critique, and immanent critique continue to be articulated and renewed through vigorous and reflexive Marxist scholarship, organization, and activist struggles to address the capitalist mode of production. This is so in vital respects, not only as dogged and realistic productive resistance and critique but also as and in pleasure and fun, too. Ambiguity, ambivalence, and irony, like the cultural forms of humor, comedy, and satire, may be deployed, following Marx's example, as productive resources, when addressing the real. They are commodifiable too, no doubt, but are also vital cultural contexts for dereification and potential devices for struggling in and for progressive class consciousness against alienation and all manner of symbolic violence. The times seem propitious once more for renewing our struggles and this book assembles wisdom and reasoned evidence aplenty for debating, analyzing, and actively challenging the value form of commodified labor power in the specific relations of the capitalist mode of production. The book is itself constitutive of educating the educators, ourselves in struggle, in consciousness, in collaborative action, dialogically working to collectively realize social justice and the fullness of human creative potential.

ANTHONY GREEN
December 2010

Acknowledgments

I would like to thank Glenn Rikowski for handing me the baton and Tony Green for his valuable support and advice. I'm grateful to Simeon Yates and Dave Waddington of the C3Ri and the Communication and Computing Research Centre at Sheffield Hallam University for providing research time, with special thanks to Kerry McSeveny and Rachel Finch for their help with the editing and indexing.

Helen Colley's Chapter 2 is reproduced here with the kind permission of Symposium Journals. It originally appeared as:

Colley, H. (2006) Learning to Labour with Feeling: Class, Gender and Emotion in Childcare Education and Training. *Contemporary Issues in Early Childhood*, 7 (1): 15–29.

Material from Paul Brook's Chapter 4 is reproduced from Brook, P. (2009) The Alienated Heart: Hochschild's 'Emotional Labour' Thesis and the Anti-Capitalist Politics of Alienation. *Capital and Class*, 98: 7–31. Copyright © 2010 by Conference of Socialist Economists. Reprinted by permission of Sage.

Anna Stetsenko's Chapter 7 is reproduced here with kind permission from Springer Science+Business Media: Anna Stetsenko, *Cultural Studies of Science Education*, From Relational Ontology to Transformative Activist Stance on Development and Learning: Expanding Vygotsky's (CHAT) Project, Volume 3, 2008, pp. 471–491.

Finally, I would like to express my appreciation to all the contributors to the volume for their hard work and enthusiastic involvement in the project. Thanks to their efforts, the Dialogue goes on!

Introduction and Overview: Marxism and Education—Dialogues on Pedagogy and Culture

Peter E. Jones

This is the third book in the Palgrave Macmillan *Renewing Dialogues in Marxism and Education* series. Like its predecessors, this volume has its origins in the Marxism and Education: Renewing Dialogues (MERD) seminar series, which started life at the Institute of Education, University of London, in 2002 as the initiative of Anthony Green and Glenn Rikowski. The present volume has arisen from the third seminar in the MERD series (Pedagogy and Culture), hosted by Green and Rikowski at the Institute on October 22, 2003. In the seven years since that seminar, however, the world has changed.

In their Introduction and Overview to the first book in the series, Green and Rikowski note that their 2002 event "emerged at a point of our recognition of a somewhat bleak time for Marxist theory, research, and discourses in regard to education, despite some indications of small-scale revival" and add that the "chapters included in this volume represent positive signs of this revival" (Green and Rikowski, 2007: 3). This revival of interest in Marxism and in the implications of Marxism for education needs to be understood, as they rightly say, in the context of "the continuing struggles for socialism in a world in which the value form of labor and commodification are central to neoliberal globalization of capital in all its educational dimensions" (Green and Rikowski, 2007: 3).

What has changed in the interim is that the "neoliberal globalization of capital" has taken a massive hit. And while the icy blasts began to ravage the very foundations of global capitalism, the Marxists had unexpectedly, unbelievably, come in from the cold.

The crunch came in 2008, about a year after the publication of the first volume. On September 25, the world woke to find the U.S. president and his Treasury secretary locked in last-minute negotiations over a bailout of the U.S. banks. In prospect, it seemed, was the collapse of the world's largest economy—just for starters. As the U.S. government threw a trillion dollars at the problem, propping up or (dare we say it?) *nationalizing* financial institutions, an example soon to be followed around the world, the acutely paradoxical, indeed, bitingly ironic, nature of the unfolding events was not lost on commentators. Ben Bernanke and Hank Paulson "have done more for socialism in the past seven days than anybody since Marx and Engels," as Larry Elliott of the UK newspaper *The Guardian* observed ("Big Finance Now Faces a Long Spell on the Naughty Step," September 20, 2008). As the UK government was preparing its own bailout, Geoffrey Robinson, one of the richest of the New Labour elite, grimaced on national TV: "We're now implementing our 1983 Manifesto pledge to nationalise the commanding heights of the economy" (BBC *Newsnight*, October 7). Neoliberal governments were shredding their own system—at the behest of the banks.

As Paul Mason puts it:

> We have lived through an event that most of us thought we would never see. In October 2008, free-market capitalism, on the edge of collapse, was rescued by the state. The alternative was oblivion. (Mason, 2010: vii)

As the crisis deepened, the sacred cows of finance and the market were fair game in the media. In Britain, for example, even church leaders queued up to take pot shots. The Archbishop of York declared that financial speculators were no better than bank robbers, while no less a figure than the Archbishop of Canterbury invoked Marx in his own attack on "unbridled capitalism."

Marxist thinkers, political activists, and economists—formerly derided or ignored—were lifted from the wastebasket of history onto prime time TV and asked for their views. Maybe old Marx had been right after all?

Two years on, the crisis has found its second wind. If the state stepped in to save capitalism, then, as Mason goes on, "the state bit off more than it could chew" and "the same poison that took down banks" has begun "to take down states" (2010: vii). The "spectre of debt restructuring and default has spread from Greece to Portugal and Spain" (2010: vii) and now, as I write, to Ireland.

If the collapse of Soviet "communism" in the 1980s and 1990s appeared to many to vindicate the actions and ideology of the free marketeers, undermining the credibility of anticapitalist thinkers and activists, then the collapse of capitalism puts the boot on the other foot. The bleak time for Marxist theory referred to by Green and Rikowski has become a propitious one. But, still, the chance to take the fight to the enemy has to be actively seized. The present volume, I would like to think, is part, even if a tiny part, of this attempt to seize the moment.

As British students, at the forefront of resistance to the cuts agenda of the new Conservative-Liberal coalition, take to the streets and occupy campus buildings to protest government plans for universities, we should note that these have been interesting times for education, too. The social transformation of educational institutions has been a crucial dimension of the Bolivarian Revolution promoted by the Chávez government in Venezuela (Cole, 2009), providing an inspiring demonstration of the potential role of radical, popular educational practices and programs in the processes of economic and political liberation. *El Sistema*—a triumph of mass participation and popular energy with its young musical geniuses and prodigies—has gained global renown and spawned innumerable imitations. At the same time, as this book and its predecessor show, educational theory and research are also changing under the influence of ideas and practices derived from, or heavily influenced by, Marxist scholarship in a range of disciplines.

It is in this context that I have the honor and the pleasure of welcoming the reader to this new volume and introducing the chapters and their authors. The three original participants in MERD III, 2003—Helen Colley, Victoria Perselli, and Peter E. Jones—are joined here by Terry Wrigley, Chik Collins, Paul Brook, Sara Carpenter and Shahrzad Mojab, Anna Stetsenko, and Peter McLaren. Paula Allman was also a participant at the 2003 seminar and her formidable intellectual presence is clearly felt in a number of the chapters that follow as well as in her contribution to the previous volume (Allman, 2007).

While the first book in the series was appropriately subtitled Openings, this third volume continues to extend the scope of the dialogue between Marxism and educational theory and practice in a number of new directions indicated by the subtitle Pedagogy and Culture. To some extent this subtitle could be said to express a marked emphasis rather than the central or explicit focus of all papers. But this depends on quite how we read the term *culture* itself. For example, we may have in mind the culture of those to be educated—the cultures (plural) of different communities or classes. We may have in mind the culture of the educators themselves—the ideology, ethics, and values of the teaching profession. We may have in mind the culture of the school or classroom itself—the cultural field where educat*or* encounters educat*ee*. Or we may have in mind the workplace more generally as a pedagogical culture in its own right. More generally, and perhaps more fundamentally, we may take *culture*, as Marx himself did, to mean human activity as the fundamental life-affirming and life-creating condition of our species. All of these "cultures" are examined in the chapters that follow. But this book is also about another, quite distinctive culture. And that is the intellectual culture of Marxist theoretical activity itself. This is a culture of commitment and vigorous critique, certainly, but it has also proved to be one of openness, dialogue, debate, diversity, self-reflection, and, not least, innovation. More to the point in this context, it is a *culture of learning*, priding itself on its ability to learn from the present, from contemporary thinkers, and from its own mistakes as well as from the past and the giant thinkers of the past. On the evidence of this volume, I hope the reader will judge that culture to be in rude health.

These variations on the theme of culture are variously represented in the three parts of the volume. Part I, "Marxism and Culture: Educational Perspectives," has perhaps the most explicit focus on issues of culture, cultural difference, and cultural tradition, both within and without the classroom. Part II, "Marxism and the 'Culture' of Educational Practice," focuses on how Marxist theory can critically illuminate, or inform, practices of education and workplace training. Part III, "Marxism and Education: Advancing Theory," deepens the discussion of the theoretical and methodological issues at stake in the analysis and understanding of pedagogical activity and learning as a social practice. These thematic divisions, however, are far from watertight. The papers are crisscrossed by a thick network of topical and thematic interconnections reflecting the interest of the contributors in relating theory to practice and practice to theory.

Part I, "Marxism and Culture: Educational Perspectives," kicks off in Chapter 1 with Terry Wrigley's "Culture, Class, and Education: A Reflective Essay." Wrigley sets out to examine some of the complex, ambiguous, and misleading ways in which the term "culture" has been used in the educational literature. In particular, he takes up the relationship of "culture" to "class," an equally troublesome concept in the educational field. Wrigley's examination spans a number of different areas, including cultural explanations of educational underachievement, the question of curriculum relevance or mismatch in relation to "working-class culture," and the hollowed-out sense of "culture" in recent school improvement literature. On the basis of this discussion Wrigley goes on to argue that concepts of "culture" and "class," when realigned to Marxist social models, are central to a struggle for social justice and emancipation.

Chapter 2, Helen Colley's "Learning to Labor with Feeling: Class, Gender, and Emotion in Childcare Education and Training," is a pioneering attempt to place the role and significance of emotion at the heart of the discussion of culture and learning. As Colley observes, the learning of feelings is rarely mentioned, let alone analyzed, in educational research and yet is a key issue in vocational education for carers. As Colley shows, there is now debate amongst early years experts as to the appropriate degree of emotional engagement between nursery nurses and the children in their care. On the basis of a detailed case study of a group of childcare students over the two years of their course, Colley shows how gendered and class-fractional positionings combine with vocational education and training to construct imperatives about "correct" emotions in childcare. Drawing on Hochschild's work on emotional labor, as well as the work of other Marxist theoreticians, Colley argues that the costs of emotional labor to the nursery nurse are due not to the consumption of her emotional resources by the children in her care but to the control and exploitation of those resources for profit by employers.

In Chapter 3, Chik Collins conveys a fresh blast of air direct from the West of Scotland in "'For a People's Clydebank': Learning the Ethic of Solidarity amidst the Wreckage of Neoliberalism in Contemporary Scotland." Collins tells the remarkable story of the Clydebank Independent Resource Centre, a local working-class organization providing services and support to local people and run by local people themselves. The most remarkable thing about the organization, as Collins argues, is that it has survived in a hostile social and political environment, something that Collins sets out to explain. He argues that the survival of the centre is due, first and foremost, to an extremely agile, informal, and collaborative learning culture rooted in a traditional ethic of solidarity in the face of the encroachment of neoliberal agendas in Scotland.

Part II, "Marxism and the 'Culture' of Educational Practice," begins with Chapter 4, Paul Brook's "Learning the Feeling Rules: Exploring Hochschild's Thesis on the Alienating Experience of Learning and Performing Emotional Labor." Brook, like Helen Colley, looks to Hochschild's development and application of alienation theory to explore the experience of learning and performing emotional labor in the workplace. Brook notes that contemporary workplaces are increasingly marked by managerial efforts to harness and mold the emotional product of employees, either as specific commodified interactive service encounters or as a generic commitment to organizational goals. In this way, organizational emotion is increasingly viewed by capital as a resource to be exploited, something that Brook notes is frequently overlooked in educational research on workplace learning. Through a critical reading of Hochschild's thesis, Brook reaffirms its contemporary anticapitalist relevance by examining the human cost incurred through the workplace learning involved in emotional labor.

In Chapter 5, Sara Carpenter and Shahrzad Mojab engage with fundamental issues of Marxist philosophy in their "Adult Education and the 'Matter' of Consciousness in Marxist-Feminism," a theoretical analysis that could sit just as easily in Part III of the volume. Noting that the theorization of consciousness has become a central component within the field of adult education, they turn to the work of Paula Allman and other Marxist writers for insights into the nature and springs of human consciousness and its relationship to revolutionary praxis. Carpenter and Mojab then take the debate further by showing how feminist interventions have contributed to the development of a more concrete understanding of capitalist social relations and of capitalism as a totality. They go on to consider the implications of this Marxist-Feminist analysis for adult education practice.

Victoria Perselli in Chapter 6, "A Little Night Reading: Marx, Assessment and the Professional Doctorate in Education," offers an unashamedly personal reflection and commentary on her experiences as a practitioner working with students doing a professional doctorate in education. Perselli is particularly concerned with the problematic role and place of theory, especially Marxist theory, in the whole process of design, preparation, and assessment of the doctoral dissertation, as well as in the relationship between student and supervisor. How could the doing of a dissertation, Perselli asks, be theorized in Marxist terms? And could Marxist theory help practitioners to enable students to make the reading of theoretical works into both a pleasure and a necessary dimension of their own self-development?

Part III, "Marxism and Education: Advancing Theory," begins with Chapter 7, Anna Stetsenko's "From Relational Ontology to a Transformative Activist Stance on Development and Learning: Expanding Vygotsky's (CHAT) Project." Reviewing the whole field of sociocultural research, Stetsenko offers a bold synthesis of dialectical views of human development and learning with an ideology of social justice and social transformation. She draws on the psychological theory of Lev Vygotsky, informed by a Marxist conception of the primacy of social practice, to create a new, unifying perspective for sociocultural approaches to mind and activity—*a transformative activist stance*—based on the view that collaborative, purposeful transformative practices constitute the very foundation and core of human nature. Stetsenko shows how such a perspective can be the key to resolving the theoretical dichotomies between individual and social and between ontology and ethics, which lie at the root of the current fragmentation of the cultural-historical and activity theory traditions.

Chapter 8, Peter E. Jones's "Activity, Activity Theory and the Marxian Legacy," is an attempt to clarify aspects of Marx's methodological principles and practice through a critical examination of the "activity theory" of Yrjö Engeström and colleagues. In particular, Jones discusses the use made by "activity theory" scholars of Marx's method of "ascent from the abstract to the concrete" in the elaboration of an original approach to the analysis and transformation of social practices. Jones argues that Marx's method has been misunderstood and misapplied within this approach, with the result that specifically capitalist social relations have disappeared altogether from its analytical radar. Jones goes on to consider the implications of this methodological divergence for an understanding of the place and function of educational institutions and practices within capitalist society.

Part III, and the volume with it, ends on a high note with Chapter 9, Peter McLaren's "Critical Pedagogy as Revolutionary Practice," based on an interview for a Peruvian journal. In a wide-ranging reflection on the state of Marxist theory and revolutionary practice, McLaren discusses the theoretical foundations of his own perspective on critical pedagogy and its revolutionary significance in the struggle against capitalist globalization. He then focuses specifically on the role of critical pedagogy in Latin America. McLaren gives his own insights into the education reforms implemented by the Venezuelan government of Hugo Chávez. In addition, he focuses at length on the work of José Carlos Mariátegui, Latin America's most prominent Marxist thinker and activist. McLaren emphasizes Mariátegui's powerful and distinctive contributions to Marxist theory in his original understanding of the relationship between race and class within capitalist conditions and in his conception of the role of indigenous peoples in anti-imperialist struggles.

References

Allman, P. (2007) The Making of Humanity: The Pivotal Role of Dialectical Thinking in Humanization and the Concomitant Struggle for Self and Social Transformation. In A. Green, G. Rikowski, and H. Raduntz (eds.) *Renewing Dialogues in Marxism and Education. Openings,* 267–78 (New York: Palgrave Macmillan).

Cole, M. (2009) *Critical Race Theory and Education. A Marxist Response* (New York: Palgrave Macmillan).

Green, A. and Rikowski, H. (2007) Introduction and Overview: Marxism and Education—Renewing the Dialogues. In A. Green, G. Rikowski, and H. Raduntz (eds.) *Renewing Dialogues in Marxism and Education. Openings,* 3–9 (New York: Palgrave Macmillan).

Green, A., Rikowski, G., and Raduntz, H. (2007) *Renewing Dialogues in Marxism and Education. Openings* (New York: Palgrave Macmillan).

Mason, P. (2010) *Meltdown. The End of the Age of Greed* (London: Verso).

Part I

Marxism and Culture:
Educational Perspectives

Chapter 1

Culture, Class, and Curriculum: A Reflective Essay

Terry Wrigley

Introduction: The Complexity of *Culture* and *Class*

Any attempt to review the use of the term *culture* in education is asking for trouble. Raymond Williams, in *Keywords* (1976: 87), claims that culture is "one of the two or three most complicated words in the English language." As part of this complexity, it can refer to "high" art, to artistic practices more broadly including popular arts, and to the whole way of life of a people or period. Williams traces the history and multiplicity of denotation and connotation of the word *culture* not in order to arrive at a singular meaning, but to enable us to hold in tension these differences of meaning or emphasis. Terry Eagleton goes even further in this rejection of attempts to pin it down, referring to the concept *culture* both as "an historical and philosophical text" and as "the site of a political conflict" (2000: 19). Rather a lot for one word to carry.

Even more perilous, then, is it to trace the extent of Marxist influence. There is the rather obvious difficulty that Marx himself hardly ever uses the word. Yet, as I will attempt to show, it is not surprising that, through those working within the Marxist heritage, the concept has acquired enormous resonance, providing us with rich resources for understanding education, its processes, and outcomes. I deliberately say "working within the Marxist heritage" rather than the shorter "Marxists," to include those such as Freire or Bourdieu who, for various reasons, preferred to avoid the suggestion of club membership.

It is not simply that both these writers and others understand that culture is deeply affected by social structures, specifically class, and by material production. Their link to Marxism goes all the way down, to an ontology that rejects the Cartesian dualism of a mind-matter split, in favor of a dynamic and dialectical materialism in which spirit (intellect, ideas, *Geist*) thoroughly inhabits and springs forth from the world we touch and see. Of course, one cannot call all nondualists "Marxists"—think, for example, of Spinoza or Dewey—but it is essential to recognize, in Williams's and Eagleton's discussion, the significance of the origins of the "culture" word: it is fundamentally nondualist.

> One of its original meanings is "husbandry," or the tending of natural growth...The word "coulter," which is a cognate of "culture," means the blade of a ploughshare. We derive our word for the finest of human activities from labour and agriculture, crops and cultivation. Francis Bacon writes of "the culture and manurance of minds," in a suggestive hesitancy between dung and mental distinction. "Culture" here means an activity, and it was a long time before the word came to denote an entity. (Eagleton, 2000: 1)

It is somewhat paradoxical therefore (though historically understandable, given Stalinist distortions) that Marxism has been accused of subordinating culture to vulgar material reality—poetry to pig iron production—a dualist and nondialectical division into mind and matter. In this model, culture is crudely equated to "the superstructure" that is "determined" by the "material base." As Williams (1980[1973]: 31–3) argues, this shows a limited grasp of both ends of the relationship as well as the link verb *determines* to convey the connection between them. He regards the architectural metaphor of base/superstructure as unhelpful, preferring Marx's earlier terminology of *social being* and *consciousness*. Williams rightly insists that "base" involves both the forces of production (the technology, materials, and so on) and the relations of production (especially class divisions), themselves often in deep contradiction with one another:

> When these forces are considered, as Marx always considers them, as the specific activities and relationships of real men, they mean something very much more active, more complicated and more contradictory than the developed metaphorical notion of "the base" could possibly allow us to realize. So we have to say that when we talk of "the base," we are talking of a process and not a state. (Ibid: 34)

Eagleton (2000: 1–2) goes further in opposing a simplistic and dualistic opposition between culture and the material world (production, society, etc.): "In Marxist parlance, it [culture] brings together both base and superstructure in a single word." Culture (seen as a "whole way of life," Williams, 1958: 16) can scarcely be viewed as ethereally spiritual; similarly (using "culture" in a more aesthetic sense), it is no longer possible, if it ever was, to write off cultural workers as economically unproductive floss who are somehow marginal to the "real working class." Thus, rather than the caricature of subordinating culture to some inert block of matter, Marxism views culture as *practice* (labor, preferably nonalienated) and the *products of practice* (everyday artifacts as well as works of art), and requires that we look for *meaning* in both.

Williams rightly argues for a lighter and less mechanistic (less *deterministic*) sense of *determine* (German: *bestimmen*), in terms of setting limits or exerting pressures, rather than a precise "prefiguration, prediction or control." The "determination" is often qualified by the rider "in the last instance."

> According to the materialist conception of history, the *ultimately* determining element in history is the production and reproduction of real life. More than this neither Marx nor I have ever asserted. (Engels, 1890)

Williams himself made a key contribution to understanding the complexity of this relationship by conceptualizing some cultures and cultural phenomena as *residual*; namely, they reflect earlier material and social circumstances but, nevertheless, have an ideological impact in the present. The Church of England, or idyllic concepts of rural England, are good examples. Conversely, Williams describes cultural phenomena that reflect the beginnings of a new social situation as *emergent* (see Williams, 1980[1973]: 40 for a more detailed discussion).

The contradictory, conflictual, and unresolved character of culture also forms a key part of Gramsci's thinking, in his discussion of "common sense" attitudes and understandings. Gramsci argues that the ideology of a subordinate class is a complex mixture of uncritical responses to social circumstances, taken-for-granted pieces of traditional "wisdom," the opinions of "minor intellectuals" (the mass media?), as well as more accurate and productive reflections on contemporary society.

> The active man-in-the-mass has a practical activity, but has no clear theoretical consciousness of his practical activity, which nonetheless involves understanding the world in so far as it transforms it. His theoretical consciousness can indeed be historically in opposition to his activity. One might almost say that he has two theoretical consciousnesses (or one contradictory consciousness): one which is implicit in his activity and which in reality unites him with all his fellow workers in the practical transformation of the real world; and one, superficially explicit or

verbal, which he has inherited from the past and uncritically absorbed. (Gramsci, 1971: 641)

When we begin to see culture as

- linking matter and meaning—matter with meaning, activities that signify
- contradictory and unresolved
- shaped by economic and social realities in complex and indirect ways

we move into a space where the concept becomes an invaluable resource for understanding educational processes and institutions in a capitalist society. We are enabled to explore the complex, dynamic, and often indirect influence of work and class on culture, and on the way culture is handed on through education. Conversely, such a complex understanding is undermined by parodies of Marxism that posit a simplistic determination of culture by production, but also by the simplistic reductionism of non-Marxists who assume that a subordinate class must therefore have an inferior culture (see, for example, the critique of Bernstein below).

It is important to recognize that the concept of class is equally problematic. (Williams calls it an "obviously difficult word.") In the *Communist Manifesto*, Marx and Engels (2005 [1848]) clearly predict the complete division of society into two major classes, with hitherto privileged groups collapsing into the proletariat. The concept of "middle class," used vaguely nowadays to refer to all white-collar and professional employees, simply doesn't fit Marx's worldview. We don't get far in understanding current industrial struggles if we fail to see that most supposed members of the "middle class" are simply different kinds of employees of capitalism, whether directly or indirectly through the state. Indeed, the supposed equivalence of "working class" and "manual workers" is doubly misleading, in that many of the self-employed are manual workers but without occupying positions (being positioned?) as employees vis-à-vis capitalism.

Unfortunately, the overwhelming tendency in educational sociology has been to distinguish between "the working class(es)" and the "middle class," using these two terms synonymously with manual and nonmanual types of work. Though a gross and damaging overgeneralization, it is arguable that people employed in clerical or professional occupations, especially those with higher levels of academic education, may tend to pass on to their children ways of speaking and a range of interests that—compared with manual workers—are closer to the discourses and subject matters of formal school learning. This has pedagogical implications, but is not a difference of class. Clarity is essential when reading educational sociology: Does "working class" refer to the entire proletariat in a Marxist sense? Or exclusively to manual workers? Or is it being used as a pseudonym for that section of the working class living in poverty? Furthermore, is it referring to a section of capitalist society, to their lifestyles, to their attitudes, or to the exercise of political agency?

Second, when the "middle class" actually materializes in many sociology of education texts, it has a tendency to take the shape of high-level professionals living in exclusive suburbs, driving their children to school in four-wheel drives by day and entertaining one another to dinner parties by night. Even Bourdieu is guilty of this dualism, implicitly portraying a society divided between impoverished indigenous or immigrant workers on the one hand and graduates of France's *hautes écoles* (elite colleges) on the other (Bourdieu, 1984).

It should be clear by now that that there are compound possibilities of misunderstanding in the relationship between class and culture, some of which are discussed below. This chapter will examine the abuses and uses of *culture* in the subfields of school development, curriculum, and pedagogy.

Culture and Managerialism

The adoption of "culture" as a keyword in the study of management and organizational change is both an opening up and a closure; the polyvalence and dynamism of the concept potentially enables management theory to transcend a monochrome and mechanistic "sociotechnical approach" (Parker, 2000: 47), but simultaneously reduces "culture" to a means of domestication and control.

This first occurred across management studies in the private sector, before being imported to educational governance. Martin Parker (2000: 59) maps an "explosion of academic interest in culture" from the early 1980s in terms of a ten- or twentyfold increase in academic papers. Deploying the word "culture" amounts to a recognition that social organizations are far too complex to be controlled and developed in simple top-down authoritarian ways; their complexity involves a multiplicity of perspectives and motivations and relationships, and crucially involves a realization that environments, practices, and relationships signify and have an impact on an organization's development. But, unwilling to take a democratic turn, theorists began to propagate new modes of analysis and "leadership." They seized on Burns's (1978) "transformational leadership" (though failing to understand the political and ethical dimension of Burns's text and concept). Management gurus such as Peters and Waterman (1982) became best sellers, while theorists with a more critical and dynamic understanding of organizational cultures such as Mats Alvesson (2002) were generally overlooked.

New organizational structures (delegated school management, a quasi-market, loosening of local authority control) opened the gates for a flood of management and leadership texts directed at schools. A culturalist model was attractive given the complexity of controlling schools and teachers and the difficulties of realigning their activity to neoliberal policy. Besides, culture had a friendly feel to it: after all, wasn't that what schooling was about? However,

> in the process, the everyday meaning of "culture" in English education was substantially changed. Culture is not now understood as a dialogic space of negotiated (or struggled-over) meanings, but rather as something that is an internal, self-created and relatively secure property of an organisation. (Jones, 2003: 146)

The English case shows how contradictory the shift of control to schools could be: a promised "liberation" from local authority "bureaucracy" was soon revealed as a concentration of power by central government (a standardized National Curriculum, Office for Standards in Education, Children's Services and Skills (Ofsted), high-stakes tests); lest anybody assumed that ordinary teachers, let alone students and parents, might enjoy democratic participation, headteachers were reconstituted as managers and trained to exercise power over those they had previously thought of as colleagues in the ways approved by a National College of School Leadership. Headteachers found themselves with a certain amount of administrative and financial autonomy, but they and their colleagues simultaneously lost control of curriculum and pedagogy.

Whereas the real staff culture was dynamic, critical, or contradictory, it was the role of managers to homogenize it. This was a recognition of the complexity of school cultures but in the same move the myth was propagated that this could be overcome through appropriate "leadership." The new managerial culturalists were right to insist, against more mechanistic paradigms, that school change requires a holistic understanding and a willingness to involve staff—a recognition neatly summed up in Fullan's slogan (actually coined by McLaughlin, 1990) that "You can't mandate what matters." There was an important truth in Fullan and Hargreaves's (1992: 71) identification of the problem of "balkanised" cultures in many secondary schools, though the structural implications of this, namely, the benefit of more coherent small schools, were sidestepped. Generally, it was uncritically assumed that headteachers and senior management teams should be able to align the various voices, and that this alignment and homogenization would be in the public's or students' best interest, particularly if the direction was determined by national government. Such confusion arises by neglecting issues of power and class.

As Ken Jones points out:

> The school is separated from its complex cultural matrix in order to be presented as a potentially homogenous organisation, and in order to be more easily managed. (Jones, 2003: 146)

Jones (2003: 148, quoting Geoff Whitty, John Dixon, and others) summarizes the cultural loss in terms of an unquestioning attitude to educational processes, a willingness to deploy ways of learning whose rationales are beyond question, and a lack of interest in other people's experiences.

Culturalist managerialism involves engineering uniformity and conformity to the aims set by governments and their test-driven accountability regimes. The central role of school principals is to "manage culture" (Deal and Peterson, 1999). They can recognize success through blandly positive indicators ("Norms of Improving Schools") such as

- shared goals—"we know where we're going,"
- responsibility for success—"we must succeed,"
- collegiality—"we're working on this together," and so on. (Stoll and Fink, 1996)

As I have argued elsewhere,

> As the Weltanschauung of school improvement, it is bland and one-dimensional, taking little account of the many contradictions, of teachers' and pupils' lives outside, and of external pressures both political and socioeconomic. There is no concession that some innovations might be ill-conceived, that professionals have a right and duty to evaluate them critically, or that some changes should be resisted. There is a warm glow about this notion of culture, emphasising a rather uncritical cohesion, which can conceal some of the turmoil outside. (Wrigley, 2008)

I am not of course arguing against highlighting cultural dimensions of school change, but that a particularly limiting and controlling usage, in favor of a managerialist homogenization, crucially misrecognizes and does violence to the conflicting voices and interests that exist in reality and that cry out for change in the direction of greater social justice.

> School improvement cannot be understood by focusing on internal processes alone but requires us to look at the interaction between internal and external cultures.... There is, within each school, a contest of different voices, which is what makes school development so interesting. Indeed, it is this that makes school development *possible*. The voice of teachers who insist upon challenging inequality, tedium, and superficial or irrelevant learning is a powerful force for change, despite attempts to silence it. The voice of the local community is crucial to the successful development of multiethnic and other urban schools.
>
> The conflicts that arise from the gap between dominant school cultures, on the one hand, and the crises of children growing up in poverty, dealing with racism or the life choices offered by mass media, on the other, can lead to a dysfunctional disengagement of adolescents from learning. The challenge for school improvers is to find creative ways of engaging with the various cultures and interests at work, and to develop a learning culture which supports achievement and social development within this context. (Wrigley, 2003: 35)

Many writers have commented on the manipulation that managerialist usages of culture give rise to. Andy Hargreaves, a leading figure in school change theory, and by no means a political radical, has consistently warned of "contrived collegiality" (1994: 229 and elsewhere). Helen Gunter (2001: 122) sums up the problem:

> The neo-liberal version of the performing school requires teachers and students to be followers, but to feel good about it.

Bennett (2001: 107–9) points out that

> the culture of an organization, then, is a construct made up of a range of expectations about what are proper and appropriate actions.... This raises two very important questions...where the expectations that define legitimate action come from and how they become part of the assumptive worlds of each organizational member.

There is a fundamental misunderstanding when culture is no longer regarded as uncertain and contested, but as "plastic, shapeable" (Jones, 2003: 147). The social, contradictory, and material character of culture is reduced to a tacit assumption that teachers can be led to assimilate to a single authorial message. By failing to recognize a range of voices, and privileging a monologic authoritarian discourse, managerialism dematerializes culture so that it floats above the popular consciousness that derives from real lives and lifeworlds.

Ironically, even this manipulative misuse of culture proved insufficient for the more impatient of New Labour's school improvement gurus. Michael Barber, who was in command of school development for many years of Blair's government, and his coauthor, Pennsylvanian School Superintendent Vicki Phillips, argue that culture can best be changed by enforcing a change of actions:

> Winning hearts and minds is not the best first step in any process of urgent change. Beliefs do not necessarily change behaviour. More usually...behaviours shape beliefs. Only when people have experienced a change do they revise their beliefs accordingly. Sometimes it is necessary to mandate the change, implement it well, consciously challenge the prevailing culture and have the courage to sustain it until beliefs shift. (Barber and Phillips, 2000: 9–11)

While this view of culture is certainly materialist, it fails to ask critical questions about the legitimate use of power, lacks any concept of class, and appears to regard culture as deadweight, overlooking the extended historical formation of a culture.

So what would be the foundations of a Marxist use of culture in the field of school change? The starting point has got to be an acceptance that we are living in a class society, in which not only the dominant ideas but also institutional norms are strongly influenced by the power of the ruling class and by hegemonic responses to inequality such as discourses of deficit. These macrocultural relationships impact in complex ways on the microculture of a school, as I attempted to outline in my book *Schools of Hope*:

> School improvement requires a more political and situated exploration of culture than we have managed so far, and specifically in relation to demands for greater democracy and the achievement of real success in inner-city schools. For example:
>
> - exploring the differences between authoritarian and cooperative cultures, including developing new rituals for cooperative and democratic learning
> - examining the cultural significance of alienated forms of learning, in which, like factory work, you are told what to write and then hand over your product not to an interested audience but to the teacher-as-examiner, for token payment in the form of a mark or grade
> - questioning the culture of target setting and surveillance which regulates the lives of pupils and teachers, and exploring more democratic

forms of educational responsibility than the present accountability culture
- examining the cultural messages of classrooms which are dominated by the teacher's voice, closed questions and rituals of transmission of superior wisdom
- developing a better understanding of cultural difference, in order to prevent high levels of exclusion
- understanding how assumptions about ability and intelligence are worked out in classroom interactions
- discovering how assumptions about single parents, ethnic minorities and "dysfunctional" working-class families operate symbolically in classroom interactions. (Wrigley, 2003: 36–7)

This is especially important if we are looking for school change to promote social justice. Unfortunately, what we might call "official School Improvement" (Hatcher, 1998) has remained inexcusably ignorant of sociological theories relating to social justice. This is ironic given that international data over the past decade have consistently shown that higher average attainment in a country crucially depends on overcoming inequalities and raising the attainment of working-class and ethnic minority students (Programme for International Student Assessment (PISA)).

Culture between School and Neighborhood

An important starting point is Bourdieu, who relates culture to a divided society in a two-directional analysis, showing how a higher class position shapes and sanctifies aesthetic taste (1984)—what counts as Culture with a capital C—but equally how culture can itself serve as "capital," complementing economic capital as a means toward higher status and higher earnings (1986).

Bourdieu's concept of *cultural capital* is key to understanding how schools reproduce social difference. Bourdieu's argument is not that higher-class families have *more* culture or even a better culture, but that their culture is *recognized* by schools, whereas the cultural interests and knowledge of working-class and ethnic minority families is either ignored altogether or viewed with disdain. As a simple illustration, consider how traditionalist schools might respond in different ways to two students, one who plays the cello and the other a bass guitar. Prior to Bourdieu, the chapter "Scholarship Boy" in Hoggart's (1957) *The Uses of Literacy* illustrates how working-class students are constrained to achieve academic success and social acceptance in higher-status schools by abandoning their family and neighborhood culture. This enforced choice, between school success and class belonging, is also a central theme of Paul Willis's (1977) *Learning to Labour*, an ethnographic study of how "working-class kids get working-class jobs." Young people at school are affected by daily border crossings between school and the lifeworld of their neighborhood. Where these diverge strongly, cultural conflict prevents many students from thriving. The process is not dissimilar to the symbolic violence that Goffman (1961) in *Asylums* describes in the context of "total institutions," for example, mental hospitals, prisons, and boarding schools, where newcomers are stripped of previous identities to become inmates (patients, convicts, pupils). If anything, the process is more problematic in normal schools since it happens on a daily basis. Conversely, in the minority of schools where the children of manual workers and ethnic minorities succeed, one often finds positive and coordinated efforts of cultural recognition.

The "Culture of Poverty" Argument

Unfortunately, some sociological theorizations of culture difference that do focus on class as formative of culture have served to encourage a deficit view of working-class and minority students and their families. The concept of a "culture of poverty" has an element of truth, in that harsh economic conditions (absolute poverty, long hours of work that make for neglect of children) do tend to bring about cultural damage. Indeed, one of Marx's few references to culture in *Capital* is a mere footnote (no. 66, citing the Fourth Report of the Children's Employment Commission) illustrating the lack of basic general knowledge on the part of children forced to work long hours in mines and factories. The danger is of a one-sided emphasis on the demoralizing impact of poverty, and that, by deploying the word "culture," one creates the impression of something permanent and unchallengeable, neglecting the potential for resistance. The classic case is Oscar Lewis's anthropological studies of Latin American societies, for example:

> The culture of poverty is not only an adaptation to a set of objective conditions of the larger society. Once it comes into existence it tends to perpetuate itself from generation to generation because of its effect on the children. By the time slum children are age six or seven they have usually absorbed the basic values and attitudes of their subculture and are not psychologically geared to take full advantage of changing conditions or increased opportunities which may occur in their lifetime. (Lewis, 1966: xlv)

While this is one strand of a complex process of adaptation and reaction to poverty, the renowned Marxist anthropologist Eleanor Leacock (1971) points out how easily such an outlook is translated into a "blame the victim" ideology, involving the most abusive denigration of poor and especially black families. She quotes, for example, Bartky's *Social Issues in Public Education* (1963) with its references to the "dregs culture" of the Chicago ghetto, with its high crime such that the law must work "fast and ruthlessly," and where even religion takes the form of a "wild cat church," which "is more of an amusement than... a moral influence." Similarly, in Moynihan's report for the US Department of Labor, *The Negro Family: The Case for National Action*, the black American family is portrayed as a "tangle of pathology" and as the "principal source of most of the aberrant, inadequate, or antisocial behavior that did not establish, but now serves to perpetuate the cycle of poverty and deprivation" (1965: 30, 47).

Leacock reminds us how quickly the seemingly fixed, fatalistic "culture" of the slums of Havana studied by Lewis was transformed by revolution. Her lasting challenge to the discourse of "cultures of disadvantage" is that

> Cultural norms do not exist outside man's living history, and they involve conflicting and contradictory goals and values, from which people choose, and which allow for change and development.
>
> Furthermore, individuals may either passively accept their cultural environment or actively seek to develop or change some part of it, and they will exhibit a wide variety of styles in the way they do either one. (1971: 14)

"Culture of poverty" arguments are, as Leacock rightly argues, a restoration of "the nineteenth-century argument that the poor are poor through their own lack of ability and initiative," which has "reentered the scene in a new form, well decked out with scientific jargon" (1971: 11). The line of this "blame the victim" ideology based on cultural deficit can be traced forward to Charles Murray's "underclass polemic" (e.g., Murray, 1990), and is identified by Levitas (2004: 5) as a strand in Blairite "social exclusion" policy on poverty. This is not to suggest that poverty has no cultural impact, including lowering aspirations as people accommodate to the possible at the "threshold of calculability" (Jenkins, 2002: 28, quoting Bourdieu), but rather it stresses the vital importance of cultural recognition and of enabling the poor "to have and to cultivate voice," in order to increase the "capacity to aspire" in a process of "bringing the future back in" (Appadurai, 2004: 62–3).

Culture and Language Deficit

One of the most subtle but damaging offshoots of this was the "language deficit" argument, transmuted by Basil Bernstein from a crudely racist North American form into a more urbane English argument on language and class. In its original form, language deficit theory was based on the linguistically ignorant belief that the frequent omission of the verb "to be" (e.g., "She no good") by African Americans and their use of double negatives ("I ain't done nothing") is "illogical" and that this supposed "illogicality" leads to unclear thinking, which is the root cause of educational underachievement. As Labov (1969) pointed out, its proponents were seemingly not aware that many languages share these features; the copula "to be" is similarly absent in Russian, and double negatives are standard in French and other Romance languages. This would presumably prevent their entire populations from thinking logically.

Bernstein's more sophisticated argument was essentially that

(i) working-class language is mainly orientated toward the familiar and toward objects and events that are physically present and visible to the speakers; and
(ii) it therefore tends to use a code that, for example, deploys pronouns rather than nouns, less complex sentences, and so on.

He called discursive patterns appropriate to circumstances where people are talking about immediately visible or thoroughly familiar referents "restricted code" and discursive patterns oriented toward more distant objects "elaborated code." Bernstein argued that "middle-class" families are capable of using both according to circumstance, but that "working-class" families are only well practiced in "restricted code," leading to educational failure in their children.

It is useful to distinguish between everyday transactional or conversational discourses that relate to what is immediately visible or closely familiar, such as family talk, and discourses that relate to more hidden, distant, or abstract matter, such as academic writing. Wertsch has helpfully termed this more abstract mode one of "decontextualised rationality" (Wertsch, 1990); this is more helpful because it suggests the possibility of discourses of contextualized rationality, but also implies (de-) that loss of context can become problematic. While it is important for schools to develop in all pupils a fluency in the academic or abstract mode of language, Bernstein (1970 and elsewhere) failed to provide proof that "working-class" families did not use the former, or that this was a cause of underachievement in school. Indeed, his attempt at experimental proof was deeply flawed: the "working-class" children whom he criticized for using "restricted code" did so to describe events in a cartoon story that remained in front of them the whole time (see Rosen, 1972: 12–13, for a more extended critique). Indeed, exceeding this, Bernstein also deployed a cruder argument that "working-class" mothers smacked their children rather than reasoning with them; this too was presented without empirical evidence. The language-deprivation arguments led to a widespread professional folklore among a generation of teachers that "working-class children are barely talked to by their parents"; that "working-class children have little experience of having their questions answered, or of hearing explanations, reasoning, predictions and projects into the experience of others"; that working-class mothers pass on to their children a failure to be explicit, that their range of topics is limited, that they do not play with their children, and that they exercise authority by force rather than reason (see critique by Tizard and Hughes, 1984: 135–55).

Harold Rosen's (1972) challenge to Bernstein's deficit view was not only based on linguistic considerations but was also grounded in his socialist engagement in class struggle. In his critique of Bernstein, Rosen highlights the rich verbal culture of militant working-class areas such as the East End of London where he grew up, or the coal-mining regions:

> No attention is paid to that vast area of critical working class experience, the encounter with exploitation at the place of work and the response to it…Collective bargaining, demonstrations, strikes and so on…can occur only if language is available which is adequate to the task. What kind of people imagine that the 1972 miners' strike, for example, was made possible merely by the incantation of a few rabble-rousing slogans? (1972)

Bernstein's explanation of school underachievement in terms of language deficit illustrates the consequences of reading off cultural features directly from class position. It is almost a parody of a vulgar Marxist position (superstructure mechanistically "determined by" base). Rather than theory providing a guide to action, it closes off possibilities of both individual achievement and social emancipation.

It also fails to recognize that, in key respects, the most typical discourse of school learning (a preponderance of low-level closed questions that are presented to test pupils rather than engage them in dialogue or explore ideas) is just as restricted as Bernstein's "working-class restricted code" and just as great a limitation on educational engagement and achievement (Cooper, 1976). Similarly, the "culture of poverty" argument fails to pick up on the many ways in which school structures, and the assumptions of many teachers about communities in poverty, serve to reproduce poverty, inequality, and disadvantage. It is clear that chronic unemployment and poverty create a psychology of shame and futility (see, for example, Charlesworth, 2000), but the normative practices of most schools may be reinforcing these rather than countering them. In other words, schools themselves are reproductive of a culture of poverty.

Culture and Curriculum

Two of the key principles of Marxism form a paradox: first, a faith in the "self-emancipation of the working class" and, second, the belief that "the ideas of the ruling class are in every epoch the ruling ideas." The contradiction is resolved only in practice, as a working class in struggle also undertakes and experiences an intellectual struggle against ideologies that hold it back.

Raymond Williams, the son of a railway worker appointed to a lectureship in English in an elite university, set about rethinking the nature of establishment culture, specifically the academic field of English literature, and its relationship to the working class. His analysis inevitably faced both ways.

One side of Williams's project was to ask questions about the "canon" of English literature: who decided what was included, and upon what principles was this selection based? Though appearing to students as if cast in stone, the literary canon had changed over time, and is, as Williams perceived, a selection based as much on class preferences as "literary quality" (Williams, 1961: 67). The (often implicit) ideologies of writers showed through in form as well as content, and criticism too provided a selective filter. Thus, Williams challenged the standard view of critics that Thomas Hardy's novels were peopled by quaintly bucolic "peasants"; Hardy is describing not peasants but an oppressed rural proletariat in a solidly capitalist economy (Williams, 1984: 100). Similarly, Williams's class perspective enabled him to notice that Jane Austen uses the word "neighbours" not to refer to "the people actually living nearby" but to

> the people living a little less nearby who, in social recognition, can be visited. What she sees across the land is a network of propertied houses and families, and through the holes of this tightly drawn mesh most actual people are simply not seen. To be face-to-face in this world is already to belong to a class. (Williams, 1985: 166)

But the other side of Williams's work was to fill the gaps, to focus on neglected works, including political and social texts that provided the essential context (not merely "background") for the canonical literary texts. This began with the book *Culture and Society* (Williams, 1958), but eventually led to the establishment of an entirely new academic field of cultural studies that would concern itself with other kinds of cultural phenomena. For Williams, culture was "ordinary." This in itself was a political challenge, given the elitist view that Culture (with a capital C) was intrinsically beyond the reach of the working class.

School Curriculum and the Selective Tradition

It was not too great a step from Williams's writing about the "selective tradition" in universities (1961) to Denys Lawton's (Lawton, Gordon and Ing, 1978) formulation about schools, "Curriculum is a selection from the culture." The term was liberating to a point, since the school curriculum no longer appeared normal or "natural," but Lawton risked losing Williams's critical edge. His statement begs some questions:

(i) The definite article suggests a singular entity, begging the question whether Lawton is referring to an authoritarian canon or a broadly accepted common culture.
(ii) It is crucial to ask why particular items are selected, who has done the selecting, for whom, and to what ends.

More radical voices, including Liverpool's director of education, Eric Midwinter (1972), sought to establish models for a curriculum that was more in tune with working-class culture. Lawton was very critical of this, condemning Midwinter for trapping working-class students in their neighborhoods of origin.

This tension can only be resolved by holding on to Williams's ideal of an education that would both respect the "ordinary" culture—in the sense of both creative activity and its products and of culture as a "whole way of life"—and provide access to (a critical reading of) the selective tradition. Indeed, Williams argued strongly in the conclusion to *Culture and Society* (1958: 307) that the small amount of "proletarian" writing and art that exists can only form a "valuable dissident element" rather than a culture; and conversely, that what we have received as "traditional culture" is always something more than the product of a single class.

> Even within a society in which a particular class is dominant, it is evi-
> dently possible both for members of other classes to contribute to the

common stock, and for such contributions to be unaffected by or in opposition to the ideas and values of the dominant class. (Ibid: 307)

This is close to Trotsky's view as expressed in *Literature and Revolution* (1960 [1923]). The point is—and Williams models this out for us in various books (1958; 1984; 1985)—to seize the assets by rereading from a different class perspective. Similarly, a popular scientific and environmental education should respect and build upon knowledge deriving from the lifeworld of students while providing a clear understanding of scientific theory. The one pole without the other provides a limited education.

This connects with more recent attempts to discover, respect, and build upon the practices and knowledges of young people, including the work of Luis Moll who refers to these as "funds of knowledge" (Moll and Greenberg, 1990). Pat Thomson (2002) uses the term "virtual schoolbag" in a similar sense. Without this bridging between ordinary and high-status culture, practical and academic knowledge, the project of the "common school" or "comprehensive school" is doomed to failure. But it is not enough, because, as Gramsci points out, everyday "common sense" knowledge, while reflecting aspects of reality, can provide misleading explanations of reality and be inadequate as a guide to action. The funds of knowledge by themselves could be extremely limiting, for example, by providing only local or archaic perspectives, being loaded with prejudice, carrying attitudes of servility, or being built on mystifying religious and unscientific models of the world.

Freire's curricular approach is based upon respect for the everyday experiences of the learners, achieved by identifying words and themes based on the familiar, but engaging learners in discussion of the political significance of the words and experiences. Williams's work on culture in many ways parallels this. As Eagleton summarizes Williams's project, "the making of a common culture is a continual exchange of meanings, actions and descriptions." It does not involve the rejection of either a low or a high culture, but rather of bringing

> the culture of the selective tradition [into] a relationship with the lived culture of a particular time and place.

This involves

> both a revaluation of established high culture . . . and a project of "releasing and enriching the life experience which the rising class brings with it" (Jones, 2009: 21–2, quoting various texts of Williams)

One particular site of struggle was the subject English in secondary schools, originating in London and involving Marxists such as Harold and Michael Rosen, Chris Searle, the Hackney-based publishing project Centerprise, as well as numerous other progressive non-Marxists, under the umbrella of the London Association of Teachers of English (LATE). This movement quickly became aware of the accelerating cultural diversity of the working class and the need to struggle against racism both in the classroom and on the streets. New pedagogies were developed, based on a commitment to the understanding that all students have the capacity for creative expression—that the working class does have culture if only schools could learn to work with it and not against it (Rosen, 1982). This movement was a particular target of the Thatcherite counterrevolution; the National Curriculum to a great extent effectively filled up all the creative spaces with the rubble of grammatical knowledge "about" English, sterilizing the ground and closing down the space for affective and critical engagement. English was seen once again as predominantly a skill for working life, rather than a space for cultural participation and articulation as part of a wider democratic struggle.

The need is equally great today for schools to promote the creation of a common culture through "the exchange of meanings, actions and descriptions" (see above), but the task is more difficult. First, as a result of deindustrialization and the defeats suffered by the labor movement in the 1980s, the "working class has been largely eviscerated as a visible social presence" and "is no longer a central reference point in British culture" (Savage, 2003: 536). The dignity attached to job stability and reliable earnings has been replaced by "the indignities of flexible and obedient labour" (Willis, 2003: 397). Culture has been increasingly commodified, removing some of the potential for creative engagement. The purposes of schooling have been redefined by neoliberalism, for society in terms of economic competitiveness and for the individual in terms of acquiring marketable labor power (Ball, 2008).

At the same time, we should be careful not to limit our meaning of "working class" to manual or industrial. The vast majority of the population, whether in blue-collar, white-collar, or "professional" occupations, belongs to the wider working class, as foreseen by Marx and Engels a century and a half ago (2005 [1848]). The cultural interests of young people of these different sections of a broader working class are probably closer than ever. The culture now available to young people has been considerably enriched by migration and international influences. New struggles have developed around such issues as the war, environment, and antifascism, helping to generate a new culture of resistance; though this is not always class conscious, it objectively unites large numbers against global capitalism. The challenge now is to rethink Williams's project in a new context, rather than engage in cultural nostalgia.

Culture and Pedagogy

For most of the twentieth century, an authoritarian and transmission-based pedagogy was underpinned and justified by the pseudo-science of behaviorism, a theory based on experimentally inculcating unnatural patterns of behavior on caged animals. Behaviorism represents a rigorously nondialectical and mechanistic materialism that eschews all reference to meaning-making, reducing interpretative capacity to the manipulative linking of one object or event to another as conditioned by reward and punishment. This served to rationalize and justify the worst practices of mass public schooling that had been developed in the nineteenth century to prepare working-class children for industrial work.

For many years, opposition to this, in the name of progressive child-centered reform, was limited by being both idealist and individualist. Even Piaget's constructivism, based on interpretation of the real world, was limited to individual operations and reflections on nature, with progress dependent on maturation, and with both teachers and language playing an uncertain part.

The rediscovery of Vygotsky's sociocultural psychology, starting in the 1960s, provided a means to overcome these limitations. Vygotsky (1978: 19–20) sought to overcome both the individualistic psychology based on the behaviorist animal metaphor and the progressive-Romantic plant metaphor with its discourse of independent "growth." He started to build a new psychology, which is three times social:

(i) It regards learning as fundamentally social before being internalized.
(ii) It emphasizes interaction with more knowledgeable or skilled coparticipants.
(iii) It places enormous emphasis on the mediating function of signs (particularly language), which are regarded as a special kind of tool (Vygotsky, 1978: 1986).

The latter idea derives directly from Marx and Engels, whose view of history places strong emphasis on technological development and the invention of new tools for transforming nature into useful objects. Vygotsky adopts this concept of tools, building a theory that language and other signs are cultural or semiotic tools that not only help us draw up plans and carry out tasks effectively through communication, but also turn inward, helping us reflect upon, regulate, and transform our own behavior and consciousness.

The notion of sign as "tool" should not be seen as a simple reflection, a static representation of an object, a mental proxy, but as potentially transformative. This goes beyond a tool's role in carrying out a physical operation on nature. Marx's explanation of the key difference between human beings and animals, well known to Vygotsky, shows that symbolic systems also provide a way of planning forward, of remaking the world, of doing things differently:

> What distinguishes the worst of architects from the best of bees is that the architect raises his structure first in imagination before he erects it in reality. (*Capital* Volume 1, Chapter 7 used as the opening motto for Vygotsky, 1925)

Semiotic tools range from the abstractions of algebra to rich experiential forms such as paintings and computer simulations. The philosopher of science, Marx Wartofsky, points out that even the least abstract, most experiential forms of representation (e.g., novels, children's dramatic play, scientific models) are *off-line*—that is, they are not reality itself. This provides the potential to reimagine and redesign the world (Wartofsky, 1979: 208–9). The concept of semiotic tools connects with a view of culture that not only inherits from the past but is technologically and politically active in creating a very different kind of future.

The interpretation of Vygotsky has suffered from various kinds of distortion, both under Stalinism and in the West. It was reduced to a more mechanistic "activity theory," under pressure from the Stalinist authorities, by Leontiev and others (Kozulin, 2005). This reduced the role of culture, including the mediating role of the sign, such that activity came to be seen as sufficient. When *Thought and Language* first appeared in English, almost all references to Marx had been removed (Daniels, 2005: 2). It is also important to understand that Vygotsky's life was cut short by tuberculosis, after only 15 years of scholarly activity, and that many of his ideas were written down in an undeveloped form only, giving enormous space for further development.

It is in the last 30 years that teachers and scholars have begun to build upon Vygotsky. The principle that learning is primarily social has led to new conceptions of mind and thinking as "stretched" between people, the environment, and language—"distributed cognition" (Salomon, 1993). This provides a basis for challenging the individualism and abstraction of traditional school learning (see, for example, Perkins, 1992; Wertsch, 1990). This is not to diminish the importance of abstract thinking or theory, but to understand that they are best comprehended when used as means of illuminating and guiding practice.

Another area of creative application of Vygotsky, drawing also on Freire and Bourdieu, relates to the need to overcome tendencies to disengagement and low achievement of many young people in working-class neighborhoods, including minorities. The "funds of knowledge" concept of Luis Moll and colleagues (Moll and Greenberg, 1990; Gonzalez et al., 2005) referred to earlier is crucial here. Again, it must be stressed that this is no one-sided cult of relevance, but a process whereby accessing and recognizing hidden community knowledge and culture, which is normally ignored or marginalized in schools, not only gives important recognition, but also provides a route for engaging with formal academic knowledge.

Conclusion: Culture and the Future

What links the above sections, on reflection, is a sense of *culture* as meaningful activities and artifacts—matter that signifies—and a struggle to bring into relationship, through practical pedagogical work, culture as a high-status aesthetic product with culture as "ordinary." This intellectual struggle has all the difficulties of counterhegemonic theorizing, given the strength throughout the bourgeois epoch of both a Cartesian dualism and a view of aesthetic artifacts as belonging intrinsically to an elite. When it is actually conceded that workers have a culture, this is often either reified as a cultural remnant (pigeons and whippets) or denigrated as a "culture of poverty."

Following Thatcher's destruction of the industrial heartlands and their communities and cultures, it is difficult to locate a "working-class culture" that might be a source of pride. The material foundations for the Grimethorpe Colliery Band have been visibly destroyed. However, the political history and cultural heritage needs to be passed on, as a cultural tool without which it may be impossible for a new generation to relate positively to new cultural elements imported through migration or surviving in a commercially captured youth culture. As Williams (1958: 313) insisted, the central cultural achievement of the British working class has been to invent organizations for struggle and to establish practices of solidarity. Future generations will lose out if the history of struggle for democracy and a welfare state, and the arguments surrounding this, are unavailable to new generations. It is also important to carry forward an understanding of the working class as knowledgeable and critical, demanding access to quality education for its children and at times creating its own sites for learning.

In the twentieth century, Marxism began to take culture seriously as an essential factor in deciding whether we would be trapped by ruling-class ideologies and hegemonic "common sense" (Gramsci, 1971), and whether our future would be socialism or barbarism (Luxemburg, 1915). However, there is little clarity among Marxists as to how this cultural struggle might relate to formal education and a great deal of pedagogical thinking to be done.

This is immensely difficult in contexts in which curriculum is tightly controlled by the state, and when even the concept of publicly provided schooling is being undermined by charter schools (United States) and academies (United Kingdom). The struggle for culture is unavoidably a question of power. It cannot be pursued without holding on to the Marxist view of emancipation as the project of the working class, which includes engaged teachers, the communities they serve, and the students.

The processes by which a capitalist ruling class has denied the working class the opportunity to develop a culture for liberation have taken many forms historically, including

- the attempt by Victorian teacher training colleges to declass and reculture academically successful young people of working-class families to turn them into teachers who would domesticate the next generation;
- the desiccation of culture into a curriculum of inert facts, and the authoritarian mode of its transmission;
- establishing competitive markets between schools, and the setting and streaming and grading within, to limit the aspirations and opportunities of working-class students; and
- outpricing higher levels of education from working-class reach, then blaming parents and students for "lack of ambition."

In these neoliberal times, educational policy making has been dominated by the perspective of economics, its prime aim being seen as the efficient production of human capital (Ball, 2008: 11). In England, the 2006 Education and Inspections Act (UK Parliament, 2006) divided 14- to 16-year-olds into an academic and a vocational track, with the latter losing the entitlement to study history or geography, a foreign language, creative and performing arts, and design and technology. This move implicitly carries the message that the established cultural heritage of academic learning is inappropriate to the working class, and, conversely, often in the name of relevance, offers them a vocationalist curriculum that is stripped bare of culture, history, politics, and critique. A similar division is occurring in primary education, where particular pressure is placed on schools in poorer neighborhoods to implement a decultured version of literacy teaching with an exclusive emphasis on phonics. The children who might have had least opportunity in early childhood to gain pleasure from books are then denied it at school.

> Nowhere in this anaemic instructional vision is there room for really connecting at a human level with culturally diverse students. When we frame the universe of discourse only in terms of children's deficits in English and in phonological awareness (or deficits in any other area), we expel culture, language, identity, intellect, and imagination from our image of the child.
>
> Effective citizenship requires active intelligence, critical literacy, and a willingness to challenge power structures that constrict human possibility...Identity, intellect, imagination and power are absent from the new regime of truth because they potentially challenge the smooth operation of coercive power structures. (Cummins, 2003: 56–8)

The most recent form of this attack is the plan of the Conservative-led UK coalition government to remove all subsidy from university teaching in the arts and humanities, so that these courses become the exclusive preserve of the rich.

Making working-class cultures available is not some kind of heritage industry. It is about recognition and identity but also about tools for critical understanding, a sense of history, conflict, and the nature of human labor. As Wexler (1982) points out, such perspectives are systematically absent from most school learning. How often is class or poverty or exploitation discussed in schools? It has become commonplace to speak of a multicultural curriculum, whereas a "working-class curriculum" (or indeed "community curriculum") is unspeakable, but the former only makes full sense within wider perspectives of class and struggle.

Some excellent models do exist of teachers within state-run schools working together to establish a socially critical curriculum that relates to students' cultural foundations. The most inspiring and wide-ranging is probably the *Rethinking Schools* collective, which has promoted the teaching of issues that are normally missing from school curricula, redefined standard topics (see the book *Rethinking Columbus*, Bigelow and Peterson, 2003), found ways of connecting subjects that are generally assumed to be unpolitical to the big issues of the day (see *Rethinking Mathematics,* Gutstein and Peterson, 2005), and conveyed a sense of the injustices of the past and present while honoring and respecting oppressed cultures in a spirit of hope for the future.

Another important model is the work of the MST (Landless Workers Movement) in Brazil, which insists that the public authorities must fund schools while the teachers and communities themselves must decide what and how to teach. The MST has created a school culture for young people who have experienced struggle against oppression, which does not seek to domesticate. They have combined an appreciation of the local with critical perspectives on the national and global context (Kane, 2001; MST, 2005).

A Marxist cultural project involves critical engagement with a range of symbolic tools, from single words to novels, from the abacus to algebra. However, it is too limited to regard these in static ways as tools for recording or classifying; they are not simple *reflections* of material reality. At the most basic level, words are inflected according to the social position and desires of those who use them (Volosinov, 1973 [1929]). Symbolic representations highlight particular features of experience but always, as Volosinov stressed, in a "partial" way, that is from particular points of view. We need to appreciate their partiality in order not to be absorbed uncritically by them. Thus, for example, the Marxist playwright Brecht (1949) sought to create in his theatre a *Verfremdungseffekt*, a distancing process whereby the audience are jolted into taking a step back from the scene, to recognize that things can be different than they are, the future can be different from the present, that cruelty and poverty and war are not inevitable. Whether reading a book or taking part in a simulation, absorption and empathy must be complemented by a critical distancing, a reediting of the text brought about by asking questions about power and authorial perspective and significant omissions. This is a critical pedagogy based on cultural reflection and reimagining and repositioning.

One of the seams running through this chapter has been the orientation of culture toward the future as well as the past, so I will return to and extend Marx's metaphor of architect and bee. Architects have the cultural tools to imagine and draw a building before construction. Their cultural resources include pens and paper, drawing techniques, and engineering knowledge, but also the broader humanistic knowledge and understanding drawing on memories of the other buildings they have seen and how people live in built environments. The most enlightened architects have a sense of how their fellow human beings are forced to live but also a vision of how they might live.

This is a wonderful metaphor of culture and what it means to be human. Worker bees are trapped in a natural cycle of serving the queen or the beekeeper, but humanity is not condemned to endless repetition of exploitation and injustice. Culture enables us to build a world to meet our own needs, not labor endlessly for our exploiters. For Marxists, culture is a resource for resistance. Culture is more than drawing on riches from the past for our present enjoyment, or utilizing technologies developed across many generations to produce for current needs. It is a set of living practices and relationships, activities and artifacts that help and inspire us to shape a radically better future.

References

Alvesson, M. (2002) *Understanding Organizational Culture* (London: Sage).

Appadurai, A. (2004) The Capacity to Aspire: Culture and the Terms of Recognition. In V. Rao and M. Walton (eds.) *Culture and Public Action* (Palo Alto, CA: Stanford University Press).

Ball, S. (2008) *The Education Debate* (Bristol: Policy Press).

Barber, M. and Phillips, V. (2000) *Fusion: How to Unleash Irreversible Change.* Unpublished conference paper, DfEE Conference on Education Action Zones.

Bartky, J. (1963) *Social Issues in Public Education* (Boston, MA: Houghton Mifflin).

Bennett, N. (2001) Power, Structure and Culture: An Organizational View of School Effectiveness and School Improvement. In A. Harris and N. Bennett (eds.) *School Effectiveness and School Improvement: Alternative Perspectives* (London: Continuum).

Bernstein, B. (1970) *Class, Codes and Control, vol. 1: Theoretical Studies towards a Sociology of Language* (London: Routledge and Kegan Paul).

Bigelow, B. and B. Peterson. (2003) *Rethinking Columbus: The Next 500 Years* (Milwaukee, WI: Rethinking Schools).

Bourdieu, P. (1984) *Distinction* (Cambridge, MA: Polity).

Brecht, B. (1949) A Short Organum for the Theatre. In J. Willett (ed.) (1964) *Brecht on Theatre: The Development of an Aesthetic* (London: Methuen).

Burns, J. (1978) *Leadership* (New York: Harper and Row).

Charlesworth, S. (2000) *A Phenomenology of Working Class Experience* (Cambridge, MA: Cambridge University Press).

Cooper, B. (1976) *Bernstein's Codes: A Classroom Study* (Brighton: University of Sussex).

Cummins, J. (2003) Challenging the Construction of Difference as Deficit: Where Are Identity, Intellect, Imagination, and Power in the New Regime of Truth? In P.P. Trifonas (ed.) *Pedagogies of Difference: Rethinking Education for Social Change* (London: Routledge Falmer)

Daniels, H. (2005) *An Introduction to Vygotsky* (London: Routledge).

Deal, T. and K. Peterson (1999) *Shaping School Culture* (San Francisco, CA: Jossey-Bass).

Eagleton, T. (2000) *The Idea of Culture* (Oxford: Blackwell).

Engels, F.(1890) Letter to J Bloch. [www.marxists.org/archive/marx /works/1890/letters/90_09_21.htm].

Fullan, M. and A. Hargreaves. (1992) *What's Worth Fighting for in Your School* (Buckingham: Open University Press).

Goffman, E. (1961) *Asylums: Essays on the Social Situation of Mental Patients and Other Inmates* (Garden City, NY: Doubleday).

Gonzalez, N., L. Moll and C. Amanti. (2005) *Funds of Knowledge: Theorizing Practices in Households, Communities, and Classrooms* (London: Lawrence Erlbaum Associates).

Gramsci, A. (1971) *Selections from the Prison Notebooks* (London: Lawrence and Wishart).

Gunter H. (2001) *Leaders and Leadership in Education* (London: Chapman).

Gutstein, E. and B. Peterson (2005) *Rethinking Mathematics: Teaching Social Justice by the Numbers* (Milwaukee, WI: Rethinking Schools).

Hargreaves A. (1994) *Changing Teachers, Changing Times* (London: Cassell).

Hatcher, R. (1998) Labour, Official School Improvement and Equality. *Journal of Education Policy*, 13(4): 485–99.

Hoggart, R. (1957) *The Uses of Literacy* (London: Chatto and Windus).

Jenkins, R. (2002) *Pierre Bourdieu* (London: Routledge).

Jones, K. (2003) Culture Reinvented as Management: English in the New Urban School. *Changing English*, 10(2): 143–53.

Jones, K. (2009) *Culture and Creative Learning: A Literature Review* (London: Creativity, Culture and Education).

Kane, L. (2001) *Popular Education and Social Change in Latin America* (London: Latin American Bureau).

Kozulin, A. (2005) The Concept of Activity in Soviet Psychology: Vygotsky, His Disciples and Critics. In H. Daniels (ed.) *An Introduction to Vygotsky* (London: Routledge).

Labov, W. (1969) *The Logic of Nonstandard English* (Georgetown Monographs on Language and Linguistics, vol. 22).

Lawton, D., P. Gordon and M. Ing (1978) *Theory and Practice of Curriculum Studies* (London: Routledge).

Leacock, E. (1971) *The Culture of Poverty: A Critique* (New York: Simon and Schuster).

Levitas, R. (2004) Let's Hear It for Humpty: Social Exclusion, the Third Way and Cultural Capital. *Cultural Trends*, 13(2): 41–56.

Lewis, O. (1966) *La Vida* (New York: Random House).

Luxemburg, R. (1915) *The Junius Pamphlet: The Crisis of German Social Democracy.* (http://www.marxists.org/archive/luxemburg/1915/junius/).

Marx, K. and F. Engels (2005 [1848]) *The Communist Manifesto* (London: Bookmarks).

McLaughlin, M. (1990) The Rand Change Agent Study Revisited: Macro Perspectives and Micro Realities. *Educational Research* 19(9): 11–16.

Midwinter, E. (1972) *Priority Education* (Harmondsworth: Penguin).

Moll, L. and J. Greenberg (1990) Creating Zones of Possibilities: Combining Social Contexts for Instruction. In L. Moll (ed.) *Vygotsky and Education: Instructional Implications and Applications of Sociohistorical Psychology* (Cambridge, MA: Cambridge University Press).

Moynihan, D. (1965) *The Negro Family: The Case for National Action* (Washington: U.S. Department of Labor).

MST [Movimento dos Trabalhadores Rurais Sem Terra, Landless Workers Movement] (2005) *Dossie MST Escola: Documentos e Estudos 1990–2001* (Sao Paulo: Expressao Popular).

Murray, C. (1990) *The Emerging British Underclass* (London: IEA).

Parker, M. (2000) *Organisational Culture and Identity: Unity and Division at Work* (London: Sage).

Perkins, D. (1992) *Smart Schools: Better Thinking and Learning for Every Child* (New York: The Free Press).

Peters, T. and R. Waterman (1982) *In Search of Excellence: Lessons from America's Best Run Companies* (New York: Harper and Row).

Rosen, H. (1972) *Language and Class: A Critical Look at the Theories of Basil Bernstein* (Bristol: Falling Wall Press).

Rosen, M. (1982) In Their Own Voice. *In Talk Workshop Group (1982) Becoming Our Own Experts*, 378–91 (London: Vauxhall School).

Salomon, G. (ed.) (1993) *Distributed Cognition: Psychological and Educational Considerations* (Cambridge, MA: Cambridge University Press).

Savage, M. (2003) A New Class Paradigm? *British Journal of Sociology of Education*, 24(4): 535–41.

Stoll, L. and D. Fink (1996) *Changing Our Schools: Linking School Effectiveness and School Improvement* (Buckingham: Open University Press).

Thomson, P. (2002) *Schooling the Rustbelt Kids: Making the Difference in Changing Times* (Stoke-on-Trent: Trentham).

Tizard, B. and M. Hughes (1984) *Children Learning at Home and in School* (London: Fontana).

Trotsky, L. (1960 [1923]) *Literature and Revolution* (Ann Arbor, MI: University of Michigan Press).

UK Parliament (2006) *Education and Inspections Act* (www.legislation.gov.uk/ukpga/2006/40, accessed Oct 2010).

Volosinov, V.N. (1973 [1929]) *Marxism and the Philosophy of Language* (Cambridge, MA: Harvard University Press).

Vygotsky, L.S. (1925) *Consciousness as a Problem in the Psychology of Behaviour* (http://www.marxists.org/archive/vygotsky/works/1925/consciousness.htm).

Vygotsky, L. (1978) *Mind in Society: The Development of Higher Psychological Processes* (Cambridge, MA: Harvard University Press).

Vygotsky, L. (1986) *Thought and Language* (Cambridge, MA: MIT Press).

Wartofsky, M. (1979) *Models* (Dordrecht: Reidel).

Wertsch, J. (1990) The Voice of Rationality. In L. Moll (ed.) *Vygotsky and Education: Instructional Implications and Applications of Sociohistorical Psychology* (Cambridge, MA: Cambridge University Press).

Wexler, P. (1982). Structure, Text and Subject: A Critical Sociology of School Knowledge. In M. Apple (ed.) *Cultural and Economic Reproduction in Education*, 275–303 (London: Routledge and Kegan Paul).

Williams, R. (1958) *Culture and Society 1780–1950* (London: Chatto and Windus).

Williams, R. (1961) *The Long Revolution* (London: Chatto and Windus).

Williams, R. (1976) *Keywords: A Vocabulary of Culture and Society* (London: Fontana).

Williams, R. (1980) *Culture and Materialism* (London: Verso). [The chapter 'Base and Superstructure in Marxist Cultural Theory' was first published in *New Left Review*, 82, Nov–Dec 1973].

Williams, R. (1984) *The English Novel from Dickens to Lawrence* (London: Hogarth).

Williams, R. (1985) *The Country and the City* (London: Hogarth).

Willis, P. (1977) *Learning to Labour: How Working Class Kids get Working Class Jobs* (London: Gower).

Willis, P. (2003) Footsoldiers of Modernity: The Dialectics of Cultural Consumption and the Twenty-first Century School. *Harvard Educational Review*, 78(3): 390–416.

Wrigley, T. (2003) *Schools of Hope: A New Agenda for School Improvement* (Stoke-on-Trent: Trentham).

Wrigley, T. (2008) School Improvement in a Neo-liberal World. *Journal of Educational Administration and History*, 40(2): 129–48.

Chapter 2

Learning to Labor with Feeling: Class, Gender, and Emotion in Childcare Education and Training[1]

Helen Colley

Introduction

Fledglings: offering care, love and education. (Advertising flyer)

The words above arrived through my letterbox one day, blazoned across a leaflet for a private nursery nearby. While the purchase of education and care has come to seem commonplace in a world of privatized services, this offer promises something more deeply significant. Here, love itself—one of the most powerful and intimate of human emotions—is one of the products for sale, a distinctive part of the total childcare package.

Simple marketing ploy though this may have been, it reflects a serious debate in early years research and practice: to what extent should the nursery represent a home-like environment and the nursery nurse play a quasi-maternal role? Opposing views on the answer to this question have been expressed by early years experts. On the one hand, Dahlberg et al. (1999) argue that the nursery cannot and should not be seen as a home-from-home, nor should the nursery nurse be regarded as a substitute parent. To portray the nursery as a place of emotional closeness and intimacy, which are inevitably *faux*, is to conflate misleadingly a public with a private sphere. On the other hand, Elfer et al. (2003) contend that such objections overstate problems that can and must be overcome in developing high-quality childcare. From their perspective, only a special relationship with a "key person" who does offer love in the nursery can provide the intimacy and closeness that they claim children both need and want.

I avow here that I am not an expert in childcare or early years education, and would therefore be ill qualified to engage in this particular
debate about "what works." My own research interests focus on postcompulsory education, but for the last four years, as part of my work
in the project "Transforming Learning Cultures in Further Education"
(TLC) in the Economic and Social Research Council's Teaching and
Learning Research Programme, I have been studying a further education (FE) college course that prepares school-leavers for employment as
nursery nurses. As an interested "intruder" in the field of early childhood, then, I propose to draw on data from that FE research to address
a different set of questions posed by the Fledglings leaflet. These are not
about "what works" in terms of nursery nurses' emotional engagement
with infants and small children but rather "how it works" in the social
practices of learning to do the job. What do prospective nursery nurses
learn from vocational education and training about emotion in childcare
work? How do they learn it? And what factors interact to determine their
success (or otherwise) in this learning? I begin by reviewing some of the
key academic contributions to understanding the learning of emotion
for personal service and caring work.

Learning to Labor with Feeling

Hochschild's (1983) seminal work, *The Managed Heart: Commercialization of Human Feeling*, was the first to address centrally the idea
that labor is not divided between the simple dualism of the manual
and the mental, but may incorporate important emotional work too.
Such work entails learning to manage one's own feelings in order to
evoke particular feelings in other people. She argues that, in social and
family life, this is an important function that contributes to civilized
relationships. But in what she terms "emotional labor," such feeling-
management is sold within the labor market. The emotional style of
providing a service—be it customer care, education, or health care—
becomes part of the service itself, since "in processing people the product is a state of mind...[It] requires one to induce or suppress feeling
in order to sustain the outward countenance that produces the proper
state of mind in others" (Hochschild, 1983: 6–7). As such, however,
it is subject to prescription and control by dominant groups who seek
to profit from it. Consequently, emotional work is transformed into
its opposite—not a source of human bonding and satisfaction, but of
alienation and eventual emotional burnout. Women, she argues, face
much higher costs in this work than do men: partly because the display
of emotion is an integral expectation of gender stereotyped "women's

work" in caring and personal service occupations, partly because of women's difficulty in escaping the socially constructed gendered role of nurturing others established early on in family life, and partly because women have to rely more on their emotional resources, lacking equity with men in economic, cultural, and social capital.

Hochschild's is a Marxist-feminist analysis, which departs from the psychological accounts of emotion that have predominated, to place it in a sociological framework concerned with the influence of social structures on individual identities, roles, and actions under patriarchal capitalism. Little headway has since been made in analyzing the role of education in facilitating emotional labor, while the literature on caring work and the ethics of care largely perpetuates assumptions that it relies on inherent capacities of women, undifferentiated by class or "race" (Thompson, 1998). Although there has been a recent revival of sociological interest in emotional labor, this has tended to be limited to descriptive accounts in different settings, from barristers (Harris, 2002) to beauty therapists (Sharma and Black, 2001).

Given the lack of sustained research and theoretical development about learning to labor with feeling, it is interesting that Hochschild's work has recently come under attack for its focus on the exploitative aspects of such work. Price (2001) objects that the commercialization of feelings is a question of individual workers' agency rather than a product of social relations in the workplace:

> The commercialisation and marketisation of emotional relations provides a relatively new and particularly pernicious "fit" with individuals' prior tendencies to adopt an instrumental stance towards the other or indeed towards aspects of the self. I do not think it is adequate to explain such instrumentalisation with reference to "capitalism" alone; and it needs explaining. I also think that Arlie Hochschild has little to say about aspects of paid work that are rewarding—not in monetary terms, but *intrinsically* so. How and why do *individuals* exploit or enrich each other in their emotional relating, as a matter of course and also of choice? (165, original emphasis)

Using examples of teachers working with small children, and a psychoanalytical framework that homogenizes a series of particular experiences, Price argues that emotional labor is undertaken with pleasure by children as well as teachers in the classroom, and is in fact a matter of

> very ordinary, universal capacities for relating to others as deserving of recognition, empathy and respect...Such emotional sensitivity is not a specialist skill or "intelligence" that can be factored off or

straightforwardly taught. This emotional labor gives a moral dimension to "human services" work. (179)

These comments appear to dismiss the concept of emotional intelligence, which is the discourse that has come to dominate current discussions of feelings in the workplace. It is epitomized in the work of Goleman (1996), who argues that emotional skills and competencies need to be recognized alongside, and connected to, other areas of competence in order to maximize productivity. It is impossible to engage in a full analysis and critique of such business management theories within the remit of this article (see Cameron, 2000; Martin et al., 2000; and Hughes, 2005). However, we can note that this discourse also constitutes a celebration of emotional labor that resists acknowledging its costs to the employee.

Notable exceptions to the turn away from critical analyses of emotion—those that focus in particular on structures of class and gender—in learning and work can be found in the work of Inge Bates (1990, 1991, 1994) and Bev Skeggs (1997). Both present evidence that substantiates Hochschild's view that the use of emotion at work is both pre-formed by social conditioning in the family and re-formed through education and training for particular occupational roles. In particular, they refute the notion that emotional labor is a universal or intrinsically human response to others.

Bates's (1990, 1991, 1994) study is of a youth training scheme (YTS) in care of the elderly. The "care girls" involved were working-class girls who had left school with few qualifications and been rejected from their preferred career options, such as childcare. They had to get used to a number of tasks they initially found very unpleasant and distressing, and much of their learning centered on coping with incontinence, violence, and death. To do this, they had to learn above all to control and manage their own feelings of disgust, anger, sorrow and fear, and reconstruct them differently. They also had to control, manage, and reconstruct the feelings of their patients.

Bates argues that vocational and educational training (VET) contributed two significant social and cultural processes to learning the labor of elderly care. First, it exercised a "screening" effect, recruiting and then further sifting those girls who had suitable dispositions. Second, it also operated in a disciplinary way to socialize suitable girls into the work, and exclude those who were unable to adapt to the prevailing vocational culture. Although their off-the-job tutors and the assessment criteria for their National Vocational Qualification conveyed an idealized and sensitive version of caring *for* people as also caring *about* them, the culture of the workplace demanded a more realistic "tough-ness," detachment, and resilience. Those who were "mardy" (i.e., too sensitive) were characterized by other trainees as "bleeding, whining Minnies," and tended to drop out. Girls who were too "tough" and, for example, reacted violently when provoked by patients, were also filtered out of the program.

Those most likely to settle into the job were from families in the most disadvantaged fractions of the working-class: girls who had already had to care for elders or siblings, and had learned in particular to engage in self-denial rather than resistance to fulfill this role. A certain classed and gendered predisposition appeared necessary, then, *but not suffi-cient*, for success in training for elder care. Processes of habituation to the vocational culture through VET both on and off the job were required for them to adjust their disposition further, become the "right person for the job," and feel that the job was "right for them."

Skeggs (1997) studied a group of young women who had entered general caring courses at a FE college as a "choice" by default, having similarly been confronted by schooling that failed them, a collapsed youth labor market that offered only unemployment as an alternative, and college "options" that were determined by professionals' percep-tions of their abilities, aptitudes, and prior experiences of caring. Like the "care girls," many of their experiences on work placements were traumatic, and to these emotional demands they brought classed and gendered predispositions. Here too, their courses framed, constrained, and produced particular selves re-formed from those dispositions.

Skeggs argues that, in a historical context where the cause of inequalities faced by working-class people is constantly represented as their own moral deviancy, dominant discourses construct working-class women either as posing a threat of further moral pollution or as a civilizing social force—depending on the degree to which they take responsibility for the moral welfare of others.

The college courses these young women follow also forge an indis-soluble association between caring for and caring about others. Being the "right kind of person" is at least as important as doing the right things: "the practices of caring become inseparable from personal dis-positions" (Skeggs, 1997: 56).

The requisite dispositions are well learned, and as in the "care girls" study, they are dominated by notions of altruism and selflessness, and of intimate social relations with those cared for and about. Emotional dispositions such as being kind and loving, warm and friendly, gentle and affectionate are universally cited by the students as qualities of a caring person. Despite the fact that here, as in the YTS, they constitute an impossible ideal, these dispositions and emotions are constructed as "natural" and "intuitive," even as much of the curriculum is devoted to teaching them:

> The caring self is produced through care for others. It is generated through both self-production and self-denial. The selflessness required to be a caring self is a gendered disposition...[C]are of the self...is the prerogative of someone who does not have to care for others to be seen as worthy of respect. [These] women...have to continually prove themselves as respectable through their caring performances. (Skeggs, 1997: 64)

With this emphasis on respectability, Skeggs adds a further layering to the understanding of education for the deployment of emotion at work by focusing on the bourgeois moral imperatives that underpin it. She shows how frequent and detailed teacher-student discussions about "good" and "bad" ways to care constantly reinforce pressure on the girls to demonstrate their suitability in terms of moral propriety: "The curriculum is organized in such a way that certain dispositions are invalidated and denied, while others are valorized, advised and legitimated" to produce a *respectable* self (Skeggs, 1997: 68).

This is key for Skeggs's analysis—and an important challenge to Price's (2001) unproblematized "moral dimension" of caring work—since aspiration to respectability historically acts as a marker of those (working-class people) who are suspected (by the middle classes) of not having it. One issue for middle-class women, of course, is that many of them rely on working-class women to provide care for their children (see, for example, Vincent and Warren, 2000). We could argue here that, as a consequence, nursery nurses face a particularly strong imperative to be—and to appear to be—"nice girls." Skeggs highlights the importance of correctly coded dress and demeanor as signifiers of "proper" moral dispositions, and although she only discusses these in terms of young women's social lives, we shall see later how crucial they were to the performance of childcare for the nursery nurses in our study.

This analysis also provides a further explanation of agency as well as social structure in the process of learning emotional labor, going beyond notions of individual occupational adjustment to reveal historical and collective processes at work. The care students embrace the disciplinary regulation of their courses, precisely because being seen to care properly for others in the public setting of the workplace allows them to gain respectability, and to rescue themselves *and others* from the mass of the nonrespectable. The initial disappointments, the low status, low pay and poor conditions, and the ongoing emotional demands of their work can therefore be experienced positively, offering pleasurable satisfaction, a sense of worth, even superiority, and Skeggs takes full account of the fact that these positive aspects dominated the students' accounts of their experiences.

Without denying that such pleasures are genuinely felt, this interpretation confronts the frequent objection to critical analyses, that women do take pleasure in caring for others, especially for small children, and appreciate the rewards that loving relationships in such contexts can bring.

Walkerdine and Lucey (1989) also address this point in the context of mothering. They express the reality of both sides of the emotional work that it entails, and argue that socially constructed imperatives are the facets of care that are misrecognized and therefore neglected:

> It might be argued that mothering is a very pleasurable activity and we are making it sound totally oppressive. We certainly agree that such pleasure is crucial and yet we would also argue...that such pleasure is also produced and regulated—correct and incorrect, normal and abnormal—and cannot be seen as given. (Walkerdine and Lucey, 1989: 30–31)

Learning to Labor in the Nursery

This returns us to the early years debate highlighted in the introduction to this chapter. In the context of the literature reviewed above, my purpose here is to investigate how the education and training of nursery nurses functions to prepare them for this work. How does it mediate their previous experiences and predispositions? What does it teach them about the "right kind of person" they have to become? I continue by discussing the learning of a group of trainee nursery nurses, almost all of them teenage girls, throughout their two-year course. In analyzing and interpreting their experiences, I draw on sociological theories of the relationship between structure and agency, including Marxist-feminist analyses, as well as the theories of Bourdieu and feminist readings of his work. Diane Reay's (2000) work on emotional capital is of special interest here, as a major contribution to new sociological theorizations of feeling.

The data presented are drawn from a case study of one of 17 learning sites participating in the TLC project. The methodological approach of the project is founded on partnership between researchers based in both universities and FE colleges, and includes the active participation of the site tutors (see Hodkinson and James, 2003). Some of the data are qualitative: repeated semistructured interviews with the tutor and a sample of six students in the first and last term of each year, and two interviews with the tutor's line manager; researcher observations of the college course and work placements three times a term; and the tutor's own ongoing reflective journal.

Other data are quantitative: a questionnaire survey of all students in the site at the start, midpoint, and end of their course, and college and national statistical data. All of the students identified themselves as white British, except one who identified herself as mixed race, and one student was male. The analysis is based on synthesizing categories emerging across the data with narratives constructed by immersion in individual students' accounts, and discussions of the interpretation with the site tutor. All personal names have been changed here, and the college is anonymized to protect confidentiality. Let us turn now to the learning site itself.

The CACHE Diploma Learning Site

Joanne Lowe is the tutor for this learning site, one of two groups who started the Level Three CACHE (Council for Awards in Childcare and Education) Diploma[2] in September 2001. This is a full-time, two-year course, half of which is taught in college and half of which comprises work placements in nurseries and primary schools. It is an overwhelmingly female group, and only one of the 20 students who originally joined Joanne's group this year is male. The course is located in the Department for Health and Social Care, and recruits mainly school-leavers. Most students originally had higher career aspirations to become professional teachers or nurses, but performed poorly in their school examinations, and became obliged to lower their ambitions. The large majority of students go on to work in private nurseries, looking after middle-class children, although most of their work placements are in the public sector, working with children from more disadvantaged families. A recent Office for Standards in Education (Ofsted), inspection rated teaching on the course as excellent, and it is held in high regard by the CACHE national examination board and by local employers.

Joanne and two of her three colleagues in the CACHE teaching team are former nursery nurses themselves, and they offer valued "insider" expertise. Joanne dedicates a great deal of time to intensive academic support for individual students, some of whom entered this advanced level course with only two passes in the General Certificate in Secondary Education (GCSE) examinations at 16 plus (the usual minimum requirement for a Level Three course is four passes), and most of whom struggle with the written work required. She also helps organize a wide variety of extracurricular activities, and provides a great deal of pastoral support for students and their parents. She is perceived as a very caring tutor, in whom students can confide. The promotion of equal opportunities and antidiscriminatory practice is central to her teaching role and to the team's ethos.

The Vocational Culture of Childcare

The site reflects the fact that childcare in the United Kingdom is a heavily gender-stereotyped occupation: 99% of nursery nurses are female. Within the broader field of early years education, it is low-status work, and nursery nurses are often subordinate to qualified teachers or health workers. They are also poorly paid, earning little more— sometimes even less—than the minimum wage in the private sector (Low Pay Commission, 2005), which has come to dominate provision and transform into an "edubusiness" (Ball and Vincent, 2000) in recent years. Nevertheless, nursery nursing is an attractive occupation to many working-class girls. This may be partly because it is seen as a kind of "labor aristocracy": work that is still highly preferable to more mundane work in worse conditions for those who are underqualified (O'Connor and Goodwin, 2002). This in turn resonates with powerful images of a more glamorous niche in childcare, in which young women from bourgeois families train at élite private colleges and travel the world as nannies to the wealthy, as Princess Diana did before her marriage to Prince Charles.

The CACHE tutors place great emphasis on their view that nursery nursing is a *profession*, and many of their efforts are devoted to raising its perceived status. All had worked previously in the public rather than the private sector, and Joanne in particular has a passionate commitment to the provision of high-quality childcare as a means of combating social exclusion in disadvantaged inner-city communities. In fact, she first became an FE tutor when she had moved to London and refused to apply for jobs in private nurseries. To a certain extent, as in health care occupations and professions such as nursing, acceptance of low pay is taken as a sign of genuine commitment to caring for others

(Frykholm and Nitzler, 1993). Although tutors recognize that nursery nurses are treated as "second-class citizens," they also argue that this means they care *about* the children they care *for*:

> *Joanne*: I mean, if you've worked as a nursery nurse, the money's rubbish. You don't do it, you know, for any other reason than you love working with children and families... Our students are really dedicated to the work.

Just as in other areas of caring work, a feminized, nurturing ideal dominates official discourses about childcare:

> There is an extraordinary international consensus among child-care researchers and practitioners about what quality child-care is: it is warm, supportive interactions with adults in a safe, healthy, and stimulating environment, where early education and trusting relationships combine to support individual children's physical, social, emotional and intellectual development. (Scarr, 1998: 102)

This ideal is enshrined in measures of quality that are widely used in childcare. Apart from various structural factors, the education of nursery nurses themselves is held to be a major determinant of quality (Blau, 1999). Consequently, one set of measures used internationally, the Caregiver Interaction Scale (CIS), focuses on the personal attributes that should be developed in the nursery nurse herself. She should display sensitivity, gentleness, enthusiasm, effort, and enjoy contact with children. Harshness and detachment are taken as contraindications of quality (see Tietze et al., 1996). This establishes a norm for the kind of person that one has to be—or to become—to succeed in childcare. The emphasis on "warmth," "supportive and trusting relationships," and the emotional development of the child, alongside these personal attributes, suggests that the deployment of emotion by the worker herself is a key part of the job. In the context of the public sector childcare where students undertake their placements, this emotional dedication is often discussed in the college classroom as a remedy for the moral deficits of working-class parents, a discourse that is quickly absorbed and reproduced by the students.

The CACHE tutors focus a great deal on this "unwritten" curriculum of developing such personal attributes in their students, especially at the start of the course. They discuss how each group is "gelling," and try to foster students' ability to "bond" emotionally with each other and with their tutors. Joanne's team leader explained the importance of this process:

> It's the nature of the job. If you're working as an early years worker, you're always going to work as part of a team, and you have to get on with people. You have to get on with other adults, not just children...I think the sort of hidden curriculum of an early years course is getting to know people and working as a team.

Joanne describes the successful "gel" exemplified by her second year group, at the same time giving a sense of how important close personal relationships with other women are for her:

> My second years, I love every minute teaching with them, and we've got some right characters in there. We get on really well, we do the work, you know, I kept every single one of them that I started with. We've got really good relationships, and it's not difficult to go in and teach them. You know, they're respectful, but we have a laugh as well...I've got a feeling this lot [*the first years*] are going to be the same. They've gelled, people that are teaching them have come in and said, like Maddie teaches both groups, "Your group have really gelled already," you know, they're chatty but they're doing the work.

However, a number of students within the group actively resisted these processes. They were mainly girls with different career aspirations, such as nursing, whose low levels of achievement in their previous school or college courses had prevented them from gaining places on other level 3 academic or health and social care courses, which all had higher entry requirements than the CACHE Diploma. Although, in theory at least, the CACHE Diploma could enable them to progress onto nurse education and training, the strong focus on nursery nursing, and the substantial work-based element of the course, did not fit their occupational intentions, nor their sense of a worthwhile occupation, and—understandably—they made little effort to "fit in." As the first-year group completed their first term, Joanne became particularly frustrated with two students, Sonya and Gaby. They led a small group who were persistently disruptive or absent, and who bullied other students, despite lengthy efforts on Joanne's part to get them to integrate better.[3] Eventually, she felt she had to set the college disciplinary procedures in motion:

> With Gaby, I just tried and tried, and it's just not worked. It's just a real clash...If they do go, I'm so looking forward to next year, because

I think that I'll really bond with the group now, and Gaby and Sonya, they've stopped me from doing that, and they've stopped the rest...I think the group will be nicer...It'll definitely be more cohesive if they go.

Developing close emotional bonds among the group is therefore seen by tutors as an essential foundation for the work that students have to learn to perform in the nursery. There is much here that resonates with mothering on the part of Joanne herself (see again Walkerdine and Lucey, 1989), in the mixture of pride and stress that accompanies a sense of total responsibility for her students, and its accents of regulatory socialization (discussed more fully in Colley, 2002). What, then, were students' own accounts of their learning during the first year of the course?

Learning the Management of Feelings

When students discussed the new skills and knowledge they had gained, they talked about practical skills (such as preparing play materials, food, displays) and more cognitive learning (such as health matters, child development theory, equal opportunities legislation) acquired at college. However, alongside this prescribed curriculum, and the unwritten curriculum of emotional bonding, a further "hidden" curriculum emerged as students talked about what they had learned as they participated in their work placements. Their narratives centered on coping with the emotional demands of the job, and revealed a vocational culture of detachment in the workplace that contrasts somewhat with the nurturing ideal that is officially promoted.

In a group tutorial discussion soon after the start of the course, following the students' first few days in placement, there were many expressions of delight at being with children. But the session also revealed events they experienced as far from pleasant: taking little boys to the toilet; finding oneself covered in children's "puke" and "wee"; and being hit by children. These responses illustrate the domination of bourgeois sensibilities, in which bodily functions, illness, and strong emotions are experienced as unpleasant and distressing.[4] Joanne was at great pains to emphasize the "correct" behavior students should display in these situations:

Joanne: Don't forget, you've got to stay cool and say, [*nonchalant tone*] "Oh, that's not a very nice thing to do, is it?," and keep your own feelings under control.

By the end of their first year, the management of feeling had become a central theme in all the female students' narratives. They often talked about the difficulties and stress of dealing with physical injuries, tears, tantrums, aggression, disobedience, and provocations:

> The morning group [of children] are still tired and maungy, and in the afternoon, they're giddy and hyper...I was so tired after a week working at nursery...I don't know if I could do it again. (Female student, white, aged 16, Year 1, interview 2)

> I asked one girl to go and get a book because we were waiting for story time. Well, she kicked up: "I'm not getting a book! I'm not getting a book, I'm staying here!" So I took her into the cloakroom and I sat down with her, and by this point she was really, really hysterical, crying because she couldn't stay outside. (Female student, white, aged 17, Year 1, interview 2)

This involves working on their own and the children's feelings to suppress extreme emotions and evoke calmer feelings. It requires conscious effort, repeated practice, and a degree of self-surveillance and self-denial on the part of the students:

> Sometimes I shout at the children, but that's just me...Cause the nursery nurses don't always raise their voice as much as I do. I could probably just tone it down a little bit, still try and realise when I'm speaking loudly, try and quieten it down. (Female student, white, aged 32, Year 1, interview 2)

> Children can wind you up! You'd say something to them, and then they're really, really cheeky. They've learned how to answer you back, so they're gonna do it. And they *can* wind you up, and suppose you've got a short temper? But saying that, I've got a short temper, but I don't let them try it. (Female student, white, aged 17, Year 1, interview 2)

As part of this process, the students' affection for small children and enjoyment of play also had to be limited, in order to take on a consciously developmental role:

> Well, like, you're taught you can't be all lovey-dovey with the children. You've got to be quite stern if they've done something wrong. (Female student, white, aged 16, Year 1, interview 2)

> That's what I've kind of learned, now...I teach, although I was playing with the children. If you went and just played with the kids and just not said owt [anything], like "How many bricks are there?", they wouldn't

really ever learn, would they? So you've just got to really think about it. Make 'em count the bricks, and say how many bricks there are, and also play at the same time. (Female student, white, aged 16, Year 1, interview 2)

In these quotations, just as for Bates's (1990, 1991, 1994) and Skeggs's (1997) care trainees, there is a mismatch between the official, idealized version of the nursery nurse conveyed by the CIS—where harshness and detachment are deemed to be negative indicators—and the vocational culture expressed in the workplace, where some degree of harshness and detachment is essential to doing the job and coping with its emotional demands. Elfer et al. (2003) acknowledge this dual orientation in their "key person" approach:

> The emotional demands are great too. The key person is in a professional role but she must develop a very personal and intimate relationship with each of the babies and children with whom she is working. There are bound to be some painful feelings involved, as the work cannot be done in an emotionally anaesthetised way...Maintaining an appropriate professional intimacy, which every child needs in order to feel special, while keeping an appropriate professional distance, requires emotional work of the highest calibre. (27)

At the same time, students were constantly encouraged by their tutors to believe that nursery nursing was a deeply worthwhile job that improved the lives of the children in their care, especially those from the most disadvantaged backgrounds. This notion of the moral worth of the enterprise is likely to have been conducive to students' commitment and their ability to come to terms with the emotional tensions they encountered in the workplace. The power of that official curriculum and students' acceptance of it is demonstrated in both qualitative and quantitative data. They show that students felt not only that the content of their course was firmly controlled by their tutors and the CACHE examination board, but they also believed strongly that it should be so.

By the start of their second year, students still agreed that working on their own and the children's emotions was a central aspect of their work. But they declared it was "easy" for them now, explaining that they simply became a "different person" when they entered into the workplace, reacting differently to provocation or distress than they would at college or at home. At the end of the course, those interviewed explained that the patience and self-control they had learned in the nursery was now part of their persona at college and at home.

They felt they had become nursery nurses. Given the focus of the project on learning cultures in FE, we have been unable to follow these students into their longer-term employment in childcare. However, another study has noted that the nursery nurses' increased affection for the infants also made them more distressed about the inadequacy of parenting that some of the infants received.

> Two young nursery staff spoke of spending sleepless weekends worrying about the happiness and safety of "their" babies. Commitment to these disadvantaged infants was achieved at considerable emotional cost. (Hopkins, 1998: 106, cited in Elfer et al., 2003: 55)

We also know from tutors' accounts of their own prior experience of working in the sector that illness due to stress and burnout are common among nursery nurses. While employers in the public sector may tolerate periods of sick leave for staff to recuperate, such tolerance is unlikely in the private nurseries where most of these students are going to work. Mentoring and supervision may help to mitigate the negative impact of emotional labor, but these require resources that private employers may also be reluctant to commit, and address the symptoms rather than the cause itself.

There is also a hint here that these working-class girls were identifying with those who oppressed both them and their charges' families, at the same time as blaming the victims of poverty and discrimination for poor parenting. We can note that, while the overwhelming majority of the trainees were white, the nurseries and schools they worked in often had significant proportions—even a majority, in some cases—of ethnic minority children, while the few ethnic minority workers observed in these settings were almost all unpaid parent-volunteers. The trainees distinguished themselves, as did Skeggs's (1997) young women, by characterizing others from working-class backgrounds as unfit to care for their own children—an assumption that often seems to underpin rationales for early childhood education.

The Role of VET in Filtering Gendered Class Fractions

The subtle processes of screening and discipline identified by Bates (1990, 1991, 1994) and Skeggs (1997) also underpin learning to labor in the nursery. Gender is crucial, and had already filtered students well before they applied for the course, notwithstanding some small success in the CACHE team's campaign to attract boys to the course. Girls had often looked after younger siblings and done part-time work babysitting or in various crèche or after-school club facilities.

Some had also had brief work experience in care of the elderly, which they described with revulsion: they would probably have been viewed as "bleeding, whining Minnies" (Bates, 1990) among the YTS care girls. Fractional locations within the working class play an important role in this regard, and (like the care girls and students above) they observed and judged one another in respect of subtle social differentiations. Nursery nurses, looking after other women's children, are supposed to be "nice girls," and one group rapidly defined themselves as "nice," while dismissing more disadvantaged students as "rough." "Nice" students described themselves as living at home with both parents, usually in the leafier suburbs of the city. Their parents were in white-collar jobs, such as clerical staff or police officers. They felt well cared for, even spoiled, and they knew that their college tutors cared for them too. But their talk about some of their fellow students reveals a process of subtle class distinction (Bourdieu, 1986):

> I come from a totally different background to some of these, because I mean, I don't know what it's like to be without a mum or a dad, I live with both my parents. A lot of them are just one parent families and it's like half of the places where they live, I've never ever heard of, or I don't even know where they are, but a lot of people say, "Oh, it's really rough, it's really rough." (Female student, white, aged 17, Year 1, interview 2)

> Some people come from different places and have different upbringings, and, you know...you just look at them and—look at them first and think, "Ooh, you know [*laughs*], don't want to be friends with *them*" [*laughs*]. If I met them on the street I wouldn't talk to them. I don't know what to say without sounding—, I seem really awful, but I don't know, it's just the mannerisms, and the way they talk and the—like some of them...I don't like swearing and they swear. (Male student, white, aged 17, Year 1, interview 2)

Such differences of location within the working class were reflected in physical appearance, in clothing, makeup, and jewelry, which are taken as signifiers of social status and moral respectability in our society (Bourdieu, 1986; Skeggs, 1997). These formed part of the surveillance and discipline that operated in both college and placements through constant discussions of the "right" and "wrong" way to appear. Students were allowed to wear what they pleased at college, and at first celebrated their release from school uniform. Joanne would comment on high-fashion items of clothing worn, sometimes admiringly, and then ask the group, "But would you wear that in placement?" Gradually, students began to tone down their appearance, and noticed those who did not:

> I don't know if you've seen Chloë, she wears all the black make-up and the big baggy pants and stuff, but then to be professional you wouldn't walk into a nursery looking like that, you'd scare the kids to death! (Female student, white, aged 17, Year 1, interview 2)

On one placement visit, after giving lots of positive feedback to an otherwise excellent student, Joanne ticked her off for wearing a revealing cropped T-shirt:

> *Joanne*: Next time, though, I don't want to see you wearing that. Not very nice for parents coming in, seeing acres of belly every time you lean across the table.

By the end of the first year, observations in college showed that almost all the remaining students had adopted a modest "uniform" of tracksuit bottoms, T-shirts, and hooded fleece tops in sober or pastel colors. (In school settings, this uniform also contrasted with the smart, formal clothing invariably worn by qualified teachers in charge, marking out the subordinate role and economic disadvantage of the nursery nurse as well as her moral suitability.)

However, as the year progressed, a number of the girls Othered as "rough"—including Gaby, Sonya, and some of their more disaffected group—had resisted developing emotional bonds with the group or with Joanne, despite her considerable patience with them and her efforts to get them to integrate. By the end of the year several of them had either left or been excluded through the disciplinary process. Those remaining were working hard to behave more collaboratively in class, but the one member who was part of our sample was reluctant to discuss what had happened, and continued to see nursery nursing as a "job with no prospects."

Meanwhile, two of the "nice" group had also quit the course. One was the student who had complained that "Children can wind you up!" and who was aware of her own short temper. She said that she had simply "had enough" of working with small children, and had been unable to motivate herself to do the written work required. Another had got into a fight outside college, was cautioned by police as a result, and when this came to light at college, decided to withdraw from the course rather than face certain expulsion. In her final research interview, she explained her view of her exclusion:

> If I look at it from [the tutors'] point of view, it's, well it's right, because I wouldn't like my kids to be looked after by someone that goes round hitting people. (Female student, mixed race, aged 18, Year 1, interview 2)

Class fractions and gender may combine rather differently in the childcare site than in care work settings, but the combination appears to operate just as effectively to include some while excluding others.

Theorizing Emotional Labor in Childcare

The experiences of the successful CACHE students match Hochschild's (1983) original definition of emotional labor well. They learned to evoke calmness or cheerfulness, and suppress anger or embarrassment within themselves, in order to project a countenance that would also calm, comfort, or discipline the small children in their care. The physicality of the work combines with its emotionality, as they care for the "undisciplined bodies" of children (and as might others care for the undisciplined bodies of elders) (Tronto, 1989). Even the most "suitable" girls have to adapt their dispositions further as they encounter the emotional challenges of the workplace. The pragmatic detachment required to cope with "puke," "pee," and punches is mitigated by the idealized image of the perfectly sensitive and gentle nursery nurse, and by the deeply caring culture created by college tutors.

Elsewhere, Colley et al. (2003), in a cross-project analysis of a variety of vocational learning sites, adapted Bourdieu's term "habitus" to develop the concept of "vocational habitus" as a way of expressing a powerful aspect of the vocational culture: the combination of idealized and realized dispositions to which students must orient themselves in order to become "the right person for the job." At the same time, we argued that such a concept must also include aspects of sensibility—of feeling and emotion—as well as the practical sense of what it takes to do a particular kind of work. But how can we theorize the nature of this emotional labor itself more clearly?

Reay (2000) has also drawn on Bourdieu's sociology in order to analyze feelings in the context of studying the (unpaid) emotional work that mothers from different social classes do to engage with their children's education. She used Nowotny's (1981) extension of Bourdieu's forms of capital—economic, cultural, and social—to include emotional capital. In this sense, emotions are regarded as resources, or a set of assets, which can be circulated, accumulated, and exchanged for other forms of capital within a particular field that allows those resources to "count." As Hochschild (1983) also argued, women typically possess greater emotional resources than men, not least because they tend to have access to fewer of the other forms of capital. Therefore emotional capital has a "looser link" with social class than Bourdieu's other forms of capital. In patriarchal capitalist society, the oppression of women makes it less likely that their resources can be fully deployed as capital, since women are generally positioned as subordinate players in all fields. This reminds us that, from a Marxist perspective at least, capital is *not* essentially an economistic metaphor, but expresses sets of *social relations* and inequalities of power.

This analysis could explain the role of VET here as allowing young women—those with particular emotional resources suited to child-care—to develop and refine these resources, but only to deploy them as *capital* within a very restricted and subordinate field. They may, for example, exchange them for economic "capital," but only for very low wages; or for more cultural capital, but only for vocational courses and at institutions that have relatively low status.

The weakness of this concept of emotional capital, however, is that it locates the exploitation of women's resources in those to whom they devote their emotional work:

> The gendered processes which make up involvement in schooling are exemplified in the complex contradictions of "a capital" which is all about investment in others rather than self—the one capital that *is used up* in interaction with others and is often for the benefit of those others. (Reay, 2000: 583, emphasis added)

This assumes that the problem of capitalism and its unequal social relations is a problem of *consumption*, and that emotions are *goods* that are generated by women, but tend to be consumed by others. Such an analysis would suggest that it is the children for whom nursery nurses care who consume their emotional work, a view that risks misplacing the root of the problem from a perspective of both class and gender. Rather than showing how structure and agency combine to produce and reproduce social inequalities, it tends to lead us back to Price's (2001) very different argument that the deployment of emotion in caring work is a matter of individual choice and morality on the part of both the carer and the cared for.

It may be more helpful to follow Heller's (1979) argument that emotions are *neither* natural/innate *nor* undifferentiated resources to which different genders or social classes have differential access and affordances. However universal, inevitable, and irresistible they appear to us, in fact quite different repertoires of feeling are available to different class fractions and genders within them. They are related to the mode of production in any given society, to multiple divisions of labor within it, and to different relationships to the means of production. In occupations like childcare and care of the elderly, the management of one's own and others' feelings is not a private adjunct to work, nor a subcategory of caring. It is a key feature of the workplace, a form of paid labor, or to be more accurate, of labor *power*—the capacity to labor, which can be ever more exploited by those who own the means of production for private profit (Marx, 1865, 1975). In Britain, while pay for nursery nurses is barely above the minimum wage, the profits for those who own nurseries are handsome: analysts Laing and Buisson (2005) estimated the childcare market in 2004 to be worth £2.7 billion, representing a fivefold increase over the last decade, and the most profitable in Europe. This suggests that the "highest calibre" emotional work expected by Elfer et al. (2003) is indeed exploited by those who sell love in the nursery.

Of course, children may benefit from the emotional labor of their carers, paid or unpaid. But this benefit is its private use-value. And as already been acknowledged, the carer may indeed find pleasure in that labor, at least until its more stressful aspects take their toll. It is only to be expected that deploying one's allocated repertoire of emotion must feel appropriate and deeply natural. It is the appropriation of emotional labor put to work for *exchange*-value—for profit—that turns it into a commodity, and a potential source of alienation. Although the limited nature of this study means that we do not have data about any eventual costs of producing themselves as "nice girls" within narrow conventional notions of femininity for successful students, the data do show how some students resisted this and found themselves excluded as a result. There is also considerable evidence from research in other contexts to support Hochschild's (1983) contention that painful experiences of guilt and stress are frequent outcomes. Moreover, in caring occupations rather than service work, these outcomes can have serious deleterious effects for the child, patient, or client (Mann, 2004).

But in childcare, as in other forms of caring work, the concept of emotional labor helps us understand how this work is learned and performed. These trainee nursery nurses were not only working upon the emotions of the children in their care, nor were they simply "handing over" emotional resources for consumption. The primary "raw material" on which these girls learned to labor was *themselves*. Successful trainees possessed particular dispositions—enjoying the company of children, creativity, outgoing personalities. They also brought with them more collective or social predispositions, in particular classed and gendered expectations of a destiny caring for children (cf. Steedman, 1982).

Disposition and predisposition are twin aspects of Bourdieu's notion of habitus, and elsewhere Reay (1998) offers a definition of gendered habitus that helps to explain the deeply embodied nature of emotional labor:

> The concept of gendered habitus holds powerful structural influences within its frame. Gendered habitus includes a set of complex, diverse predispositions. It involves understandings of identity premised on familial legacy and early childhood socialization. As such it is primarily a dynamic concept, a rich interfacing of past and present, interiorized and permeating both body and psyche. (141)

The habitus that students brought with them to their VET course was necessary, but not sufficient, to become a nursery nurse, and exemplifies this dynamic. They had to mobilize existing dispositions and predispositions, but also work further on their own feelings in order to learn to labor appropriately. This process is facilitated by the occupational or vocational culture (Bates, 1994): a "guiding ideology" of practice (James, 1989) that organizes the norms and expectations of a particular sphere of work. The "international consensus" about quality childcare (Scarr, 1998) indicates one such vocational culture. Furthermore, it combines with broader cultural imperatives that construct emotional labor as one of the few ways for working-class women to work at proving their moral respectability and worth (Skeggs, 1997). In fact, this may be a prime example of the form of gender oppression that Bourdieu (2001) terms "symbolic violence"—a form of violence that is not directly physical or visible, and may even become imperceptible to those who suffer it, but that assures their subordination nonetheless. It is likely to continue as long as capitalist edubusiness has an interest in making profits by offering motherly love for sale in the nursery.

Conclusion

The final conclusion I draw relates to the FE arenas in which nursery nursing is learned, and the responsibilities of those who manage that business and educate girls for it. For all the enthusiasm that surrounds many discussions of emotional work in childcare, when we think about how the capacity to labor on feelings is learned, we need to consider it in the context of historical changes that have taken place in VET in recent years. The solutions posed today by the Equal Opportunities Commission (Miller et al., 2005) focus on providing better information and guidance to encourage girls to enter nontraditional careers. Yet, as long as 20 years ago, Griffin (1985) argued that, in the face of trajectories that were highly structured by class, gender, and other inequalities, such responses were inadequate. Girls do not need directing toward male-dominated occupations that most will quite rationally resist because of the discrimination and harassment they may face. Instead, they need opportunities to understand why they desire the destinies they pursue; to ask critical questions about what those destinies both offer and demand; and to ask why their education contributes so often to the reproduction of social inequality.

However, the spaces for young women to explore such issues in VET have receded rather than expanded. As post-16 curricula have increasingly become dominated by narrow and often behaviorist approaches focused on skills, competencies, and economic instrumentalism, social and political education has been virtually eradicated. There is little scope in 16–19 education for young people to engage with these critical questions in emancipatory ways. Instead, much of what they learn, as on the CACHE Diploma, reproduces docile subjectivities and uncomplaining caregiving.

Most young women today find themselves caught up in a disempowering paradox. They believe equal opportunities exist, but still experience stereotyping and discrimination, and so they tend to believe that these are personal rather than collective or political issues. Like Griffin's (1985) "typical girls," they too need opportunities to recognize and analyze their own gendered experiences and the vocational conditions of other women in terms of structural inequities, examining their personal experience and disposition as socially constructed and collectively shared through political and economic currents. (Fenwick, 2004: 181).

Those who, unlike myself, *are* experts and practitioners in the field of early childhood might also use this evidence to pursue other questions that it raises: whose responsibility is it to initiate change? What can policy-makers, employers, course tutors or the CACHE awarding body do to make visible, support, and advocate better rewards for the emotional skills demanded of nursery nurses? Who else might have responsibility for initiating change? In respect of the debates reviewed at the start of this chapter, there are also more general questions to be answered: Why is attachment valued so highly in the care of children? Why is *vicarious* attachment valued so highly? Which factors interfere with attachment, and have these changed over time? Further research is also needed to explore how girls originally learn about attachment, *what* they have learned about it, and how their experiences influence their development as caregivers. It would also be useful to research other aspects of emotional labor in childcare, such as interactions with parents, which are central to the work of qualified nursery nurses, but in which these trainees were only marginally involved.

In a context where policy-makers have now opened up vocational pathways from the age of 14 (Department for Education and Skills, 2005), there is an urgent need for those involved in occupations like childcare, and in education and training for them, to think more critically about learning to labor with feeling—and for more research to understand both the processes of such learning and its consequences in subsequent employment.

Acknowledgments

The project "Transforming Learning Cultures in Further Education" was funded by the Economic and Social Research Council, Grant L139 25 1025, in the Teaching and Learning Research Programme. I am grateful for the contribution of the entire project team to discussions on the analysis of the data. I am very grateful to Joanne Lowe and her students and colleagues for their generous participation in the research. My thanks are also due to Inge Bates, Carole Vincent, Diane Reay, and Ann-Marie Bathmaker, as well as to the editor and anonymous referees of this special issue of the journal, for their helpful comments on previous drafts of this chapter.

Notes

1. This chapter originally appeared as Colley (2006).
2. CACHE used to be known as NNEB—the Nursery Nursing Education Board. The diploma is one of the most commonly recognized qualifications for entry into nursery nursing, which is a registered occupation in the United Kingdom.
3. The sample of students was selected at the cohort's entry to the course in discussion with Joanne Lowe. It is interesting that, as the group evolved, only one of our sample turned out to be in the less integrated group, and she was unwilling to discuss differences in the group.

4. This is not to suggest that working-class people do not experience such reactions, but to argue, following Heller (1979), that such sensibilities are constructed and imposed by dominant social groupings and their cultural norms. These might also be seen as particularly strong in advanced capitalist countries—it is interesting to note that the Latin American artist Frieda Kahlo lampooned the hygienic obsessions of U.S. society in a painting depicting a toilet on a pedestal.

References

Ball, S.J. and C. Vincent, C. (2000) "Educare" and Edubusiness: the Emergence of an Imperfect and Classed Market in Childcare Services? Paper presented at the British Educational Research Association Annual Conference, University of Cardiff, September 8–10.

Bates, I. (1990) No Bleeding, Whining Minnies: the Role of YTS in Class and Gender Reproduction. *British Journal of Education and Work*, 2: 91–110.

Bates, I. (1991) Closely Observed Training: an Exploration of Links between Social Structures, Training and Identity. *International Studies in Sociology of Education*, 1: 225–43.

Bates, I. (1994) A Job Which is "Right for Me"? Social Class, Gender and Individualization. In I. Bates and G. Riseborough (eds.) *Youth and Inequality*, 14–31 (Buckingham: Open University Press).

Blau, D.M. (1999) The Effect of Child Care Characteristics on Child Development. *Journal of Human Resources*, 34: 786–822.

Bourdieu, P. (1986) *Distinction: a Social Critique of the Judgement of Taste* (London: Routledge).

Bourdieu, P. (2001) *Masculine Domination* (Cambridge: Polity Press).

Cameron, D. (2000) *Good to Talk? Living and Working in a Communication Culture* (London: Sage).

Colley, H. (2002) From Childcare Practitioner to FE Tutor: Biography, Vocational Culture and Gender in the Transition of Professional Identities. Paper presented at the British Educational Research Association Annual Conference, University of Exeter, September 12–14.

Colley, H., D. James, M. Tedder, and K. Diment (2003) Learning as Becoming in Vocational Education and Training: Class, Gender and the Role of Vocational Habitus. *Journal of Vocational Education and Training*, 4: 471–96.

Dahlberg, G., P. Moss, and A. Pence (1999) *Beyond Quality in Early Childhood Education and Care: Postmodern Perspectives* (London: Falmer Press).

Department for Education and Skills (2005) *White Paper on 14–19 Education and Skills* (London: The Stationery Office).

Elfer, P., E. Goldschmied, and D. Selleck (2003) *Key Persons in the Nursery: Building Relationships for Quality Provision* (London: David Fulton).

Fenwick, T. (2004) What Happens to the Girls? Gender, Work and Learning in Canada's "New Economy." *Gender and Education*, 2, 169–86. (http://dx.doi.org/10.1080/09540250310001690564)

Frykholm, C.U. and R. Nitzler (1993) Working Life as a Pedagogical Discourse: Empirical Studies of Vocational and Career Education Based on Theories of Bourdieu and Bernstein. *Journal of Curriculum Studies*, 5: 433–44.

Goleman, D. (1996) *Emotional Intelligence: Why It Can Matter More Than IQ* (London: Bloomsbury).

Griffin, C. (1985) *Typical Girls* (London: Routledge).

Harris, L.C. (2002) The Emotional Labour of Barristers: an Exploration of Emotional Labour by Status Professionals. *Journal of Management Studies*, 4: 553–84. (http://dx.doi.org/10.1111/1467-6486.t01-1-00303)

Heller, A. (1979) *A Theory of Feelings* (Assen: Van Gorcum).

Hochschild, A.R. (1983) *The Managed Heart: Commercialization of Human Feeling* (Berkeley: University of California Press).

Hodkinson, P. and D. James (2003) Introduction: Transforming Learning Cultures in Further Education. *Journal of Vocational Education and Training*, 4: 389–406.

Hopkins, J. (1988) Facilitating the Development of Intimacy between Nurses and Infants in Day Nurseries. *Early Child Development and Care*, 33: 99–111.

Hughes, J. (2005) Bringing Emotion to Work: Emotional Intelligence, Employee Resistance and the Reinvention of Character. *Work, Employment and Society*, 3: 603–25. (http://dx.doi.org/10.1177/0950017005055675)

James, N. (1989) Emotional Labour: Skill and Work in the Social Regulation of Feelings. *Sociological Review*, 1: 15–42.

Laing and Buisson (2005) Statistics and Information: Childcare. (http://www.laingbuisson.co.uk/statisticsinformation/childcare/tabid/73/default.aspx, accessed March 10, 2005).

Low Pay Commission (2005) The Effects of the National Minimum Wage on Specific Sectors and on Small Firms: Childcare. (http://www.lowpay.gov.uk/lowpay/lowpay2005/c3_childcare.shtml, accessed March 10, 2005).

Mann, S. (2004) "People-work": Emotion Management, Stress and Coping, *British Journal of Guidance and Counselling*, 2: 205–21. (http://dx.doi.org/10.1080/0369880410001692247)

Martin, J., K. Knopoff, and C. Beckman (2000) Bounded Emotionality at the Body Shop. In S. Fineman (ed.) *Emotion in Organizations*, 115–40 (London: Sage).

Marx, K. (1865, 1975) *Wages, Price and Profit* (Moscow: Progress Publishers).

Miller, L., E. Pollard, F. Neathey, D. Hill, and H. Ritchie (2005) *Gender Segregation in Apprenticeships* (Manchester: Equal Opportunities Commission).

Nowotny, H. (1981) Women in Public Life in Australia. In C. Fuchs Epstein and R. Laub Coser (eds.) *Access to Power: Cross-national Studies of Women and Elites,* 149–65 (London: George Allen and Unwin).

O'Connor, H. and J. Goodwin (2002) "She Wants to Be Like Her Mum?" Girls' Transitions to Work in the 1960s, Unpublished Paper, Centre for Labour Market Studies, University of Leicester.

Price, H. (2001) Emotional Labour in the Classroom: a psychoanalytic perspective. *Journal of Social Work Practice*: 161–80. (http://dx.doi.org/10.1080/02650530120090610)

Reay, D. (1998) Cultural Reproduction: Mothers' Involvement in Their Children's Primary Schooling. In M. Grenfell and D. James (eds.) *Bourdieu and Education: Acts of Practical Theory,* 55–71 (London: Falmer Press).

Reay, D. (2000) A Useful Extension of Bourdieu's Conceptual Framework? Emotional Capital as a Way of Understanding Mothers' Involvement in Their Children's Education. *The Sociological Review,* 4: 568–85. (http://dx.doi.org/10.1111/1467-954X.00233)

Scarr, S. (1998) American Child Care Today. *American Psychologist,* 53: 9–-108. (http://dx.doi.org/10.1037/0003-066X.53.2.95)

Sharma, U. and P. Black (2001) Look Good, Feel Better: Beauty Therapy as Emotional Labour. *Sociology,* 4: 913–32.

Skeggs, B. (1997) *Formations of Class and Gender* (London: Sage).

Steedman, C. (1982) *The Tidy House: Little Girls Writing* (London: Virago).

Thompson, A. (1998) Not the Color Purple: Black Feminist Lessons for Educational Caring. *Harvard Educational Review,* 4: 522–54.

Tietze, W., D. Cryer, J. Bairrao, J. Palacios, and G. Wetzel (1996) Comparisons of Observed Process Quality in Early Child Care and Education Programmes in Five Countries. *Early Childhood Research Quarterly,* 4: 447–75. (http://dx.doi.org/10.1016/S0885-2006(96)90017-4)

Tronto, J. (1989) Women and Caring: What Can Feminists Learn about Morality from Caring? In A.M. Jaggar and S.R. Bordo (eds.) *Gender/Body/Knowledge: Feminist Reconstructions of Being and Knowing,* 172–88 (New Brunswick and London: Rutgers University Press).

Vincent, C. and S. Warren (2000) Education for Motherhood? In C. Vincent (ed.) *Including Parents? Education, Citizenship and Parental Agency* (Buckingham: Open University Press).

Walkerdine, V. and H. Lucey (1989) *Democracy in the Kitchen: Regulating Mothers and Socialising Daughters* (London: Virago).

Chapter 3

"For a People's Clydebank": Learning the Ethic of Solidarity amidst the Wreckage of Neoliberalism in Contemporary Scotland

Chik Collins

Here the ethic *is to bring local people on, and the Centre* does *that—not for the sake of meeting "employability" targets, but for the sake of the folk themselves.*

Patricia Rice, Clydebank, Scotland
December 2007

Introducing Patricia Rice

Patricia Rice passed away about a year after I interviewed her. Actually, she would have laughed at my calling it an interview. In late 2007 she came to *talk* to me about the Clydebank Independent Resource Centre. After her retirement—following a lifetime of activism in the town of Clydebank—Patricia had played an important role in the organization. I had been asked to write a report about the centre by Oxfam—a UK-based NGO that campaigns against poverty. Oxfam was interested in the centre for its relevance to the NGO's UK Poverty Programme. Patricia and her colleagues hoped the report would also have some immediate local value in an ongoing battle to sustain their organization.

Patricia was a picture: her white hair perfectly set against her finely featured face; her clothes tasteful and elegant. She was already frail—though with her wheeled walking frame she still zipped along. Mentally sharp, she had a bright and penetrating eye. And there was no shortage of fire in her belly. She was incandescent about what had been—and was being—done to her town and to its people.

Initially, there was a polite, slightly formulaic, quality about her approach to our exchange; but, as our conversation developed, I sensed that she felt that there was hope for me; that her breath might not be entirely wasted. She started to lay it out slowly and clearly, smiling, making eye contact, placing the necessary emphasis on key words and phrases, watching to make sure I was *getting it*, repeating where needed. This, she seemed to understand, was how one must communicate with the overeducated—or at least such of those as show meaningful signs of hope.

Speaking to Patricia that day, I did not actually *get it*. But subsequently I found that to produce that report for Oxfam I had to excavate the roots of her organization and its culture, and trace its development and struggles, so that I ended up in a position where I *did get it*. At least that was Patricia's considered opinion. By that stage, the intended report had become something much more like a book (Collins, 2008).

The Brief

My research brief had been straightforward. The centre had demonstrated a resilience and longevity that seemed close to—if not actually—unique in contemporary Scotland. Other community organizations had proven sadly vulnerable to manipulation and destruction at the hands of other agencies in the preceding years. What was it about this one that meant that it had survived, preserved its independence, and continued to serve its community? What might be learned from its experience?

In trying to meet this brief I was led to reflect on education and learning at a number of levels: first, in terms of the processes of self-education and learning built into the fabric of the organization that were at the root of its resilience; second, in terms of the stark contrasts between the nature and quality of these educative processes and those that have more commonly and conventionally been seen as appropriate for community organizations in Scotland; third, in terms of what could be learned and disseminated from the process of trying to grasp what had gone on in this organization. In what follows I will seek to convey this in and through a summary account of the centre's story. This is prefaced by an account of how I came to encounter it in the first place—which is also highly relevant.

Finding the Clydebank Centre

Clydebank is today a town of around 45,000 people, immediately to the west of Glasgow on the north bank of the River Clyde. It emerged as a kind of industrial new town in the late nineteenth century. By the early twentieth century it was well known for its mammoth Singer sewing machine factory and for the vessels produced by the John Brown Shipyard. The town suffered terribly amidst the mass unemployment and austerity of the 1920s and especially the 1930s, and local people participated extensively in the activities of the National Unemployed Workers Movement of that period. The town was then, in March 1941, almost destroyed, and many lives lost and scarred, by the *Luftwaffe* (Hood, 1988; MacPhail, 1974).

"No going back to the thirties"

The people of Clydebank rebuilt their town in the spirit of "no going back to the thirties." But by the early 1970s they feared that the British government would undermine all their best work—by forcing the closure of the Upper Clyde Shipbuilders (UCS) consortium, of which the John Brown shipyard was then part. Mass unemployment again loomed. However, the workers of the UCS embarked on a 14-month-long "work-in" to defend their "right to work." It was—remarkably—successful, and the yard remained open. In fact, such was the level of support for the UCS workers across society that the Conservative government of the day—led by Edward Heath—made its infamous "U-turn," abandoning its proto-neoliberalism and embracing a then more familiar kind of "consensus politics" (Foster and Woolfson, 1986; Collins, 2000).

However, unemployment remained, by postwar standards, very high—close to 10% (Lever, 1988: 137–8). Many local people found themselves ill-served by the welfare system to which they had long paid their dues. Some of them, deprived of their "right to work," set up an Unemployed Action Group (UAG) to try to secure what was later to be called welfare rights. For them, the struggle for the "right to work" was already giving way to the struggle for "the right to exist." They acted at the prompting, and with the support and encouragement, of the Clydebank and District Trades Union Council, and drew on the still vivid folk memory of the 1930s.

I had written about the struggle for the "right to work" many years before finding out about the struggle for the "right to exist" (Collins, 1996). This meant that I at least understood something about the context in which the latter had emerged when I actually encountered it in 2006.

Neoliberalism and Community Education

In the period between the 1970s and 2006, formerly industrial communities had suffered the damaging impacts of a neoliberal policy agenda—first under the International Monetary Fund (IMF)–inspired cuts implemented by Labour after 1976, then under the Conservative governments of 1979–1997, and later under the New Labour administration of Tony Blair. Forced deindustrialization, loss of skilled manual employment, ongoing attacks on local government in general and public sector housing in particular, disempowerment of trade unions, the development of a low-wage, service-orientated flexible labor market, and intensifying attacks on benefit claimants all generated growing poverty and inequality, and a growing crisis of both health and morale in the worst affected areas (Foster, 2003). Clydebank was amongst them.

In the later 1970s, Labour Party–controlled local and regional government in Scotland, notably in the westerly Strathclyde Region, had elaborated its own system of community education and community development. This had aimed to build the capacity of the worst affected communities in dealing with the early impacts of neoliberalism. The idea was to "help the community to organise" (Strathclyde Regional Council, 1983). There were both radical—including neo-Marxist—and reformist interpretations of this "community work," though they coalesced very often in practice (Craig, Derricourt, and Loney, 1982). Many of the community organizations that had emerged in the wave of "community action" from the later 1960s became linked to this policy—and were supported by it. Many others were developed specifically through it. They were encouraged to organize, to learn, to develop, to participate, and to campaign in pursuit of collectively agreed goals.

However, by the millennium this policy and practice was almost entirely gone. The ideas of learning, development, and participation had increasingly been appropriated for the purposes of implementing the neoliberal agenda (Reclaiming Social Purpose Group, 2008). Symptomatically, campaigning was discouraged to the point of virtual prohibition. Many of the local organizations that community workers had supported found themselves losing resources, and/or led into dubious new relationships with external agencies, which led to the organizations' "restructuring" and not infrequently to their dissolution. Their dependence on a "local state" (Cockburn, 1977) system of education and development, albeit one that had initially seemed progressive and even humanistic, had rendered them susceptible to a regressive trend of manipulation and control.

In this context there appeared a new generation of workers, across a range of agencies, with job titles focused on community education, participation, learning, and development (Craig, 2008). Increasingly they focused on adapting individuals to the requirements of a flexible labor market. The emphasis was on knowledge and skills—though not knowledge about the real circumstances of people's lives, or the skills to challenge the injustices that scarred them.

In the Scottish government agency formed at this time—Communities Scotland—a Scottish Centre for Regeneration (SCR) was established with its own "Knowledge Manager" and a dedicated team producing "learning resources" for local communities in the poorest areas. Their activity sought to establish and to police what might be called *approved learning* for communities about the past, the present, and the possibilities of the future. Soon, the SCR was to attempt to generate its own Scotland-wide community *front* organization—the Community Voices Network. In the spirit of the neoliberal agenda it was serving, it even contracted the task to a private firm (Collins, 2007).

Independent Learning

So it was that those community organizations that were still functioning in the years after the millennium, and seeking to engage with the substantive concerns of the communities they represented, came together on an *independent* basis. What was to become a series of community conferences around the west of Scotland began toward the end of 2004 in the Govan area of Glasgow (Govan Community Council, 2004). The event attracted encouraging participation from other communities, some of which then undertook to hold two further conferences in 2005 and 2006. I attended all of these conferences and was an invited speaker at two of them—speaking on the experience of government-led *regeneration*.

Something significant seemed to be happening at these conferences. Some local community organizations, albeit coming from a very low base, seemed to be (re)discovering a capacity for *independent* organization, learning, and development. Other organizations had developed at some distance from the local state over many years, and so had never lost that capacity in the first place. The result was that the processes of organization, learning, and development at these events were radically different from those being sponsored by official agencies. The impetus came from within local communities, rather than from external agencies. There was an attempt to look beyond the purely localized experience of particular communities, but no attempt to refute its validity or relevance. There was a place for particular knowledge and specialized experience of contributors; but there was no privileged voice speaking *through* other individuals or organizations. There was no attempt made to limit knowledge and learning to that which external agencies viewed as *valid* or *approved*. And, finally, the trade union movement was present and making a contribution—connecting the concerns of local communities to the concerns and capacities of organized labor.

These processes and connections were the hallmarks of a kind of community organization that had managed to stay clear of the distorting effects of official community work in the preceding decades, and they seemed now to be in the process of being learned and relearned.

Another organization that displayed the hallmarks of independence was the Clydebank Unemployed Community Resource Centre (UCRC)—the direct descendant of the UAG, which had emerged in 1971. In 2006 it was continuing the struggle for "the right to exist" initiated by its forebear. In the preceding period it had found itself embattled in its locality. Certain elements wanted the centre's role to be taken by other bodies that would conform to the *adaptation orientation* required by the neoliberal agenda.

For this reason, the centre hosted the fourth in the series of community conferences. The conference was entitled: "For a People's Clydebank or Sold 'Doon the Watter'[1]: What does the 'regeneration' of our town mean for ordinary working-class people?" I was again invited to speak.

Getting the Clydebank Centre I

At the Clydebank conference, the processes of organization, learning, and development that had characterized the previous conferences were even more prominent. Overwhelmingly, the contributions pointed toward the process of "regeneration" not as a solution to the problems but as a process that was bound up with and indeed implementing, in an increasingly intensive manner, the kinds of policies that had *created* the problems. While communities were being encouraged by such as the SCR to learn about how "regeneration" had worked elsewhere and could work for them, here it was being learned that regeneration had in fact everywhere failed to deliver its ostensible aims. Where it had delivered "outcomes" and benefits, these were often for people who were neither poor nor working class. It had also generated some paradoxically counterproductive consequences. Not least of these was the extensive destruction of the "social capital" it had for many years been claiming to develop—all those community organizations that were no longer there.

On the premises of the Clydebank Centre at this time there was a display that tried to tell the history of the organization—a collection of clippings, photographs, records of activities and achievements, and so on. It was very simple, but also very powerful. It began with a cutting from a national newspaper from 1972 about the local UAG. It quickly became apparent that this local organization had survived in various guises for 35 years, through radically changing contexts and changeovers of key personnel, while most other organizations like it had ceased to exist. Moreover, it was continuing to do what its creators had intended—serving the needs and interests of a community experiencing the havoc of neoliberal-inspired restructuring. It was on the basis of this conversation that I was later approached and asked if I would be prepared to accept the brief outlined earlier. I agreed and set aside twelve-and-a-half days for the work. It ended up taking rather longer than I had imagined.

The 1970s: The Unemployed Action Group

First I researched the transitions that linked the UAG of the 1970s to the UCRC as it then stood. The former had emerged in the context of an early crisis of expectations. The full employment of the postwar years was giving way to substantial structural unemployment—reaching 1 million across Britain in this period. The Clydebank and District Trades Union Council, particularly through a certain Eddie Kelly, had responded by initiating the local UAG. Its activities were duly featured in national media. From a surviving recording of a current affairs TV program, we can hear its Chair, John Nicholson, explain what it was about:

> We demand the right to work, we're just bein' refused it. We've got six or seven factories in Clydebank daein *nuthin*, we've got Scotland West Promotions promisin' to find work, the council, the government are all promisin' us work, and the fact of the matter is there's naebudy daein *anything* fur us.

So, in the meantime, the people were doing something for themselves:

> In the meantime we're tryin to do the best we can, defendin' people…We're just trying to get a decent standard of living for the people on the buroo [welfare benefits].

This meant maintaining a continual presence at the entrance to the local "employment exchange":

> There's always one of us here every day, continually, day in, day out, there's somebody comes out of these exchanges wi' a problem.

The group built up detailed knowledge of the welfare system, and the skills to hold it to account—by fighting individual cases and establishing more general precedents. The group aspired to "become a branch of the trade union movement." And it was clearly *dogged*—"every day, continually, day in, day out." That doggedness was just as clearly driven by an *ethic* of solidarity—an ethic that Patricia Rice had been at pains to explain to me, in similarly unpretentious terms, some 35 years later. Defending the gains of previous struggles meant connecting to the knowledge and experience of those who had won them—the unemployed workers of the 1930s, the trade unionists of the post-war period, the shipbuilders who had conducted the recent "work-in." It meant learning from their contributions, and establishing what new learning and development would have to take place to contribute anew in the present.

In all of this Clydebank was by no means unique. But, on closer investigation it became apparent that its particular history had generated some distinct qualities (Hood, 1988). The town had been thrown together in an industrial boom. It was from the outset very much a working-class town. It had forged itself as a *community* through the adversity of the early twentieth century. Struggles against rapacious landlords had been a particular feature, as well as the struggles of the unemployed. And in this context the local community developed a particularly strong tradition of independent organization, in which socialist and trade union activists played a prominent role, focused on meeting local needs. The need to rebuild the devastated town after the 1941 blitz seemed to further galvanize the solidaristic ethic—embodying it in the physical, and the sociopolitical, fabric of the town. In all of this there was a profound respect for learning and development—wherever that served the practical needs and purposes of the community. The ethic of solidarity in the UAG of the 1970s—and its doggedness—was clearly carrying forward this tradition. So too was its commitment to learning and development.

The 1980s: The UB40 Centre

The UAG operated through the 1970s. But come the end of the decade, as neoliberal shock treatment unfolded across the United Kingdom, local closures—particularly that of the Singer factory—"threatened to wipe out the town's economic base" (Kennedy, 1988: 205). By 1981 unemployment, at 20%, was more than double what it had been a decade before (Lever, 1988: 137–8). The town began to hemorrhage population.

The central government responded by designating an Enterprise Zone in the town. Clydebank was to become a test-bed for new, Thatcherite, free-market orientated, "regeneration" policy. Community organizations responded in a range of ways, one of which saw the evolution of the UAG into the Clydebank Unemployed and Unwaged Group. Again, Eddie Kelly and the local Trades Council were to the fore. The aim was now to form a center, with its own premises, dedicated to the needs of the unemployed—an Unemployed Workers Centre (UWC). Such centers were then emerging across the United Kingdom (Bagguley, 1991). The Clydebank Centre was to be staffed initially by volunteers, and governed by a management committee consisting of delegates from the Clydebank Trades Union Council, from local government, together with unemployed users of the facility. Thereafter it would seek funding through the central government's Urban Programme. It secured that funding in 1983.

Soon, the Clydebank UWC was to find itself occupying premises at the heart of the new Enterprise Zone. This serves to highlight the conditions of the centre's existence during the 1980s. It sought to maintain a tradition of independent organization, learning, and development in a national policy context that was deeply inimical—in fact overtly seeking to destroy that tradition and the values that underpinned it. Symptomatically, the centre soon found itself facing eviction from its Business Park premises. Its basic existence was called in question.

A rearguard action, with "covering fire" from the Trades Council and its supporters in local government, was mounted to ensure an orderly retreat. It was also used as a tool to generate sympathy and support locally, which in turn would allow a "counterattack"—when a move to new premises was finally arranged.

Speaking to me in 2007, Danny McCafferty, a longtime centre supporter, explained that many of the people who were to become prominent in the wider community—both in Clydebank and beyond—"learned their trade and their skills, and acquired confidence and self-respect, through their involvement in the Centre in the 1980s." There certainly seems to have been the scope for that. Surviving the "eviction" from the Enterprise Zone became the launching pad for an expansive period in the organization's history. Activities included welfare rights services, a high-quality newspaper, a women's group, a video group, a drama group, a writers' group, an outdoor group, an angling group, a woodwork group, a local history group, an unemployment and health group, a café, and a job-seeking support service. There were plans for a crèche, and ongoing participation in campaigns for social justice. A report to the centre's management committee in 1988 put it thus:

> The last 12 months have arguably been the most successful since the Centre's inception. The Centre has never before offered such a comprehensive range of services and facilities to the unemployed and unwaged in the Clydebank area and this has been reflected in the dramatic increase in the Centre's usage…It would be fair to say that our profile in the community has radically changed. There should not be one person in Clydebank who has been unemployed for any length of time who does not know what the Centre has to offer. Also our contact with the trade union movement has radically improved and this too has paid dividends for the Centre.

But there was no complacency:

> It is quite clear that the Centre's strategy of development has been successful. However, we must not be complacent; there have been some projects which have been less successful than others. The weaknesses of these projects should be analysed and appropriate lessons must be learned for the future.

A young firefighter, David McPhail, who found his way to the centre during this period—in a time of personal need—found "new hope" in the solidarity and conviviality he witnessed:

> I saw in these unemployed people new hope. They may have been unemployed but they were still active within a community of their own peers and still enjoying life. I never saw drugs or alcohol abuse within the groups and every group seemed to support the other. If there was a play the fishermen would go and if there was a fishing trip the actors would reciprocate.

From these quotations it is possible to divine some of the reasons for the ongoing survival of the organization. The ethic of solidarity remained crucial, was still being carried forward, and underpinned an ongoing commitment to education and learning. But essential to the practice of the ethic was an ongoing and always collaborative intellectual engagement focused on learning about the conditions of the organization's existence, the emerging challenges it faced, and how they should be responded to, in light of available resources and support mechanisms. Failing that, the centre may not have survived the mid-1980s; and it almost certainly would have fallen irretrievably in the attack that was just about to come.

Getting the Clydebank Centre II

In 1990, Urban Programme funding for the centre expired. The most local form of government—the Clydebank District Council—was keen, not least given the centre's impressive contribution to a town with many needs to serve, to keep the organization going. The regional government—in Strathclyde Regional Council (SRC)—saw things otherwise. It was then in the early stages of implementing the notorious central government–imposed "poll tax." This was a massively regressive system of local taxation designed to radically weaken local and regional government—prior to wholesale reorganization. It met with a tide of opposition—which contributed very substantially to the removal of Margaret Thatcher as prime minister in 1990. It was abolished within a few years, but in the meantime the Regional Council, in fear of breaking the law, was implementing its collection.

The problem was that the centre could reasonably be anticipated to be a prominent contributor to a campaign of mass nonpayment. So SRC was unwilling to help finance the centre's survival. Without that contribution, the centre would not be viable and duly it had to close. But its supporters refused to let it die, and a campaign for its "regeneration" ensued.

David McPhail now repaid his dues and more. He played a key role in galvanizing others through a protracted campaign. In the process he encountered a certain Mary Collins—an experienced trade union activist who had recently been made unemployed. Writing to me in 2007, McPhail, by then in Australia, recalled:

> Mary was seated in the back garden of her friend's house, puffing on a cigarette. She looked up at me and asked if I wanted some help with the fight to reopen the centre in Clydebank. She seemed genuinely interested

in the fight and looked neither tired nor afraid of the Council. In fact she looked like she wanted to roll her sleeves up and get into the ring with the rest of us.

Soon Collins was chair of the organization—and bringing her skills to bear on the problem of reestablishing a functioning centre.

The Clydebank
Unemployed Community Resource Centre

Collins led the organization through a protracted series of negotiations with the local and regional government, and delicately "reframed" the work of the organization to enable it to access funding. The abandonment of the poll tax at the national level had removed a major impediment to that. A survey was conducted within the town to demonstrate the need and demand for a center. At the same time Collins and her colleagues developed links and alliances across a range of organizations and agencies. A sympathetic local firm provided excellent premises at a modest rent. And on this basis the Clydebank UCRC was in operation as of July 1992—in the midst of another protracted recession (1990–1994).

The centre's position remained highly tenuous—funding was minimal, short-term and fragile. That had to be grappled with on an ongoing basis. The task was complicated by the wholesale reorganization of local government in the mid-1990s—involving the abolition of the regional tier, and situating Clydebank within a new local council area (West Dunbartonshire Council) with a severely limited tax base.

The centre was also constantly threatened by a developing neoliberal agenda that was hostile to the basic practices of solidarity and resistance that remained the *essence* of the organization. This was to prove to be as true of the New Labour years after 1997 as it had been of the period of Conservative rule under John Major from 1990. But where other organizations responded to that threat by resisting and campaigning rather *less*, the centre opted for the reverse course. With the local Trades Union Council, it initiated the Clydebank Fights Back campaign. Only in this way, it was calculated, would the centre retain the kind of relevance to real problems required to sustain any kind of *independent* existence. The course being taken by other organizations, it was rightly anticipated, would lead to the diminution of such relevance, and a growing reliance on the "benevolence" of those with other agendas. On this basis the centre was to survive and to continue to serve its community on terms set from within its community, past the millennium.

The scale of this undertaking—and what it entailed in terms of education and learning—could all too easily be underestimated. All of the various difficulties, obstacles, challenges, and issues had continually to be apprehended, brought to the attention of the collective, wherein they had to be engaged—both intellectually and practically—in order that they might be comprehended and successfully negotiated. It entailed a sustained process of collective self-education and colearning, driven by that ethic of solidarity, and committed to the defense of the gains of previous struggles.

It had also required that a new generation of activists be socialized and educated in the ethic of solidarity, and the culture of struggle and resistance. Eddie Kelly was by now becoming elderly. John Nicholson was long gone. David McPhail had gone to his new life in Australia. Most of those who had "learned their trade" at the centre during the 1980s had moved on, and many had lost touch. New people had taken their places and were now contributing in their stead. Yet they continued to do so in ways that showed that they had absorbed the culture of their forebears. And a key role in this respect seems to have been played by the continuing connection to the Clydebank Trades Union Council, and by the daily interaction between "inductees," "apprentices," and the more experienced contributors, including Mary Collins and Patricia Rice.

Collins had become the full-time "co-ordinator" of the centre from the time of its launch in 1992. Other staff had tended to emerge from the ranks of centre users and volunteers. This bred understanding and commitment. Indeed, a consultant, commissioned to produce a profile of the Centre for Communities Scotland in 2004, highlighted this as a key "learning point" for others:

> Employing local people with experience of and empathy for the situations of the people they work with will result in greater commitment and understanding of the ethos of the project. Progression routes from centre user to volunteer to staff are useful in maintaining the ethos and user led focus of the project.

This understanding and commitment was to prove vital in dealing with the next major threat to the centre's existence.

The Growing Threat of "Worklessness"

This threat was produced by the coming together of developments in local politics in West Dunbartonshire and policy development at the national level. Together, these created a potent challenge to the basic philosophy of the centre. Collins had laid the latter out in the annual report of the UCRC for 1993–1994:

> The UCRC over the past two years…has been a lifeline for many individuals…Locally, nationally and internationally we continue in recession and the problems which beset so many in our community grow seemingly ever more entrenched. It is against this background that the Clydebank UCRC strives to provide some hope and practical help for the unemployed… *It is a demanding task which calls above all else for a proper sense of the individuality of those we serve*, and for an understanding of their various needs ranging from the most basic assistance towards self confidence and self-esteem, to the most complex of vocational advice. It is fair to say that a centre such as ours, with local community volunteers and groups operating on a sympathetic scale, and perceived rightly as non-threatening, has many advantages when it comes to this. (emphasis added)

The above can be seen as an elaborated version of the ethic that Patricia Rice explained to her "over-educated" interlocutor in 2007: "The *ethic* here is to bring people on…for the sake of the folk themselves." The missing clause here, however, is "not for the sake of meeting 'employability' targets." And this clause indicates the very pointed challenge that had emerged from around 2002–2003.

> The Centre's existence had, until that point, been defended on the grounds that neo-liberal policies had caused havoc in towns like Clydebank. People were seen to have suffered due to forces which were beyond their control. Conservative governments had sought to shift this perception, and to "blame the victims." But longitudinal survey data in the *British Social Attitudes* series demonstrated a clear public resistance to that. (Jowell et al., 1996)

It was New Labour that began to shift that resistance. The *British Social Attitudes* reports show this clearly (Park et al., 2005). If in the past people had fought for the "right to work," it was suggested that now they needed to be confronted with their "duty to work." Fundamentally, the "workless," it was now maintained, needed to accept the responsibility to become "employable" in the new "flexible labour market," and the welfare system would now be moved increasingly in the direction of enforcing that responsibility. Organizations that expected to be resourced to work with the poor and unemployed would henceforth be required to meet targets for implementing this approach (Carmel and Papadopolous, 2003).

Had such thinking been likely to lead to good outcomes for its community, the centre would have signed up to the targets and been resourced to the hilt. But increasingly it was clear that the reality was of poor and vulnerable people being coerced into inappropriate training and poor-quality, short-term, low-paid, nonunionized work. Indeed, there was not even enough of that kind of work around to occupy a fraction of the "workless" population. People who did find such work were experiencing financial crises induced by delays in receiving income when coming off and going back on benefits, often leading to borrowing at very high rates from dubious lenders. Demonstrably sick and incapacitated people were being made to endure crassly insensitive medical assessments leading to withdrawal of essential benefits (Collins, Dickson, and Collins, 2009). And increasingly those who did find themselves in employment still remained in poverty (MacInnes, Kenway, and Parekh, 2009).

It was now apparent that the centre would find itself under pressure to abandon its fundamental "ethic"—to treat the ordinary people of Clydebank, not as "ends in themselves," but as "means" to meet "employability targets." The centre was not prepared to submit to this pressure. Collins laid this out very clearly in a discussion with the consultant reporting to Communities Scotland in 2004:

> It can be difficult to obtain funding for the work that your community wants and needs. Other funding packages are available, but these may lead you to compromise the work you want to do and create a tension between the needs of funders and the needs of service users. It is better to refuse potential lucrative funding that does not serve your objectives and do what you can with the funding which does.

A Little Local Difficulty

Historically, the centre could have hoped to mobilize a broad coalition of forces against the pressure it was under. An important ally would generally have been local government. However, the emergence of New Labour had also shifted the local political terrain.

New Labour, headed by Tony Blair, was predicated on the success of Thatcherism in forcing deindustrialization and weakening the labor movement. These processes had "hollowed out" the Labour Party, rendering it susceptible to conversion from a still broadly social democratic party, to a vehicle for the continuation of the neoliberal project (Heffernan, 2001).

But the party was susceptible to takeover by minorities with their own agendas locally as well as nationally. Such a takeover occurred in West Dunbartonshire in the period around the millennium. The people at the centre—including Collins, Rice, and McCafferty, all of whom were members of the party—stood out against it. For a time they played a role in preventing the problematic elements—and just how problematic they were we will soon see—from controlling West Dunbartonshire Council. But from 2003 these elements took control of that entity. And this meant that local government would not be defending the centre from the implications of the "worklessness" agenda, but specifically trying to use it to put the centre out of business. Even the centre's most optimistic supporters were doubtful about surviving this challenge.

But the centre did survive, and it did so by grappling collectively with the challenge, responding practically on the basis of its tried and tested understanding of what was at stake, finding out more about the precise dimensions of the threat, and moving iteratively through repeated cycles of learning and practice, education, and action. While doing this, the centre continued to deliver services and meet needs arising from within the community—not least because if this were to cease, it was believed, the centre would be even more vulnerable.

In this manner it proved possible to absorb some blows, and to soften or parry others. In times of acute crisis, influential allies, including leading figures in the Scottish Trades Union Congress (STUC), or broader community support, were mobilized. The centre accepted a nomination for a national award for service to its community. It duly won the award and used that to raise its profile.[2] But even then, attacks on the centre could be presented, not as attacks, but as an attempt to align an old, perhaps recalcitrant, organization with the new "best practice" for helping people—the "employability" agenda. If the centre did not want to cooperate with that, it could be implied, perhaps it was time for new organizations that would?

Breathing Space

In due course the centre found itself positioned menacingly within a Council review of funding for local service provision. The clearly intended outcome was the centre's elimination. However, within the structure of that review the people at the centre were able to detect some breathing space, and beyond that a horizon for significant change in the local political landscape. First, there were no other credible providers that could perform the centre's role in Clydebank in the short term. The Council could not simply withdraw the service—not least as a local election was looming in May 2007. The time required to engineer an alternative provider meant *breathing space*.

The election was one thing on the horizon. The other was the public report of an audit by a central government agency of the performance of the local authority itself. Early indications were that it would clearly highlight the deeply problematic nature of the element that had been running the authority since 2003. This, it was grasped, could lead to the discrediting and collapse of the leadership of the Council. The clear imperative was simply to endure while this event horizon neared.

This was the context in which I encountered the centre—at the community conference toward the end of 2006. Within a month of that event the context was shifting dramatically. A public hearing on the findings of the audit of West Dunbartonshire Council was conducted in Clydebank Town Hall, in advance of publication. The hearing was reported in *The Herald*, the main broadsheet newspaper in the west of Scotland, as follows:

> The commission is likely to report next week, and while it would be wrong to pre-judge its findings, some free advice to the council's political and official leadership is to take a good look at the recruitment section in *The Herald*…[Witnesses] were confirming reports of bullying, harassment, skewing council finances to benefit favoured wards and punish enemies, unminuted decisions involving tens of millions of pounds, council officials too close to councillors; and they were followed by trade union representatives saying the bullying culture is widespread, with daily complaints and no confidence in the grievance procedure. (Douglas Fraser, *The Herald*, December 8, 2006)

The Town Hall is down by the river in Clydebank. *The Herald* writer reported that on leaving the hearing there, one "quietly satisfied woman" said: "It's true what they say, you know. Wait by the river long enough, and eventually all the bodies of your enemies will float by." What seems most significant in the story of the centre, however, is that its people had the kind of collective learning process that enabled them to ensure that the centre had not itself been "sold doon" the River Clyde, in cadaverous form, some time ahead of the bodies to which this local wit was now alluding.

The centre had survived to fight another day. Duly the Management Committee decided that it would be best positioned to do that under a new name, one that emphasized an aspect of the centre's long-standing operation that local people seemed to value highly. It thus became The Clydebank Independent Resource Centre.

Learning in the Story of the Clydebank Centre

The preceding sections have, in narrating the concrete process of the centre's development and survival, sought to highlight the essential role of a particular kind of education and learning in that process. It is a kind that is thoroughly collective, deeply rooted in the traditions and culture of the community that created the organization, and is underpinned—driven—by an entrenched and resilient ethic of solidarity that is the legacy of the community's past experiences and struggles. Within the organization, this education and learning is clearly understood *as* education and learning, but not of a "bookish" kind. It entails a dislike for jargon and verbosity, and generates a capacity to detect and pierce such very quickly. It is understood as a process of collaborative, practical engagement with pressing problems and issues, requiring maximum information and extended dialogue and exchange about it, primarily within, but often also beyond, the organization and its immediate circle of friends and allies. The latter in particular requires a capacity to assess the nature and character of organizations and individuals prior to developing links and relationships. The organization's people have then been the primary repositories of the learning—the knowledge and understanding accumulated. This has then been transmitted to new people—inductees and apprentices—orally and experientially in the context of their own emerging, practical contributions to the work of the organization.

The preceding sections have also sought to contrast these educative processes with those more commonly and conventionally seen as appropriate for community organizations in Scotland. The contrast with those that have corresponded to the "adaptation orientation" of the neoliberal agenda is very clear and needs no further comment. However, the contrast with the forms of community education and development, prominent from the later 1970s and earlier 1980s, would seem to bear further consideration. As we have seen, these sought to build assertive organizations that could campaign on behalf of poor communities and resist regressive developments. But they did so by fostering a dependence on local and regional government employees. And it was organizations that developed such a dependence that subsequently proved vulnerable when the tide in local and regional government turned from one of limited resistance to neoliberalism toward an embrace of the "adaptation agenda." The subtleties of neo-Marxist theorization of community work as "in and against the state" (London-Edinburgh Weekend Return Group, 1980) gave way to a practice that was increasingly "for and on behalf of the state" in implementing the neoliberal agenda. The organizations that had *not* become reliant on local government community education and development proved less susceptible to such co-option and redirection, and so less vulnerable to outright destruction and replacement. These were the kinds of community organizations that, from the later part of 2004, were coming together in the series of community conferences discussed earlier.

Cumulatively, these kinds of considerations pose for us the question of *why* the centre was able to maintain its independence, while also sustaining the kind of long-term processes of education and learning, and the network of contacts and allies, which kept it alive through its many battles and its various "near death experiences." This was the key question posed by the Oxfam research brief—indicating the key matter for learning and dissemination.

A tempting answer, and one which at an early stage I was inclined to give, was that the centre had the good fortune to benefit from the services of some rather special and talented people. However, it also soon became apparent that this was not simply good fortune. It reflects, first, the deep and long-standing connections of the centre with the trade union movement. This has meant access to vital experience in—and *nous* about—what is involved in organizing and leading ordinary people in promoting and defending their interests. This, moreover, highlights how the centre's independence is not some pristine isolation, or lack of relationships and connections, but rather has required relationships and connections of a kind that have facilitated and supported an enduring sense of identity and consistency of purpose.

The "good fortune" analysis would also tend to neglect the fact that the centre has always emphasized the training and development of *its own* workers—both voluntary and paid. The talents that the centre has benefited from have been nurtured and developed by the organization itself and it is this that has allowed it to develop in its own fashion, without overreliance on workers employed by other organizations whose agendas have proven highly changeable.

All of this is in no way intended to diminish the remarkable achievements of the individuals who have served the centre over the years. Rather, the point is to highlight how other organizations might become better placed to emulate their achievements—by creating the kinds of links and processes conducive to recruiting, producing and supporting the kinds of workers they need.

Conclusion:
Learning from the Story of the Clydebank Centre

This, then, is what was, above all, learned from the story of the centre. Clydebank is the kind of place where the links between the trade unions and community organizations have been rather stronger than elsewhere. But if such links were to be developed and strengthened in other towns and cities, some of the achievements that have been seen in Clydebank could realistically be expected to be broadly replicated. And this, it was concluded, would require a renewal of the kind of positive, mutual relationship between trade unions and local community organizations that was in the past an almost defining aspect of the trade union movement in Scotland (Aitken, 1997).

This learning was then disseminated—partly through Oxfam, which published 1000 copies of the centre's story (Collins, 2008). The NGO made these freely available, while promoting the findings in national media. It also made "the report" available on the NGO's website. The learning was also disseminated in the ongoing series of community conferences that had brought me to the centre in the first place. By this time—2008—the STUC was itself, in large part due to the community conferences, becoming aware of the ways in which the members of its affiliated unions were being challenged and threatened by "regeneration" and "employability" initiatives. And the result of this was a one-day conference organized and hosted by the STUC itself, in September 2008, on "Communities, Regeneration and Democracy." The conference specifically highlighted the need to support and renew the trade union councils in the other towns and cities of Scotland, and their role in connecting the resources and capacities of the trade union movement to the interests and concerns of local communities.

Of course it is one thing to advocate this and quite another to achieve it in practice. But its advocacy has, nonetheless, been an important development. It has come about in large part through the collaborative learning practices of independent, grassroots organizations, who have nurtured and taken forward the "ethic" of solidarity through some very inauspicious times. Theirs has been a process of organization, education, and learning that one hopes will be kept alive, and perhaps will even find new life, in the darkening days, which, as this contribution is being written, can be seen to lie ahead.

Notes

1. "Doon the watter" is a way of saying "down the river" in the everyday language of ordinary Scots. The phrase "sold down the river" is

commonly used in the British labor movement to describe a deal that
betrays the interests of ordinary people.
2. It was on this basis that the centre became the subject of the consultant's
profile commissioned by Communities Scotland, which was referred to
earlier.

References

Aitken, K. (1997) *The Bairns O' Adam: the Story of the Scottish Trades Union Congress* (Edinburgh: Polygon).

Bagguley, P. (1991) *From Protest to Acquiescence? Political Movements of the Unemployed* (Basingstoke: MacMillan).

Carmel, E. and T. Papadopolous (2003) The New Governance of Social Security in Britain. In J. Miller (ed.) *Understanding Social Security* (Bristol: Policy Press).

Cockburn, C. (1977) *The Local State* (London; Pluto Press).

Collins, C. (1996) The Pragmatics of Emancipation, *Journal of Pragmatics*, 120: 791–817.

Collins, C. (2000) Developing the Linguistic Turn in Urban Studies, *Urban Studies*, 37: 2027–43.

Collins, C. (2007) "The Scottish Executive is Open for Business." In A. Cumbers, and G. Whittam, (eds.) *Reclaiming the Economy: Alternatives to Market Fundamentalism in Scotland and Beyond* (Biggar: Scottish Left Review Press).

Collins, C. (2008) *The Right to Exist: the Story of the Clydebank Independent Resource Centre* (Glasgow: Oxfam).

Collins, C., J. Dickson, and M. Collins (2009) *To Banker, from Bankies. Incapacity Benefit: Myth and Realities* (Glasgow: Oxfam).

Craig, G. (2008) The Politics of Community Development 40 Years on. A paper presented at the Word Power/Edinburgh Radical Book Fair, Edinburgh, October 30, 2008.

Craig, G., N. Derricourt, and M. Loney (eds.) (1982) *Community Work and the State* (London: Routledge and Kegan Paul).

Foster, J. (2003) The Economic Restructuring of the West of Scotland: 1945–2000. In G. Blazyca (ed.) *Restructuring Regional and Global Economies* (Aldershot: Ashgate).

Foster, J and C. Woolfson (1986) *The Politics of the UCS Work-In* (London: Lawrence and Wishart).

Govan Community Council (2004) Poverty, Deprivation and Development in Working Class Communities (Glasgow: Govan Community Council).

Heffernan, R. (2001) *New Labour and Thatcherism* (London: Palgrave).

Hood, J. (ed.) (1988) *The History of Clydebank* (Cornforth, Lancs: Parthenon).

Jowell, R., J. Curtice, A. Park, L. Brook and K. Thomson (1996) *British Social Attitudes* (Aldershot: Dartmouth).

Kennedy, G. (1988) The New Clydebank. In J. Hood (ed.) *The History of Clydebank* (Cornforth, Lancs: Parthenon Publishing Ltd).

Lever, W. (1988) Shipbuilding in Decline. In J. Hood (ed.) *The History of Clydebank* (Cornforth, Lancs: Parthenon).

London-Edinburgh Weekend Return Group (1980) *In and against the State* (London: Pluto Press).

MacInnes, T., P. Kenway and A. Parekh (2009) *Monitoring Poverty and Social Exclusion* (York: Joseph Rowntree Foundation).

MacPhail, I.M.M. (1974) *The Clydebank Blitz* (Glasgow: Cordfall).

Park, A., J. Curtice, K. Thomson, C. Bromley, M. Phillips and M. Johnson (2005) *British Social Attitudes* (London: Sage).

Reclaiming Social Purpose Group (2008) *Reclaiming Social Purpose in Community Education* (Edinburgh: The Reclaiming Social Purpose Group).

Strathclyde Regional Council (1983) *Social Strategy for the Eighties* (Glasgow: Strathclyde Regional Council).

Part II

Marxism and the Culture of Educational Practice

Chapter 4

Learning the Feeling Rules: Exploring Hochschild's Thesis on the Alienating Experience of Emotional Labor[1]

Paul Brook

> *I use the term* emotional labor *to mean the management of feeling to create a publicly observable facial and bodily display; emotional labor is sold for a wage and therefore has* exchange value. *I use the synonymous terms* emotion work *or* emotion management *to refer to those same acts done in a private context where they have* use value.
>
> Hochschild, 1983/2003: 7

> *Being the "right kind of person" is at least as important as doing the right things.*
>
> Colley, 2006: 17–18

Hochschild's Politicization of Emotion Work

Contemporary workplaces are increasingly marked by managerial efforts to harness and mould the emotional product of employees, either as specific commodified interactive service encounters or through securing workers' personal "commitment" to organizational goals (Brook and Pioch, 2006). This is not confined to private service companies, as public sector services, such as local government and health care, increasingly mimic the competitive, "customer-orientation" management practices of the commercial sector (Bolton, 2005). As such, capital increasingly views organizational emotion (Fineman, 2007) as a resource to be extracted, refined, and exploited (Hochschild, 1983/2003). As such, the process of teaching workers to emotionally labor is a core management task in contemporary workplaces (Callaghan and Thompson, 2002; Seymour and Sandiford, 2005; Colley, 2006).

Marxist-oriented analyses of the development and deployment of workers' emotions as interactive service encounters have invariably drawn on Hochschild's (1983/2003) pioneering theorization of emotional labor, as an additional aspect to labor power (alongside physical and mental labor) (Brook, 2009b) within the wider capitalist labor process (Braverman, 1974; Rikowski, 2002; Warhurst and Nickson, 2009; Thompson and Smith, 2010). Hochschild principally develops the emotional labor concept in her seminal book, *The Managed Heart* (1983/2003). For Marxists, what is striking is her core application of Marx's alienation theory, thereby generating an analysis that exposes the profound harm wrought by the expanding demand for the commodification and exploitation of emotions in the workplace (Brook, 2009a).

Hochschild's notion of emotional labor as an aspect of labor power is now widely accepted[2] to varying degrees (see Bolton, 2005; Korczynski and MacDonald, 2009) and especially so within the highly influential Marxist-derived Labor Process Analysis (LPA) tradition (see Brook, 2009b; Warhurst et al., 2009; Bolton, 2010). More recently, writers outside of the sociology of work in related areas, such as health care, nursing studies, and education studies (e.g., Price, 2001; Colley, 2006; Theodosius, 2008), have sought to utilize the emotional labor concept. However, many writers adopting it have either downplayed or ignored Hochschild's core application of Marx's alienation theory, even going so far as to condemn her analysis as "one-dimensional" and "ultimately absolutist" (Bolton and Boyd, 2003; Bolton, 2005) for its emphasis on the harm of performing emotion work. Instead, they commonly argue that service interactions are double-edged in that they possess the potential to be satisfying as well as distressing for the worker (Wouters, 1989; Tolich, 1993; Price, 2001; Korczynski, 2002), especially for those in roles, such as nursing and teaching, where the worker possesses the autonomy to choose whether to give compassion and personal commitment (Bolton, 2010). In essence, this position rejects Hochschild's central argument that the experience of learning and performing emotional labor is intrinsically alienating by virtue of being a commodified aspect of labor power, in the same way as physical and mental wage labor (Brook, 2009b; Cohen, 2010). In addition, such arguments obscure the contemporary relevance of Hochschild's "anti-capitalist" style sentiments (Brook, 2009a) evident in her pointed emphasis on the human cost of emotional labor in so-called "consumer capitalism" (Lodziak, 2002).

Nevertheless, since the publication of *The Managed Heart*, Hochschild's emotional labor thesis has inspired an immense range of studies that reach far into the world of work beyond her original study of flight attendants and debt collectors. These include studies of nurses, Disneyland workers, retail and childcare workers, schoolteachers, psychotherapists, holiday representatives, call-center workers, bar staff, waiters, and sex workers (see Steinberg and Figart, 1999; Bolton, 2005; for extensive reviews). While these studies vary in the degree to which they follow Hochschild in her explicit condemnation of the human cost of emotional labor, they tend to contain an implicit acceptance of its exploitative and subordinating nature. Also central to debates on emotional labor is the extensive development of an explicit feminist dimension, which centers on the socially reproduced, gendered commodification of emotion in organizations, and on the related feminization of most service work as it is women who are more commonly employed in "emotion rich" jobs (Fineman, 2005; Colley, 2006; Grugulis, 2007; Lewis and Simpson, 2007). One notable pioneer of a feminist-oriented application is James (1989, 1992) through her studies of cancer nurses' emotional labor, which focused on management's exploitation of gendered "compassion" in the "caring workplace."[3]

In a study of childcare education and training, Colley (2006/this volume) notes that few researchers have specifically investigated the learning of feelings for caring occupations. Indeed, there are relatively few specific studies of workplace learning of feeling rules and skills in commercial services. Those studies that exist have tended to focus as much on the informal process of workplace socialization as on formal training. For example, Seymour and Sandiford's (2005) study of the learning of emotion rules in a chain of UK public houses offers an analysis that highlights how emotion rules are in turn learned, internalized, controlled, and monitored. In addition, these studies reveal that employers' recruitment and selection processes often play a formative role in ensuring a steady supply of compatible employees for subsequent workplace learning schemes, such as customer orientation programs (Rikowski, 2002; Brook and Pioch, 2006). Hence, service organizations frequently prioritize the possession of an appropriate personality and attitude when recruiting frontline workers rather than "hard" technical skills (Filby, 1992; Callaghan and Thompson, 2002; Wright, 2005; Townsend, 2006; Tyler, 2009). Employers believe that this enhances the effectiveness of corporate socialization and training of the requisite "soft skills" (Grugulis, 2007). Furthermore, the highly gendered, "feminine" content of such "soft skills" (Grugulis and Vincent, 2009; Payne, 2009; Scholarios and Taylor, 2010) means that women continue to dominate the vast bulk of UK service employment (Warhurst and

Nickson, 2007). Moreover, much interactive service work in the commercial sector requires that workers possess not only a suitable personality but also a physical appearance that "embodies" the corporate or brand image (Pettinger, 2005). Indeed, this can also require a degree of sexualized display and behavior (Filby, 1992; Warhurst and Nickson, 2009). What is common to all forms of emotional labor is the high degree to which it is both formally learnt and informally inculcated in the workplace, irrespective of whether the worker is a highly qualified "professional" or a part-time sales assistant.

Despite a myriad of studies and theoretical developments since its publication, it is difficult to overestimate the enduring importance of Hochschild's (1983/2003) pioneering theorization of emotional labor, its reproduction, management, and effects. This is especially so for those within the Marxist tradition, as she offers a damning analysis of the cost of capitalism's wholesale exploitation of workers' emotional labor power. In addition, for those of us wanting to understand the function of workplace learning within the capitalist labor process, she reveals its pivotal and extensive role in enabling employers to harness the "right attitude" amongst employees by inculcating, training, regulating, and cajoling service "feeling rules." Equally importantly, Hochschild's account reveals managerial control is not complete, as workers' response to management's emotional prescription and labor intensification is frequently indifference and resistance, which often takes the form of a "war of smiles" where meaningful emotional display is damaged, dimmed, or withdrawn.

Despite the enormous strengths of Hochschild's thesis, her application of Marx's alienation theory is partial and overemphasizes the deleterious individual experience at the expense of the ameliorative role of the wider workplace. This is principally because she restricts her explicit theorization of alienation to the two of Marx's (1975 [1844]) four dimensions that are specific to the workplace: product alienation and labor process alienation. The first deals with workers' loss of control over and ownership of their labor product, and the second with the removal of their control over the labor process. However, while alienation has its source at the point of production, Marx's remaining two dimensions relate to the wider corrosive effects of alienation in society, and should not be separated from the first two (Yuill, 2005). These dimensions—human nature alienation and fellow beings alienation (including commodity fetishism)—deal with the way the suffusion of the commodity form and market relations through society severely distort our self-knowledge, social relations, and understanding of the world. While these dimensions are occasionally implicit in Hochschild's analysis, she does not explore them as wider social dimensions of alienation contributing to and compounding the direct commodification of workplace emotions. In not doing so, she stops short of theorizing alienation as generic to capitalist society (Mészáros, 2005 [1970]; Billig, 1999). Furthermore, *The Managed Heart* is devoid of an explicit class analysis. This undermines Hochschild's argument in explaining individual and collective responses, including resistance by workers to their emotional subordination. She compounds this weakness with an insufficiently dialectical analysis (Rees, 1998) whereby she is unable to capture the contradictory and complex nature of the labor process (Sturdy, 1998; Taylor, 1998). Therefore, Hochschild inadequately theorizes the way workers are shaped by alienation but for all that are not blinded to the reality of capitalism (Lukács, 1974).

Although Hochschild's application of Marx's alienation theory is partial[4] and overemphasizes the deleterious individual experience at the expense of the ameliorative role of wider workplace relations, it offers a damning and convincing analysis of the cost of capitalism's wholesale exploitation and commodification of workers' emotional labor. Her study reveals how employers seek to recruit and harness the "right attitude" by inculcating, training, and regulating prescribed service "feeling rules." In addition, because of the tendency of emotional labor power to be more indeterminate than its physical and mental counterparts (Bolton, 2005; Brook, 2010), learning to labor with feeling is an ongoing process, where management continually seeks to reinforce and amend its "feeling rules" to increase emotional effort and enhance "emotional displays" in response to competitive market pressures.

This chapter explores the experience of learning and performing emotional labor through the lens of Hochschild's application of alienation theory to her study of flight attendants in *The Managed Heart*. In so doing, what follows is a critical defense of the analytic and political value of Hochschild's original formulation as the basis for a more thorough theorization of the reproduction of emotional labor power within contemporary workplaces. Therefore, this chapter seeks to reassert and strengthen Hochschild's central argument that all frontline service workers, irrespective of whether they work in a commercial service industry, such as air travel, or in a public sector service, such as education, experience profound alienation because of the loss of ownership and control of their emotional product. Therefore, employers[5] require workers to suppress and deny their "true selves," which is compounded by their formal subordination to the "customer" as well as their manager. Such an analysis also sheds light on the scope and role of learning under capitalist conditions more generally. This is because the example of employer-led workplace learning, with its growing emphasis on inculcating "customer-oriented" values, lays bare the increasing need of capital to create widespread acceptance, even enthusiasm, within society for the daily reality of engaging in the alienating social relations that comprise contemporary "consumer culture."

Emotional Labor in Play

The Managed Heart's opening lines set the analytic and political tone for what is to come. Hochschild begins by citing the case of the young boy in a wallpaper factory discussed by Marx in *Capital*. She notes Marx's point that the boy is no more than an instrument of labor, and expresses a fundamental concern at the human cost. Hochschild then makes a direct comparison between the boy in the nineteenth-century wallpaper factory and a flight attendant over a century later:

> The work done by the boy in the wallpaper factory called for a coordination of mind and arm, mind and finger, and mind and shoulder. We refer to it simply as physical labor. The flight attendant does physical labor when she pushes heavy meal carts through the aisles, and she does mental work when she prepares for and actually organizes emergency landings and evacuations. But in the course of doing this physical and mental labor she is doing something more, something I define as "emotional labor." This labor requires one to induce or suppress feelings in order to sustain the outward countenance that produces the proper state of mind in others. (1983/2003: 7)

Here Hochschild is laying the foundations for her argument that the human cost of performing emotional labor is as harmful as that of the physical and mental labor discussed by Marx. This is because "beneath the difference between physical and emotional labor there lies a similarity in the possible cost of doing the work: the worker can become estranged or alienated from an aspect of self—either the body or the margins of the soul—that is 'used' to do the work" (ibid.: 7).

The early introduction of alienation theory is joined by another equally fundamental use of Marx's critique of wage labor, namely, the distinction between exchange value and use value in the commodification of emotions. This is integral to Hochschild's primary definition of emotional labor as "the management of feeling to create a publicly observable facial and bodily display; emotional labor is sold for a wage and therefore has 'exchange value.' I use the synonymous terms 'emotion work' or 'emotion management' to refer to those same acts done in a private context where they have 'use value'" (ibid.).[6]

Hochschild's analysis rests on this distinction between emotion work and emotional labor. Emotion work is the process of managing and presenting emotions in the private sphere of our lives, such as amongst family and friends and even as a customer. Emotional labor, in contrast, involves the transmutation of a worker's "private sphere" feelings into a package of commodified emotions that is consumed by the customer as a service interaction. The process has the effect of alienating frontline workers from their emotional product through management's wresting of formal ownership and control from workers of the form, timing, giving and withdrawal of feelings, moods, and the display thereof.

Two other aspects compound this loss of control. First, there is an unequal relationship with the service recipient: "the customer is always right." This is in contrast to our private lives, where we tend to experience a much greater level of assumed and/or near equality in our emotional interactions:

> In private life, we are free to question the going rate of exchange and free to negotiate a new one. If we are not satisfied, we can leave; many friendships and marriages die of inequality. But in the public world of work, it is often part of an individual's job to accept uneven exchanges, to be treated with disrespect or anger by a client, all the while closeting into fantasy the anger one would like to respond with. Where the customer is king, unequal exchanges are normal. (ibid.: 85–6)

Second, management imposes codified *feeling rules* on emotional laborers in order to ensure the delivery of the requisite quality of service. These rules dictate the form, content, and appropriateness of emotional displays, thereby separating workers from the design and control of the labor process. Workers, therefore, are estranged from their emotional product and the process of emotion production.

Hochschild argues that employers' *feeling rules* increasingly go further than demanding behavioral compliance, which she calls *surface acting*. This is because management frequently strives for emotional workers to internalize the feelings they are required to display, not only to enhance the "quality" of the emotional display, but also to diminish the likelihood of *emotive dissonance* (Jansz and Timmers, 2002), caused by the strain of continuously bridging what is really felt with what has to be feigned over long periods. Hochschild argues that the response of many emotional laborers is to "try to pull the two closer together either by changing what we feel or by changing what we feign" (1983/2003: 90), which she calls *deep acting*.

Deep acting is the result of a worker seeking a more comfortable space for herself, free from the dangers of emotive dissonance (Jansz and Timmers, 2002) through what Hochschild refers to as a process of *fusion* between her real and acted emotional labor. However, despite fusion's apparent benefits, there is "a cost to be paid" (1983/2003: 119), since it is a condition that requires a systemic suppression of the real self, thereby deepening the individual's subordination to her commodification. However, as a contradictory and unstable condition, it can transform into a nascent form of resistance:

> Often the test comes when a company speed-up makes personal service impossible to deliver because the individual's personal self is too thinly parcelled out to meet the demands made on it. At this point, it becomes harder and harder to keep the public and private selves fused . . . The worker wonders whether her smile and the emotional labor that keeps it sincere are really hers. Do they really express a part of her? Or are they deliberately worked up and delivered on behalf of the company? (ibid. 133)

Alienated from What?

Underlying Hochschild's concept of emotional labor is what she calls her "social theory of emotions." Such a theory, she argues, has to possess both social and psychological dimensions in that it needs to be able to ask how the construction of social interaction for profit influences an individual's personality. Hence, while employers' "feeling rules run deep . . . so does the self that struggles with and against them" (ibid.: 229).

Hochschild states that to manage feeling is to strive consciously to alter a preexisting emotional state that is indicative of a *given self.* Yet this notion of a psychological given self does little to articulate its relationship with the socially constructed dimension of emotion. For this, Hochschild turns to Freud's notion of the *signal function* of emotion, whereby messages such as anxiety, delight, hope, and despair signal to the individual that there is the presence of danger, pleasure, and so forth from within or external to the individual. Signal function achieves the integration of the social and the psychological dimensions by being a manifestation of the innate self that is profoundly contingent upon socially constructed *prior expectations*:

> The idea of prior expectation implies the existence of a prior self that does the expecting . . . Most of us maintain a prior expectation of a

continuous self, but the character of the self we expect to maintain is subject to profoundly social influence. Insofar as the self and all we expect is social . . . the way emotion signals messages to us is also influenced by social factors. (ibid.: 231–2)

Hochschild's theory of emotion, therefore, binds together the psychological and the social into an interdependent and dynamic unity that is akin to Marx's ontology of the dialectical unity of the mind and body (Marx, 1975 [1844]; Mészáros, 2005 [1970]). It does this by integrating the notions of emotion as a signal function—a biological sensory function—with socially constructed prior expectations as indicative of the given self. Without such a conceptualization, it would be incoherent to theorize alienated emotional labor, for without a theory of human nature, how is it possible to identify an alien condition that violates the individual?

Hochschild's given self, like Marx's theory of "human nature," appears to oppose the common-sense idea that each individual possesses a common, discrete, and fixed human nature independent of society (Ollman, 1976 [1971]). While Hochschild does not provide an explicit anthropology of the given self, her implied conceptualization is not incompatible with Marx's materialist conception, which argues that the only nature-imposed condition of all human existence is the requirement to labor on the environment in order to satisfy human needs. As sentient beings, humans are different from other animals—we are reflective and imaginative in the abstract before concretely acting on our natural environment (Marx, 1976 [1867]). Marx calls our capacity for conscious labor *species being*. This is not just a theory of individual human nature: species being is inherently social because in order to survive, individuals have to enter into collaborative, interdependent relationships.

For Marx, the source of alienation in capitalist society is the necessity for the overwhelming majority of people to labor for a wage in order to ensure physical survival and a semblance of emotional dignity, where a minority, the ruling class, owns and controls the means of production. A worker, therefore, hands over ownership and effective control of his or her labor—in other words, his or her species being. For Marx, this essential relationship between worker and capital generates alienation in capitalist society:

The fact that labour is *external* to the worker, i.e. it does not belong to his essential being; that he therefore does not confirm himself in his work, but denies himself, feels miserable and not happy, does not develop free physical and mental energy but mortifies his flesh and ruins his mind. Hence, the worker only feels himself when he is not working. (Marx, 1975: 326)

Here, Marx explicitly refers to the ruination of body and mind. This understanding of mind and body as an interrelated dialectical unity (Yuill, 2005) is crucial to the task of interpreting the efficacy of Hochschild's argument that the experience of emotional labor is alienating in the same way as the production of physical commodities.

The Human Cost of Emotional Labor

Marx (1975), as indicated above, identified four dimensions of alienation, with the first two—product alienation and labor process alienation—dealing with the immediate conditions of workplace relations. The second two, fellow beings alienation and human nature alienation, encompass capitalist society as a whole. These dimensions are not separate processes with discrete sets of symptoms, but are rather aspects of a generic process that is endemic to capitalism. This is because the whole of humankind is alienated, in that it suffers a loss of control because the power of capital is embodied as an alien force that confronts individuals and society as a hostile and potentially destructive power (Mészáros, 2005 [1970]). How thorough and adequate, then, is Hochschild's application of alienation theory, and what are its consequences for her theorization of emotional labor? Equally, how does she then provide a concrete, empirical account of the alienating experience for cabin crew of learning and performing emotional labor?

Product Alienation

The worker is alienated from the product of her labor by the simple fact that it is not she who owns or controls its disposal, but rather the capitalist. The consequence is that the product of her labor is objectified and appears as external to herself rather than as an affirmation of herself, her species being. Thus while the worker invests her energies and life in the production of the commodity, it is a one-way relationship—a "one-sided enrichment of the object" (Ollman, 1976 [1971]: 144)—for which she receives only money. The creative power, energy, thought, and consideration that is required in order to make something "vanishes into the object of alienated production, which in turn is not replaced by other revitalising creative power" (Yuill, 2005: 135). Hochschild concurs with the idea of a "one-sided enrichment" when she states that when the product "is a smile, a mood, a feeling, or a relationship, it comes to belong more to the organization and less to the self" (1983/2003: 198). This is because for the cabin crew in Hochschild's study, their smiles "were seen as an extension of the make-up, the uniform, the recorded music, the soothing pastel colours of the airplane decor, and the daytime drinks, which taken together orchestrate the mood of the passengers" (ibid.: 8). Hochschild, like Marx, sees this estrangement from the product of labor as having a human cost for emotional laborers. While Marx makes the general point that alienated labor "mortifies the flesh and ruins the mind," Hochschild is more specific and identifies emotive dissonance amongst many cabin crew where they experience "burnout" and "emotional deadness" and feel "phoney" (see Jansz and Timmers, 2002).

Emotive dissonance is the result of a worker investing emotionally in her performance over a prolonged period. The cumulative effect is that she suffers an emotional "malnourishment" caused by an insufficient revitalizing return on her investment. Hochschild argues that there comes a breaking point between the real and acted self, and that as a matter of self-protection she is forced to "divide": "some workers conclude that only one self (usually the non-work self) is the real self. Others, and they are the majority, will decide that each self is meaningful and real in its own different way and time" (1983/2003: 132).

Hochschild appears to argue that emotional labor elicits a more profound form of alienation than even Marx imagined. This is because the majority of workers can only cope with their estrangement by "fusing" their commercialized selves with their real, "private sphere" selves. Hochschild's argument, therefore, implies that Marx underestimated the potency of alienation when he stated that "the worker only feels himself when he is not working" (1975: 326).

Labor Process Alienation

Closely allied to product alienation is labor process alienation, wherein workers lack control over the process of production—that is, the conditions under which we work, how our work is organized, what we produce, and the effect it has on our health (Cox, 1998). For Marx, by wresting control of the labor process, capital denudes us of our intrinsic capacity to work creatively and transforms it into its opposite. Thus a worker experiences "power as impotence . . . [and his] own physical and mental energy, his personal life . . . as an activity directed against himself, which is independent of him and does not belong to him" (1975: 327).

Another dimension to labor process alienation is the fact that work is under the control of forces hostile to us. This is because owing to the competitive nature of capitalism, managers are under constant pressure to extract more value from the worker, thereby cheapening the worth of the individual to capitalism. As capitalism develops and corporations grow larger, there is a general tendency for work to be designed to achieve ever-greater economies of scale, unit efficiencies, and labor productivity, thereby enhancing the importance of the productive process, its logistics, and technologies over the skills and value of the individual. The result is that "the special skill of each individual, insignificant factory operative vanishes as an infinitesimal quantity before the science, the gigantic physical forces, and mass of labour that are embodied in the factory mechanism" (Marx, 1976 [1867]: 548), and the "idiosyncrasies of the worker appear increasingly as *mere sources of error*" (Lukács, 1974: 89).

Hochschild echoes Marx and Lukács when she argues that contemporary service jobs "are now socially engineered and thoroughly organised from the top" (1983/2003: 8). Yet management's control of workers' display and performance is contradictory and unstable. She details how, during cabin-crew training, airlines seek to suppress workers' negative emotions, which are largely born of their experience of the service labor process where they are "treated with disrespect or anger by a client, [yet] all the while closeting into fantasy the anger one would like to respond with" (ibid: 85–6). For her, companies' efforts to control the service labor process is an estranging experience in which "the more seriously social engineering affects our behaviour and our feelings, the more intensely we must address a new ambiguity about who is directing them (is this me or the company talking?)" (ibid.: 34). Moreover, Hochschild is at pains to highlight the alienation that derives from the progressive devaluing of a worker's creative contribution through the increasing rationalization of the labor process. Hochschild shows how the worker is no more than an appendage to the externally imposed smile factory system, and her personal, defensive responses are treated by employers as "mere sources of error," such as offering "a thin crust of display" (ibid.: 21) in order to cope with management's ever-increasing service targets.

For Hochschild, new forms of deskilling compound the alienation generated by the corporate control of the labor process, and the ever-greater competitive pressures to rationalize the service production system. Following Braverman (1974), she argues that there is a tendency for the "mind" of the work process to "move up the hierarchy leaving jobs de-skilled and workers devalued" (1983/2003: 119). For example, cabin-crew training on how to deal with angry passengers is a form of deskilling. This is because the "mind of the emotion worker, the source of the ideas about what mental moves are needed to settle down an 'irate' has moved upstairs in the hierarchy so that the worker is restricted to implementing standard procedures" (ibid.: 120).

In summary, Hochschild's theory of emotional labor explicitly argues that workers are systematically alienated from their service product and the labor process that determines the form and timing of its manufacture. However, while her explicit theorization peters out beyond the immediacy of workplace relations, she does provide a partial analysis of the impact of emotional labor on wider capitalist social relations. As a result, it is possible to argue that her thesis, rather than rejecting the remaining two dimensions of Marx's theory of alienation, instead possesses the potential for their acceptance and integration.

Human Nature Alienation

Human nature alienation is that aspect of alienation that addresses the damaging and distorting effects of capitalist society on our species being. For while capitalism has immeasurably enhanced our collective capacity to transform the world through medicine, travel, communication, modern agriculture, and so on, in the interests of all, this capacity is thwarted. This is because capitalism suppresses our potential to realize our collective species being, based as it is on an anarchic drive for profits, competition, class division, and exploitation. Hochschild appears to hint at an understanding of the way capitalism's capacity to meet the needs and desires of humanity is thwarted by its need to put profit before all else. At most, her position on this feature of alienation is ambiguous:

> Massive people-processing—and the advanced engineering of emotional labor that makes it possible—is a remarkable achievement. It is also an important one, for a good part of modern life involves exchange between total strangers, who in the absence of countermeasures and in the pursuit of short-term interest, might much of the time act out suspicion and anger rather than trust and good will... But like most great achievements, the advanced engineering of emotional labor leaves new dilemmas in its wake, new human costs. (ibid.: 187)

Hochschild, however, is openly contradictory as to whether the alienating costs of emotional labor can be removed by simply reorganizing its production process or instead requires the systemic replacement of capitalist social relations. At several points, she seems to suggest that workers can avert alienation by successfully managing their "true self": "When feelings are successfully commercialized, the worker does not feel phoney or alien; she feels somehow satisfied in how personal her service actually was. Deep acting is a help in doing this, not a source of estrangement" (ibid: 136).

This is a shift away from Marx's theorization of alienation as a systemic dimension of capitalist relations of production, and toward one that posits it as primarily an individualized, pathological condition that can be "treated" within capitalist social relations. Indeed, subsequent writers have drawn on this inconsistency to argue that it is possible to remove the alienating psychological costs of emotional labor by redesigning the work to ensure greater autonomy and control for the individual (Wharton, 1996; Ashworth and Humphrey, 1993). In short, Hochschild's ambiguous theorization and her inconsistencies on the nature of alienation and its existence beyond the immediate realm of workplace relations serve to blunt her overall critique of the generic commodification of human feelings.

Conversely, Hochschild also suggests that capitalism's deepening and spreading market relations have a cumulative spillover effect into wider society. In her 2003 afterword to *The Managed Heart*, she refers to the increasing take-up of "personal services" and the way private life is progressively invaded and shaped by commodified emotional labor, suggesting a "vital link between larger social contradictions and private efforts to manage feeling" (ibid.: 202). These contradictions, she states, which generate emotional strain between the real and false selves, now exist not only at work but also at home, and increasingly "in between" work and home. Thus, she tentatively hints at the possibility of an analysis that would highlight emotional labor's alienating, corrosive effects beyond the workplace.

Fellow Beings Alienation and Commodity Fetishism

Fellow beings alienation refers to social relations between individuals that increasingly take the form of relationships between commodities. In a society based on the production and consumption of commodities, the pervasiveness of commodities can seem an inevitable, even a natural state of affairs (Lukács, 1974; May, 2006). Marx states that under capitalism, the wealth of society appears as an "immense collection of commodities," with the commodity becoming a "universal category of society as a whole" (Marx, 1976 [1867]: 125).

For Marx, this generates a multidimensional phenomenon throughout capitalist society, which he calls "commodity fetishism" (1976 [1867]). Consequently, we experience relationships with each other not as individuals, but as if we were extensions of capitalism (Ollman, 1976 [1971]). As capitalism develops, commodification encroaches and invades our lives to the point at which a life outside market relations and independent of commodities is unimaginable. This is because marketers and advertisers ensure we are confronted perpetually by their messages and images that connect the consuming of things and experiences (from washing machines to dating agencies to air travel) with gaining success, respect, beauty, and happiness. The result is that our daily lives, aspirations, and self-concepts are indelibly inscribed by our unavoidable relationship with commodities. Consequently, even as consumers, we are alienated because of our enmeshed dependence on the market, where "the very character of man is at the mercy of his products, of what they make him want and become in order to get what he wants" (Ollman, 1976 [1971]: 146).

Individuals also relate to each other in society as objectified bearers of the commodities that they produce, possess, and consume. The consequence is that commodities acquire social and human characteristics, as with "cool," "sophisticated," and "sexy" brands, owing to our entering into unequal social relationships based on the amount (especially the amount of money) and quality of commodities we possess (Lodziak, 2002). Our social interactions are also determined by our place and function in the market as managers or managed; service workers or customers; "professionals" or clients; employed or unemployed; and so on. Indeed, this market-structured inequality and competitiveness also suffuses noncommercial service interactions, such as between teacher and student (Harvie, 2006), and medic and patient (Yuill, 2005). Thus, we encounter each other in competitive market relationships in which we are either in an inferior or in a superior position (Cox, 1998). In other words, we are reified individuals and enter into reified relationships as the bearers of economic relations. As such, we are the personification of the commodities we possess (Lukács, 1974).

Reification necessarily generates an obscuring of the actual social relations that lie behind the production of any commodity. We connect with our fellow humans through the lens of commodities, where all knowledge of and understanding of how and why our fellow humans produced the thing is submerged beneath a fetishized embrace of a commodity's assumed and claimed properties (Ollman, 1976 [1971]).

One example of a fetishized embrace is that of customer service. As customers, we expect sales staff to be trained to respect and value us irrespective of whether that respect and value is sincere. Thus commodity fetishism is the process whereby human relationships are reified as exchange values, human qualities are invested in material commodities, and real social relations of production are obscured to the point at which the world of markets and commodities appears to be almost independent of human design.

Hochschild does not acknowledge fellow beings alienation and commodity fetishism as being a dimension to Marx's theory, nor to her own. However, as in the case of human nature alienation, her theorization does not close off its existence. Indeed, *The Managed Heart* is replete with references to and examples of commodity fetishism. She shows how cabin crews' existence as commodified labor power generates a fetishized discourse on their worth as things. Managers continually remind them of their disposability due to competition for cabin-crew jobs. Even more starkly, managers refer to them as "bodies for the flight" and "breakage" when they are too ill to work (ibid.: 136). Hochschild recognizes this as reification when she explains that "surface and deep acting in a commercial setting...make one's face and feelings take on the properties of a resource...to be used to make money" (ibid.: 55). She further explains that a broader managerial discourse, based on a corporate logic in the airline industry, underpins this. This discourse makes "a series of links between competition, market expansion, advertising, heightened passenger expectations about rights to display, and company demands for acting" (ibid.: 90), thereby generating an ideological justification and pressure for the codification and learning of ever-more feeling rules. Thus, Hochschild recognizes that management continually seeks to inculcate amongst workers a reified, "taken for granted" perspective on the naturalness of their being treated as things. Moreover, she recognizes that this managerial process is heightened in conditions of increasing completion and/or expenditure reduction when employers seek labor intensification.

While Hochschild's arguments are largely consistent with the concept of commodity fetishism at the level of workplace relations, her position is ambiguous as to the extent to which it exists in other spheres of commodified social relations. Her ambiguity, however, does not preclude the occasional tantalizing commentary on the damaging impact of emotional labor in wider society:

> Estrangement from display, from feeling, and from what feelings can tell us is not simply the occupational hazard of a few. It has firmly established

itself in the culture as imaginable. All of us know the commercialization of human feeling at one remove—as witness, consumer, or critic—and have become adept at recognizing and discounting commercialised feeling. "Oh, they have to be friendly, that's their job." (ibid.: 189–90)

The significance of Hochschild's ambiguity is that she leaves open the theoretical door to the argument that away from the immediacy of workplace relations, capitalist society possesses spaces free from alienation, whereas Marx's commodity fetishism theory makes plain that in a society based on commodity production, there is no escape from alienation. As Mészáros explains, "selling is the practice of alienation [as] alienation is characterized by the universal extension of 'saleability' [and] by the conversion of human beings into 'things' so that they could appear as commodities on the market" (2005 [1970]: 35).

Commodity Fetishism, Class Consciousness, and Resistance

Commodity fetishism is central to Marx's theory of class consciousness and class struggle. This is because commodity fetishism produces the appearance "that class exploitation is not a social product but the inevitable and unalterable result of the functioning of the market" (Rees, 1998: 95). Class distinctions are also submerged by the common experience of being a customer. This is particularly acute in contemporary "consumer capitalism" thanks to the ideological elevation in status of consumers over producers through the "myth of consumerism" (Lodziak, 2002), wherein workers and billionaires appear to possess, in equal measure, "customer sovereignty." Commodity fetishism, therefore, is the harbinger of a distorted ideology peculiar to capitalism in which "all men and their circumstance appear upside-down as in a camera obscura" (Marx and Engels, 1970 [1845]: 47). As such, under capitalism "widespread social beliefs become so distorted that they are insufficient for understanding the social conditions which have produced such beliefs" (Billig, 1999: 314).

Commodity fetishism may dominate the everyday consciousness of workers, but it is not an "iron cage" of ideological distortion. This is because the wage-labor relationship comprises a central contradiction that acts as a countertendency to commodity fetishism. Thus, although capitalists treat workers' labor power as if it were another purchased tool to be exploited intensely, it is unlike any other commodity, for it is not possible to separate the worker from the labor power itself (Rikowski, 2002; Thompson and Smith, 2010). When an item is bought from a shop, full ownership and control of the commodity passes to the consumer. However, the price, content, and duration of labor power are subject to continual haggling. Moreover, the "worker brazenly accompanies his labor power right into the workplace and stands protectively by it while arguing 'about the terms of its sale' " (Rees, 1998: 221). For Lukács (1974), this central contradiction corrodes and prises open the grip of commodity fetishism. This is because while the reified "laws" of labor market relations may accept as normal, even understandable, the daily struggle (antinomy) over the terms on which labor power is sold, capitalism is unable to resolve this most profound of all structural contradictions. Accordingly, this contradictory experience continually presents workers with the potential power and opportunity to question capital's ideological hegemony and exploitative social relations, and their own reification as commodities (Rees, 1998).

Workers, therefore, are compelled to address the social reality of their commodification and its exchange as a struggle for justice and dignity against exploitation and abuse by employers. Through this experience, nascent working-class consciousness emerges and begins to oppose the distortions of commodity fetishism, with the potential for workers to collectively "use this insight to unravel all the other mystifications of human relations that have taken on the appearance of relations between things" (Rees, 1998: 222). Thus, a contradictory consciousness exists within classes and individuals, comprising a dialectical relationship between commodity fetishism as bourgeois ideology and class consciousness. Alienation, therefore, is never a complete process but is instead a contradictory one that generates the potential for conscious resistance by workers to commodity fetishism and its underpinning, dehumanizing social relations.

The Managed Heart offers argument and evidence that supports this analysis of the relationship between commodity fetishism and class consciousness, without itself utilizing either concept. Hochschild's "transmutation of feelings" is an unstable state, vulnerable to the contradictions of capitalist accumulation processes, as she explains: "When an industry speed-up drastically shortens the time available between flight attendants and passengers, it can become virtually impossible to deliver emotional labor. In that event, the transmutation of emotion work, feeling rules, and social exchange will fail" (1983/2003: 121). The instability of transmutation arises, for the most part, from the central contradiction intrinsic to the wage-labor relationship: the daily struggle over the terms of sale of workers' emotional labor, particularly in an increasingly competitive environment:

> The companies worry that competitors may produce more personal service than they do, so they continue to press for "genuinely friendly" service. But they feel compelled to keep the conveyor belt moving faster and faster. For workers, the job of "enjoying the job" becomes harder and harder. Rewards seem less intrinsic to the work, more compensation for the arduousness of it. (ibid.: 125)

Hochschild explains that when management is seeking to intensify emotional laborers' work, there is a corresponding reaction by many workers that undermines any such efforts, and protects the workers' perceived value of their labor power:

> The company exhorts them to smile more, and "more sincerely," at an increasing number of passengers. The workers respond to the speed-up with a slowdown: they smile less broadly, with a quick release and no sparkle in the eyes, thus dimming the company's message to the people. It is a war of smiles. (ibid.: 127)

Hochschild's "war of smiles" can be seen as a breach in the wall of commodity fetishism that allows class consciousness to emerge. As management imposes ever-more feeling rules and demands greater effort, trade unionism gives expression to workers' "accumulated resentment and discontent" (ibid.: 126). This burgeoning class consciousness is also evident in reactions to those workers who respond positively to management's work intensification: they "become the 'rate-busters' who are resented by other workers" (ibid.: 130). Thus Hochschild acknowledges that the commodification of emotional labor is a contradictory process that tends to generate resistance to management's control of the labor process:

> As one veteran put it, "The more the company sees the battle, the tougher they get with the regulations. They define them more precisely. They come up with more categories and more definitions. And more emotionalizing. And then, in time, we reject them even more." (ibid.: 130)

Hochschild's analysis, therefore, interprets resistance to exploitation and subordination—and its accompanying undermining of commodity fetishism—as being generated by the contradictory nature of wage (emotional) labor.

"Crippled Actors" or Resistive Agents?

Hochschild's account of resistance demonstrates that she understands that workers are reflexive and possess the agency to begin to challenge their alienation. This contradicts a commonly made criticism of her thesis, namely, that she presents emotional laborers as "crippled actors" in that their "transmutation of feelings" implies they cannot exert an active and controlling force in relationships with management and customers (Bolton and Boyd, 2003; Bolton, 2005). This is because Hochschild is said to imbue management's feeling rules with such dominance that the performance of service interactions becomes an atomized experience for the worker, where emotional reassessment is anaesthetized by alienation. This is evidently not the case, for Hochschild clearly theorizes workers' transmutation of feelings as being inherently unstable owing to the daily playing out of the struggle at the frontier of control of emotional labor power. Equally, she is able to explain how the breakdown of "transmutation of feelings" frequently transforms itself into conscious, organized resistance. Nevertheless, such is the frequency of the "crippled actors" charge and its milder form of being too "one-dimensional" (Callaghan and Thompson, 2002: 248) that her account of resistance requires more detailed critical assessment.

Since *The Managed Heart*, competition, restructuring, and work intensification have fuelled unionization and militancy in the airline industry globally (Blyton et al., 2001), and the resistive "emotional labor" of cabin crew has proved a rich source of empirical study (e.g., Linstead, 1995; Tyler and Taylor, 2001; Bolton and Boyd, 2003). Indeed, Linstead's (1995) account of the 1993 strike by Cathay Pacific cabin crew against staff cuts and the consequent speeding up of work appears to take up the "story" where Hochschild leaves off. In it, he captures the contradictory struggle between management's normative (and gendered) feeling rules, and the class-conscious nature of resistance to them: "In the advertisements, the Cathay girls fix [a] sultry smile then avert their faces with Asian humility . . . This servile image has been smashed by the perfumed picket line which has shown itself to be tough, resilient and well orchestrated" (Linstead, 1995: 200).

While the airline industry represents the best example of militant trade unionism by emotional laborers, there is also evidence that in their day-to-day activities, cabin crew "remain very aware . . . that they are offering an *empty performance* . . . without ever *buying-in* to the norms set by the company" (Bolton and Boyd, 2003: 301). Moreover, there exists a plethora of evidence from other service industries of day-to-day, informal individual and collective resistance, irrespective of a union presence (e.g., Ogbonna and Harris, 2004; Sandiford, 2007). Thus in call centers, Mulholland found that "sales sabotage, working to rule, work avoidance, absenteeism and high turnover are expressions of a workplace antagonism rooted in and against the social relations of production" (2004: 720). Moreover, workers invariably direct their resistance against customers as well as against managers. In betting shops, Filby (1992) found that while women are employed for their "figures," their "personality," and their "bums," they exploited their sexualized emotional labor to assert informal control by developing a culture of sexual humor to ridicule and humiliate male managers and unpleasant "punters." Likewise, Taylor and Bain's (2003b) call-center research found that workplace activists used a culture of humor to subvert antiunion managerial authority in their campaign for trade union recognition. Thus, Taylor (1998: 99) is correct to argue that workers experience an "incomplete transmutation," and that as a resource for the creation of surplus value, the emotional labor of service employees is a "double-edged sword" (Filby, 1992). While in the public sector there is widespread opposition by service workers to the creeping "marketisation" (and privatization) of education, health, and other services, where commercial values of competition and profit undermine employment conditions and the principles of egalitarian public service provision (Ogbonna and Harris, 2004; Harvie, 2006; and Taylor and Cooper, 2008).

Studies on resistance among emotional laborers, in a range of service settings, tend to highlight the triadic nature of the labor process in which the core relationship for analysis is expanded to include the service recipient (in varying degrees) alongside the employer and employee (Korczynski, 2002; Sandiford, 2007). Likewise, many point to the existence of shifting boundaries at the "frontier of control" (e.g., Tyler and Taylor, 2001; Taylor and Bain, 2003a), where "management control of emotional labor can be partial, incoherent and often contradictory" (Taylor, 1998: 100). This is due to the "exacerbated" labor indeterminacy of emotional production (Bolton, 2005: 62), as management struggles to control the thoughts, feelings, and behaviors of workers during service interactions. This in turn is further exacerbated where there is a greater degree of "professional" autonomy such as in classrooms (Harvie, 2006) and in hospital wards (Theodosius, 2008) and where there is little or no formal supervision, as with the example of nannies (Isserles, 2010). Consequently, service regimes are marked by a process of informal, "continual negotiation and re-negotiation [with management and service recipients] over the transformation of emotional labor power into a serviceable product" (Callaghan and

Thompson, 2002: 251). This relies, in turn, on an informal process of workplace socialization, outside of direct management control, through which workers share and inculcate knowledge of the "renegotiated" feeling rules (Korczynski, 2002; Seymour and Sandiford, 2005).

It is not surprising, therefore, that Hochschild's notion of a "successful transmutation of feelings" should risk appearing to consign workers to a disabling, fetishized state. This is a consequence of her partial application of Marx's theory of alienation, which results in her being unable to generate a dialectical account of emotional labor in which workers' consciousness is conceptualized as contradictory and their agency as constrained. This in turn would allow her to understand workers' experience of emotional labor as comprising an antagonistic tussle between the contradictory possibilities of assimilating management's feeling rules and collective resistance. Such a theorization would enable an explicit explanation of how workers retain and exercise sufficient control over their emotional labor to alleviate their day-to-day working lives—or even to exert a counter controlling force in relationships with management and customers (Callaghan and Thompson, 2002).

While Hochschild does not, in her theory, close off the potential for the type of daily *getting by* and *getting back* activities outlined above, she largely omits an explicit analysis of them. Moreover, her lack of a theorization of class means that she does not possess the conceptual armory to account for them as preconditions and precursors to more class-conscious acts of resistance, in contrast to more recent Marxist-oriented LPA studies of emotional laborers (e.g., Taylor, 1998; Taylor and Bain, 2003a, 2003b; Mulholland, 2004). These studies have sought to overcome this weakness by arguing for the integration of the emotional labor concept with LPA's theorization of relations of production as antagonistic and contradictory, thereby producing "a complex interplay of compliance, consent and resistance" (Taylor, 1998: 100). Nevertheless, to date there has not been a detailed and systematic assessment of Hochschild's theoretical adequacy from within the LPA tradition.

Finally, it should be noted that Hochschild explores the experience of emotional labor principally through the individualized, conceptual lens of her distinction between individuals' surface and deep acting and the "transmutation of feelings" (Bolton, 2005). By focusing on the immediacy of the individualized commodification process, in contrast with the LPA approach, she insufficiently locates her analysis in the wider context of workplace class relations. Thus, she underemphasizes the basis, form, and significance of collectively forged organizational space for worker agency and activity outside and within the commodification process. Yet, a lack of emphasis is not the same thing as a theoretical closure, as Bolton and Boyd (2003) and Bolton (2005) have argued. Rather, Hochschild's portrayal of the emotional labor workplace is one in which consent, indifference, and conscious resistance by workers are ever present, but are unduly overshadowed by her conceptual foregrounding of the deleterious impact on individuals from the commodification of their emotions.

Conclusion:
Reasserting the Human Cost of Emotional Labor

The Managed Heart may suffer from theoretical ambiguities, inconsistencies, and gaps but its core arguments remain tenable within the context of a classical Marxist analysis (Rees, 1998). Hochschild convincingly argues that learning and performing emotional labor requires the formal commodification of a worker's emotions. Commonly, this process commences with employers recruiting and selecting employees with the right attitude and personality as prerequisites for delivering the form and style of service demanded by management. However, in order to realize this potential and sustain it, an ongoing process of workplace learning is frequently employed to inculcate workers with the desired customer-oriented values and behaviors, which Hochschild refers to as "feeling rules." The result is that their emotion work is then subjected to management design and control, which in turn is subject to labor intensification as employers continually search for enhanced performance. Equally importantly, she reveals the contradictory and antagonistic nature of the experience. Consequently, she is also able to begin to account for why and how workers learn to ameliorate and resist the loss of control and ownership of their emotional labor.

For Hochschild, emotional labor is an acutely alienating variant of wage labor that systemically throws workers into a daily struggle to secure a dignified sense of self. It also increasingly involves management deploying workplace learning strategies in an attempt to secure adequate soft skill levels, behavioral compliance, and corporate acculturation. Hochschild's account of reproducing emotional labor in the workplace begins to reveal in stark fashion how all learning in contemporary capitalist society invariably possesses a cultural dimension that to a greater or lesser degree plays some part in fostering belief in the primacy of the customer, marketized social relations, and the desirability of today's consumer culture. Hochschild's legacy, therefore, is twofold. First, her emotional labor concept is invaluable for our understanding of the experience of working and living in "consumer capitalism." Second, her account of learning the feeling rules illustrates that, for "consumer culture" to reproduce itself both in the workplace and in wider society, some degree of inculcation of customer-centered values is likely to be a feature of all learning under contemporary capitalist conditions.

Notes

1. This chapter is an adapted version of Brook (2009a).
2. The widespread academic, public policy and general interest in the concept is revealed by the combined figure for Google searches of "emotional labour" and "emotional labor," which generates approximately 80,000 results (July 8, 2010).
3. Hochschild makes a foray into the gendered nature of emotional labor (1983/2003: 162–84) but it is largely theoretically unintegrated with her emotional labor concept.
4. Hochschild's partial application may be a consequence of her narrow understanding of Marx's concept. After reading an earlier version of this chapter, she commented, "It really made me think about alienation in a larger way" (2007). She is not alone in offering a partial rendering of alienation, for example, Barbalet (2001) and Lodziak (2002).
5. Cohen's (2010) study of self-employed hairdressers reveals another dimension of emotion work alienation. She reveals how engaging in the immediate market relations required to build and sustain a small hairdressing business generates a level of alienation in which there is a severe blurring of temporal, physical, and relational boundaries between working and private life.
6. Hochschild is vague on whether all forms of wage labor comprising emotional displays constitute alienating emotional labor. She suggests that the all-important distinction is whether there is "exploitation of the bottom by the top." Therefore, "it is not emotional labor itself but the underlying system of recompense that raises the question of what the cost of it is" (198/2003: 12). Yet, Hochschild does not attempt to theorize what might constitute an exploitation of emotional labor.

References

Ashworth, B.E. and R.H. Humphrey (1993) Emotional Labor in Service Roles: The Influence of Identities. *Academy of Management Review*, 18(1): 88–115.
Barbalet, J. M. (2001) *Emotion, Social Theory and Social Structure* (Cambridge: Cambridge University Press).

Billig, M. (1999) Commodity Fetishism and Repression: Reflections on Marx, Freud and the Psychology of Consumer Capitalism. *Theory and Psychology*, 9(3): 313–29.

Blyton, P., M.M. Lucio, J. McGurk, and P. Turnbull (2001) Globalization and Trade Union Strategy: Industrial Restructuring and Human Resource Management in the International Civil Aviation Industry. *International Journal of Human Resource Management*, 12(3): 445–63.

Bolton, S.C. (2005) *Emotion Management in the Workplace* (Basingstoke: Palgrave).

Bolton, S.C. (2010) Old Ambiguities and New Developments: Exploring the Emotional Labour Process. In P. Thompson and C. Smith (eds.) *Working Life: Renewing Labour Process Analysis,* 205–24 (Basingstoke: Palgrave).

Bolton, S.C. and C. Boyd (2003) Trolly Dolly or Skilled Emotion Manager? Moving on from Hochschild's Managed Heart. *Work, Employment and Society*, 17(2): 289–308.

Braverman, H. (1974) *Labor and Monopoly Capital* (New York: Monthly Review Press).

Brook, P. (2009a) The Alienated Heart: Hochschild's "Emotional Labour" thesis and the Anti-Capitalist Politics of Alienation. *Capital and Class,* 98: 7–31.

Brook, P. (2009b) In Critical Defence of "Emotional Labour": Refuting Bolton's Critique of Hochschild's Concept. *Work Employment and Society*, 23(3): 531–48.

Brook, P. (2010) An Indivisible Union? Assessing the Marriage of Hochschild's Emotional Labour Concept and Labour Process Theory. *International Journal of Management Concepts and Philosophy*, 4(3): 326–42.

Brook, P. and E. Pioch (2006) Culture Change Management. In R. Lucas, B. Lupton, and H. Mathieson (eds.) *Human Resource Management in an International Context*, 89–116 (London: CIPD).

Callaghan, G. and P. Thompson (2002) We Recruit Attitude: The Selection and Shaping of Routine Call Centre Labour. *Journal of Management Studies*, 39(2): 233–53.

Cohen, R.L. (2010) When It Pays to be Friendly: Employment Relationship and Emotional Labour in Hairstyling. *The Sociological Review*, 58(2): 197–218.

Colley, H. (2006) Learning to Labour with Feeling: Class, Gender and Emotion in Childcare Education and Training. *Contemporary Issues in Early Childhood*, 7(1): 15–29.

Cox, J. (1998) An Introduction to Marx's Theory of Alienation. *International Socialism Journal*, 79: 41–62.

Filby, M. (1992) The Figures, the Personality and the Bums: Service Work and Sexuality. *Work, Employment and Society*, 6(1): 23–42.

Fineman, S. (2005) Appreciating Emotion at Work: Paradigm Tensions. *International Journal of Work Organisation and Emotion*, 1(1): 4–19.

Fineman, S. (ed.) (2007), *The Emotional Organization: Passions and Power* (London: Wiley Blackwell).

Grugulis, I. (2007) *Skills, Training and Human Resource Development: A Critical Text* (Basingstoke: Palgrave).

Grugulis, I. and Vincent, S. (2009) Whose Skill Is It Anyway? Soft Skills and Polarization. *Work, Employment and Society*, 23(4): 597–615.

Harvie, D. (2006) Value Production and Struggle in the Classroom: Teachers within, against and beyond Capital. *Capital and Class*, 88: 1–32.

Hochschild, A.R. (1983/2003) *The Managed Heart: Commercialization of Human Feeling* (London: University of California).

Hochschild, A.R. (2003) *The Commercialization of Intimate Life: Notes from Home and Work* (London: University of California).

Hochschild, A.R. (2007) personal correspondence, April 22.

Isserles, R. (2010) Caring for and about the Work We Do: The Dialectics of Alienation, Emotional Labor and an Ethic of Care. Paper presented to the *International Labour Process Conference*, Rutgers University, New Jersey.

James, N. (1989) Emotional Labour in the Regulation of Skill and Feeling. *The Sociological Review*, 37(1): 15–42.

James, N. (1992) Care = Organisation + Physical Labour + Emotional Labour. *Sociology of Health and Illness* 14(4): 488–509.

Jansz, J. and M. Timmers (2002) Emotional Dissonance: When the Experience of an Emotion Jeopardizes an Individual's Identity. *Theory and Psychology*, 12(1): 79–95.

Korczynski, M. (2002) *Human Resource Management in Service* Work (Basingstoke: Palgrave).

Korczynski, M. and C.L. MacDonald (eds.) (2009) *Service Work: Critical Perspectives* (London: Routledge).

Lewis, P. and R. Simpson (eds.) (2007) *Gendering Emotions in Organizations* (Basingstoke: Palgrave).

Linstead, S. (1995) Averting the Gaze: Gender and Power on the Perfumed Picket Line. *Gender, Work and Organization*, 2(4): 192–206.

Lodziak, C. (2002) *The Myth of Consumerism* (London: Pluto).

Lukács, G. (1974) *History and Class Consciousness* (London: Merlin).

Marx, K. (1975) Economic and Philosophical Manuscripts (1844). In *Karl Marx: Early Writings* (London: Penguin/New Left Review).

Marx, K. (1976 [1867]) *Capital, Volume 1* (London: Penguin/New Left Review).

Marx, K. and F. Engels (1970 [1845]) *The German Ideology* (London: Lawrence and Wishart).

May, C. (2006) The Denial of History: Reification, Intellectual Property Rights and the Lessons of the Past. *Capital and Class*, 88: 33–56.

Mészáros, I. (2005 [1970]) *Marx's Theory of Alienation* (London: Merlin).

Mulholland, K. (2004) Workplace Resistance in an Irish Call Centre: Slammin', Scammin', Smokin' an' Leavin'. *Work, Employment and Society*, 8(4): 709–24.

Ogbonna, E. and L. C. Harris (2004) Work Intensification and Emotional Labour among UK University Lecturers: An Exploratory Study. *Organization Studies*, 25(7): 1185–203.

Ollman, B. (1976 [1971]) *Alienation: Marx's Conception of Man in Capitalist Society* (Cambridge: Cambridge University Press).

Payne, J. (2009) Emotional Labour and Skill: A Reappraisal. *Gender, Work and Organization,* 16(2): 348–69.

Pettinger, L. (2005) Gendered Work Meets Gendered Goods: Selling and Service in Clothing Retail. *Gender, Work and Organization,* 12(5): 460–78.

Price, H. (2001) Emotional Labour in the Classroom: A Psychoanalytic Perspective. *Journal of Social Work Practice,* 2: 161–80.

Rees, J. (1998) *The Algebra of Revolution: The Dialectic and the Classical Marxist Tradition* (London: Routledge).

Rikowski, G. (2002), Methods for Researching the Social Production of Labour Power in Capitalism. *School of Education Research Seminar,* University College Northampton, March 7.

Sandiford, P. (2007) Emotional Labour and Emotional Resistance in Service Work: The Case of the UK Public House Sector. Paper presented at *Manchester Metropolitan University Business School, HRM and OB Seminar Series.*

Scholarios, D. and P. Taylor (2010) Gender Choice and Constraint in Call Centre Employment. *New Technology, Work and Employment,* 25(2): 101–16.

Seymour, D. and P. Sandiford (2005) Learning Emotion Rules in Service Organizations: Socialization and Training in the UK Public-House Sector. *Work, Employment and Society,* 19(3): 547–64.

Steinberg, R. and D. Figart (1999) Emotional Labor since The Managed Heart. *ANNALS–AAPSS,* 561: 8–26.

Sturdy, A. (1998) Customer Care in a Consumer Society: Smiling and Sometimes Meaning it. *Organization* 5 (1): 27-53.

Taylor, S. (1998) Emotional Labour and the New Workplace. In P. Thompson and C. Warhurst (eds.) *Workplaces of the Future,* 84–103 (Basingstoke: Palgrave).

Taylor, P. and P. Bain (2003a) Call Centre Organizing in Adversity: From Excell to Vertex. In G. Gall (ed.) *Union Organizing,* 153–72 (London: Routledge).

Taylor, P. and P. Bain (2003b) Subterranean Worksick Blues: Humour as Subversion in Two Call Centres. *Organization Studies,* 24(9): 1487–509.

Taylor, P. and C. Cooper (2008) It Was Absolute Hell: Inside the Private Prison. *Capital and Class,* 96: 3–30.

Theodosius, C. (2008) *Emotional Labour in Health Care* (London: Routledge).

Thompson, P. and C. Smith (2010) Debating Labour Process Theory and the Sociology of Work. In P. Thompson and C. Smith (eds.) *Working Life: Renewing Labour Process Analysis,* 11–28 (Basingstoke: Palgrave).

Tolich, M.B. (1993) Alienating and Liberating Emotions at Work. *Journal of Contemporary Ethnography,* 22(3): 361–81.

Townsend, K. (2006) Recruitment, Training and Turnover: Another Call Centre Paradox. *Personnel Review,* 36(3): 476–90.

Tyler, M. (2009) Growing Customers: Sales Service-work in the Children's Culture Industries. *Journal of Consumer Culture*, 9(1): 55–77.

Tyler, M. and S. Taylor (2001) Juggling Justice and Care: Gendered Customer Service in the Contemporary Airline Industry. In A. Sturdy, I. Grugulis, and H. Willmott (eds.) *Customer Service: Empowerment and Entrapment*, 60–78 (Basingstoke: Palgrave).

Warhurst, C. and D. Nickson (2007) Employee Experience of Aesthetic Labour in Retail and Hospitality. *Work, Employment and Society*, 21(1): 103–20.

Warhurst, C. and D. Nickson (2009) Who's Got the Look? Emotional, Aesthetic and Sexualized Labour in Interactive Services. *Gender, Work and Organization*, 16(3): 385–404.

Warhurst, C., P. Thompson, and D. Nickson (2009) Labour Process Theory: Putting the Materialism Back into the Meaning of Service Work. In M. Korczynski and C.L. Macdonald (eds.) *Service Work: Critical Perspectives*, 91–112 (London: Routledge).

Wharton, A. (1996) Service with a Smile: Understanding the Consequences of Emotional Labour. In C.L. Macdonald and C. Sirianni (eds.) *Working in the Service Society*, 91–112 (Philadelphia: Temple University).

Wouters, C. (1989) The Sociology of Emotions and Flight Attendants: Hochschild's Managed Heart. *Theory, Culture and Society*, 6: 95–123.

Wright, D. (2005) Commodifying Respectability: Distinctions at Work in the Bookshop. *Journal of Consumer Culture*, 5(3): 295-314.

Yuill, C. (2005) Marx: Capitalism, Alienation and Health. *Social Theory and Health*, 3: 126–43.

Chapter 5

Adult Education and the "Matter" of Consciousness in Marxist-Feminism

Sara Carpenter and Shahrzad Mojab

In teaching adult education courses, a major challenge for us is to make students articulate the sources of their knowledge about themselves or the world. We ask them to think through these questions: "How do you know what you know?" "Where does your knowledge come from?" There are some immediate and predictable answers such as personal experience, accumulated academic, or work-related knowledge, or social learning through culture, tradition, media, personal, or group interaction. We encourage them to go deeper in their explanation and interpretation of social relations and their role and location in them. This, we have come to realize, is not an easy process, in part because, in our understanding, the way to answer these questions is to articulate the relationship between self and the social world as well as between consciousness and the material world. Often students are neither able to name this relationship nor are fully capable of articulating their location in these social relations. Thus, as teachers, we have found it necessary to delve deeper into the problematic of dissociated self and society. In this chapter, we undertake an exploration of the relation between consciousness and the material world from the perspective of Marxist-Feminism.

The theorization of consciousness is a central component of the field of adult education and has grown in recent years through the work of authors such as Paula Allman, Wayne Au, John Holst, Helen Colley, Peter McLaren and Nathalia Jaramillo, and the continued exploration of Freire's seminal works (Allman, 2007; Holst, 1999; Au, 2007a; Colley, 2002; McLaren and Jaramillo, 2010). The transformation of consciousness is an important aim of the field's historical legacy of social movement mobilization, popular education, and trade union organizing (Rikowski, 1996, 1997). Despite this centrality, the theorization of consciousness largely takes place in other arenas of social theory and, noticeably, almost exclusively by radical scholars from feminist theory, psychoanalytics, critical race theory, and Marxism. We observe that in adult education consciousness is often treated as an object of pedagogical intervention; the phrases "critical consciousness," "consciousness raising," and "conscientization" are expressed as outcomes, process, methods, or goals. The outcome of this practice is to disconnect consciousness from its theoretical roots and, ultimately, to deradicalize the purpose of talking about consciousness in the first place. Part of this problem may be found in educators confining their reading on consciousness to Freire as well as reading Freire in an essentially liberalized or pragmatic vision, divorcing the work from its roots in Marxist humanism (Allman and Wallis, 1990; Au, 2007a). As Marxist-Feminist researchers and educators, we find the theorization of consciousness to be essential not only to our imagination of pedagogical possibilities but to understanding the realities of the social relations and conditions we research and try to explain.

We begin this chapter from Paula Allman's argument that Marx's theorization of consciousness is central for critical education theory, as well as for understanding the role of education in the reproduction of labor and capitalist social relations (Allman, 1999, 2001, 2007). For Allman, the Marxist theorization of consciousness is in fact the theorization of praxis. However, we seek to go further into the social relations elucidated in Allman's work by providing a reading of consciousness from a Marxist-Feminist perspective. To do this, we have organized this discussion in three parts. First, we review Marx's original articulation of the theory of consciousness. This review, which draws heavily from Allman's as well as Derek Sayer's work, positions our reading of consciousness dialectically and historically (Sayer, 1979, 1987). Second, we provide a historical review of the development of the theorization of consciousness in the field of adult education in order to give our reader a sense of how this theorization has evolved as part of the ongoing political struggles of Marxism, feminism, and antiracism. Third, we examine feminist-materialist expansions on Marx's theory of consciousness and argue that through these feminist interventions we can see more deeply into Marx's notion of social totality and into the complex and changing organization of capitalist social relations. We conclude by sketching some of the implications of a Marxist-Feminist perspective for consciousness in the field of adult education.

Consciousness in Marx

Marx's discussion of consciousness began with what, from our vantage point, may appear as an abstract philosophical debate. In the wake of Hegel's death a group of young, radical philosophers began their academic and activist lives, calling themselves "the Young Hegelians." Initially Marx was one of these young men committed to freeing human consciousness from the strangleholds of religious and secular monarchy (Callincos, 1999). However, Marx eventually broke from this group over an extremely important question: Who makes history or how is history made? In the Hegelian framework, history was made, determined, and advanced through the development of human rational consciousness. This consciousness existed only in the human mind or spirit; Hegel referred to this consciousness as "absolute." Hegel's argument was a pure form of idealism, in which the existence of objective reality is only made possible through human consciousness. In this schema, consciousness determines life (Warminski, 1995).

The Young Hegelians exchanged this absolute idealism for what they knew as "materialism," an inversion of the Hegelian reliance on "the spirit." Rather, they argued, the relation between the ideal and the material had to be inverted; the material determined the ideal (Arthur, 1991). In this formulation, human consciousness was treated as an effluence; it is the thing that comes after and corresponds to its precursor (Allman, 2001). Beginning in the mid-1840s, Marx and Engels began a series of critiques of Hegel and his successors. This critique developed from *A Contribution to the Critique of Hegel's "Philosophy of Right"* (1843) (Marx, 1977), to *The Holy Family* (1844) (Marx and Engels, 2002), *The German Ideology* (1845–1846) (Marx and Engels, 1932), and *The Poverty of Philosophy* (1847) (Marx, 2008). In these "early" texts, Marx and Engels systematically dismantled the arguments of the Young Hegelians. Marx commented on this relation:

> My inquiry led to the conclusion that neither legal relations nor political forms could be comprehended whether by themselves or on the basis of a so-called general development of the human mind, but that on the contrary they originate in the material conditions of life, the totality of which Hegel, following the example of English and French thinkers of the eighteenth century, embraces within the term "civil society"; that the anatomy of this civil society, however, has to be sought in political economy. (Marx, 1970a: 20)

Marx and Engels, in their critique of philosophical idealism, conferred on matter a determining role, although in their critique of mechanistic materialism they insisted that the relationship between consciousness and matter could not be understood as one of determination (Marx and Engels, 1932). This relation of "determination," however, is extremely complex and forms the central feature of the base-super-structure debate. From a dialectical position, the two enter into relations of unity and struggle of opposites, meaning that the ideal and the material mutually determine one another through an inner relation. To establish this inner relation, Marx and Engels needed to refute Hegel's emphasis on the "absolute" ideal at the same time that they refuted the "absolute" materialism of the Young Hegelians. Establishing this dialectical relation poses a significant challenge to Marxist thinkers.

This dialectic was not seen by the Young Hegelians, such as Feuerbach, for whom reality was only considered as "*the object of contemplation*, but not as *sensuous human activity, practice*, not subjectively" (Marx, 1970b: 121). The relation between the ideal and the material was essential to Marx because of its implications for human practice. In both the "subjective idealism" of Hegel and the "contemplative materialism" of Feuerbach, human agency was subtext rather than the "engine" of history. History and reality moved around and passed people, as if people were passive observers of a world moving without them. For Marx, history and social reality were "sensuous human activity" (ibid.). Thus, in direct opposition to the dogmatic interpretation of Marxism as a science that obliterates the subject, Marx insisted on the power of people to transform the world. For Marx, our consciousness is nothing less than conscious life, meaning that consciousness and matter are locked in a dialectical relation with one another in which they constantly form and transform their essence and appearance through struggle and movement. This dialectical unity of opposites, a major organizing principle of Marx's philosophy and science, is conditioned by a kind of materialism in which the sensuous activity of people *over time* is central to its conception. Marx argued that the social life of people, understood as the ways in which they produce and reproduce themselves materially and socially, was historically specific. Everyone, he argued, must contend with history. We act, we think, we resist, we organize ourselves, but not under conditions of our choosing (Marx, 1972).

Marx's understanding of consciousness is complex and related to another important formulation: social reality. Marx's ontology, which he and Engels put forward in *The German Ideology*, is based not only on historical specificity but on the notion of human cooperative activity (Marx and Engels, 1932). For Marx and Engels, human life would not exist without humans living and working in "cooperative" social relations in order to produce and reproduce their lives. These "cooperative" relations were not necessarily peaceful, but rather cooperative in the sense that humans live and reproduce socially, their existence is evidence of the social nature of life, and language is the most indelible proof of this connection (Marx, 1988; McNally, 2001). However, one of the central characteristics of life within a capitalist mode of production is that we do not experience our lives as "social" or "cooperative." Rather, we work under the conception that we are individual, independent, and self-sufficient (Wilde, 1994: 1175). One of the easiest ways to understand this tension is to take a moment and think about where your food comes from. For some of us, we may be able to say that we grew our food on our own land. The rest of us will acknowledge that our food arrives on our table through a vast network of human relations in which active human labor takes place at every level. This cooperative behavior demonstrates the social organization of the relations of production. It also demonstrates that we do not experience the world on a daily basis as the subjective reality that reflects these complex relations. When we go to the grocery store we do not think about all the people whose lives are found in the product that winds up in the cereal aisle. Rather, we just think about the objects of human labor and, frankly, we do not think of other people as part of the same social relations as ourselves. They disappear in the objectification of social life we experience every day. For Marx, this relation of objectivity and subjectivity is intrinsic to the explanation of the relation between consciousness and matter. Consciousness exists in both subjective and objective forms, as does matter. The objectification takes place on the level of consciousness and in real everyday life. It is this objectification and its formation in consciousness that Marx and Engels refer to in their famous analogy of the camera obscura, in which "men [sic] and their circumstances appear upside-down" (Marx and Engels, 1932).

In other terms, the relation between consciousness and matter can be understood as the relation between epistemology and ontology. Ontology, which we have discussed above, refers to the theorization of actually existing reality. For Marx, reality does objectively exist, but it exists dialectically in the cooperative labor of people *and* their forms of consciousness. What is of the utmost importance for the theorization of consciousness is how this reality can be *known*. These are the questions we ask our students in class and with which we began this chapter. How do we know what we know? Where does our knowledge come from? The philosophical articulation of this relation has extremely important implications for the practice of revolutionary struggle. For instance, Mao Zedong's contribution to this debate, in the context of the Chinese revolution, was to argue that in the realm of ontology it is impossible to differentiate between consciousness and matter (Mao, 2007). However, on the terrain of epistemology we can come to know "the mechanism by which thought can have access to and come to know objectively the realm of reality" (Knight, 2005: 175). What is established in the ontology-epistemology relation is the philosophy of praxis, which Mao referred to as "practice-based epistemology," and which unites consciousness and matter in a dialectical relation in which consciousness can come to know reality *and* move beyond the experiential and situated appearances of matter (ibid.: 175).

In a way similar to Mao and Gramsci, Paula Allman has argued that Marx's theory of consciousness cannot be understood as anything other than a philosophy of praxis (Knight, 1990; Thomas, 2009; Allman, 2001). Understanding the relation between consciousness and matter within capitalist social life is very tricky, and Allman has done an invaluable service to educators by developing a heuristic tool to help us think about the relation between praxis, human agency, and historical change. For Allman, the logical extension of Marx's argument is that human praxis can exist in two very divergent forms. On the one hand, we can live in such a way that reproduces the violence, oppression, and exploitation of capitalist life. This form of praxis, which Allman calls reproductive or uncritical, does not interrogate the roots of social relations. It may be able to describe the effects or consequences of capitalist social relations, but it cannot locate their source and, further, it cannot move beyond the *appearance* of these relations. An alternative is critical or revolutionary praxis. This form of praxis requires seeking out the forms of consciousness that dig below the surface of capitalism's appearances and into its *essences*, the dialectical contradictions that form the relations of everyday life.

Paula Allman provides a useful and astute organization of what she refers to as the "characteristics" of uncritical/reproductive praxis (Allman, 2007). Another way to refer to these characteristics is to describe them as terms of engagement with the *phenomenal forms* of capitalism, capitalism's appearance, or, rather, its ideologically objectified forms of social consciousness (Sayer, 1987). These characteristics reproduce the separations and inversions of capitalist social relations that obliterate the visibility of dialectical contradictions in everyday life. Each of these forms of consciousness, or ways of thinking, is part of what "Marx describes as the 'violence of *abstraction*,' when one's thinking reproduces the separation of the opposites that constitute a unity of opposites, an internal relation, when it 'violently abstracts,' it distorts one's understanding" (Allman, 2007: 35). Consciousness formed through abstraction, which Marx referred to as "the imagined concrete," ultimately happens because of the very nature of social life within capitalism. We do not often experience daily life in such a way that the relations between phenomena are seen; in fact, we often experience these relations, such as violence against women and labor exploitation, temporally and in spatially disparate ways and, thus, we see their "appearance" in capitalist social relations although not their "essence" (Colley, 2002). Thus, it is equally important to remember that these forms of consciousness are not "errors" in logic as much as they are "grounded in capitalism's phenomenal forms, the ways in which the social relations of bourgeois society present themselves to the consciousness of its participants" (Sayer, 1987: 130).

Many of the concepts Allman describes as "characteristics" are related to the larger social relation of *alienation* (Allman, 2007). Alienation is not essentially a pathological emotional state, although in its extreme forms it may emerge as such. An excellent example of this process can be found in the memoir *Rivethead: Tales from the Assembly Line*, in which the author painstakingly details the emergence of physical and psychological self-abuse as a response to the violence of factory life (Hamper, 1992). Alienation is in fact a social process and relation in which individuals are divorced from their humanist vocation, the "process of becoming" in Marx's terms, by giving up or surrendering their power and potential to an external force (either a person or a thing) that in turn uses that power against the individual. Once given away, human power appears to us as something outside ourselves and alienation becomes manifest in the appearance of opposition between individuals and things, rather than as a struggle rooted in the relations of alienation.

Alienation is often manifested in *dichotomized thought*. Dichotomies, so often the target of critical analysis, are pervasive in reproductive praxis because they obliterate the existence of relations, particularly inner relations, and complexity in social life. In a dichotomy, something cannot be logically understood as two things at the same time as opposed to a dialectical relation in which a phenomenon is composed of mutually determining components locked in struggle. At their center, dichotomies are an expression of the ongoing experiential separation of contradictory social relations. A second process that contributes to this experiential separation is the tendency toward *reification* in bourgeois thought. Reification is simply taking social processes and relations and making them into "things." We sometimes find it helpful to remind ourselves that the verb "reify" is akin to "petrify"; both take something alive and turn its movement into stasis and lifelessness. In a particularly grotesque about-face, an extreme characteristic of reification is personification. A classic example is Marx's analysis of money, which he argues is essentially a commodity expressing a number of complex human relations. Within the historical development of capitalist relations, money becomes a "thing," which can be hoarded. It even becomes a person, given agency and power in society. As such, "money talks." In its most developed form, reification becomes "a form of distortion where the attributes and powers, the essence, of the person or the social relation appear as natural, intrinsic, attributes or powers of the 'thing'" (Allman, 2007: 37). This is *fetishism*, "the ultimate objective and subjective expression of alienation in human practice" (ibid.). In capitalist society, we believe that the value of money is intrinsic to its material form. We see money as an end in itself rather than symbolic of the labor of billions of people, reduced to the exchange of commodities mediated by the universal commodity, money. Allman argues that fetishism is the dialectical relation of alienation. As we produce within capitalism we negate ourselves through the labor-capital relation; as we consume we also negate ourselves and everyone else.

As we can see, the dialectical formation of consciousness and matter is rife with complexity. The ultimate outcomes of bourgeois thought are to make this complexity invisible in order to naturalize and normalize capitalist social relations. A simple way to do this is through *conflation*, which "involves a futile attempt to eliminate complexity by taking entities that are separated and reuniting them by equating them, or in philosophical terms, establishing an immediate identity between them" (ibid.: 38). Conflation is easily seen in the bourgeois claim to the transhistorical nature of market-based social relations.

> To Marx, conflated thinking was both simplistic and distorted, particularly because it encouraged people to ignore historically specific differences as well as the essential internal relations, i.e. the internally specific (but not identical) nature of various entities and processes. (Ibid.)

By eliminating history and contradiction, conflation, in concert with other forms of reproductive praxis, performs a second level of violent abstraction. Not only is the unity of dialectical relations ruptured, but the social relations of material life are broken up into composite parts. Relations such as gender, race, sexuality, and class are divorced from one another and appear as autonomous. The feminist theorizing of "intersectionality," "interlocking oppression," or "matrices of domination" demonstrates the role of conflation in consciousness; having artificially separated these social relations they are reunited in a "mystical" way (Aguilar, 2010). These two kinds of abstraction, the separation of life and relations, and their reunification through unknown processes constitute the core of the method of ideological knowledge production. However, while all consciousness requires some kind of abstraction, not all abstractions must be ideological. Marx and Engels argued that through the method of dialectical historical materialism, abstraction could be used in order to fully explicate the essence of dialectically contradictory relations. It is this form of consciousness, as we will show below, that has become the epistemological imperative of the Marxist theorization of education and learning.

The Roots of "Critical Consciousness"

Our purpose in this section is to historicize, albeit briefly, a component of the theoretical underpinnings of the approaches to consciousness used in critical education. We recognize that it would be a separate undertaking to expand this section to include the full scope of authors on this subject; thus we have limited this discussion to those who have been most significant to adult educators, including Lenin, Vygotsky, Lukács, Mao, and Freire. It is important that adult educators be familiar with this historical trajectory in order to guard against a tendency in social science to disconnect theoretical categories from their full social development, a tendency implicated in the larger project of ideological knowledge production (Smith, 1990). We draw on the contributions of feminist theory, particularly Dorothy Smith's work on consciousness, in the latter part of this chapter. We have observed that there are three important threads that run through this body of knowledge: the relation between consciousness and matter, the everyday versus the scientific, and the processes of abstraction and generalization.

After Marx the theorization of consciousness became deeply embroiled with the question of revolution. While this connection, that is, the problem of how to transform human consciousness for the purposes of revolution, may appear obvious on the surface, the debates about this relation have been deep and far-reaching. A major turning point in this debate was set by Lenin's "What is to be done?" (1902) (Lenin, 1967). Lenin's discussion provides an excellent starting point for tracing the nuances in the theorization of consciousness as he sets out the central problematic of the debate. "What Is to Be Done?" was a response to the ongoing debate in the late nineteenth and early twentieth centuries about the strategic development of revolution in Russia, particularly the role of consciousness in the transformation of organized action. Lenin focuses his discussion on the theorization of the proletariat's responses to the abuses of capital. He differentiates between what he sees as "spontaneous" forms of consciousness, which take the form of revolts, riots, or uprising, and "conscious" action, which takes the form of organized working class struggle. He argues,

> Taken by themselves, these strikes were simply trade union struggles, not yet social-democratic struggles. They marked the awakening antagonism between workers and employers; but the workers were not, and could not be, conscious of the irreconcilable antagonism of their interests to the whole of the modern political and social system, i.e. theirs was not yet social-democratic consciousness. (1967: 122)

Lenin argues that while the conditions of work had spurred the workers on in rebellion, the consciousness driving their activity was not formulated in terms of the dialectical relations of labor-capital nor in a particularly historical way. His central challenge is to argue that this latter form of consciousness is imperative for socialist mobilization to move beyond reactionary forms. In this way, Lenin identified dialectical and historical analysis as components of what we might call "critical consciousness."

The premises of Lenin's discussion are taken from Marx (Harding, 1996).[1] As philosophical concepts, Lenin understands consciousness to be in a dialectical relation with matter, meaning that the two stand in unity and struggle. For Lenin, matter includes everything outside of our bodies, including the consciousness of other human beings. In this way, the relation of consciousness and matter is also the relation of the individual to the social whole. Lenin's problem, and that of the communist movement, is that while the consciousness of workers is based on observing and experiencing labor conditions, the experience of it does not necessarily lead to a theoretical understanding of the conditions themselves. Lenin points out, as many of us may have recognized ourselves, that most workers will not arrive, through their own experience, at the same conclusions to which Engels and Marx came. However, Lenin observes an important contradiction. Engels, a factory owner, did not begin his intellectual life as a socialist or communist; he was a factory owner and, like many other members of his class, was expected to justify the exploitation of the working class. That he was able to change sides and advocate the interests of workers was primarily because of his study of theory and history and due to a political decision to change the world. Lenin used a dialectical understanding of the relation between consciousness and matter, one in which human agents are not psychically or intellectually trapped in the conditions they find themselves. This dialectical relationship has been expressed in different ways in Marxist literature, including in Mao Zedong's (1968: 136) statement that "matter can be transformed into consciousness and consciousness into matter."

Lenin formulated his terminology through the concepts of "spontaneous" and "conscious." By spontaneous, Lenin referred to the consciousness of life formed through everyday experiences. "Spontaneous" consciousness must exist as, given Marx's dialectical formulation, life cannot be anything other than conscious life. Spontaneous consciousness, so often cast in a pejorative light, is of the utmost importance to Lenin. Spontaneity, however, is understood as somehow different from "conscious" activity. It is important to recognize that Lenin and Marx are using the terms "consciousness" and "conscious" in different ways. Marx is entering the German Idealism debate about the relationships between matter and consciousness. He is demonstrating how consciousness is dialectically related to social organization of life and exists in both objective and subjective forms. Lenin is talking about consciousness in relation to the formation of a political agenda necessary to revolution. Thus, to be "conscious" is to have the kind of consciousness that relates to revolutionary practice. Lenin is moving into the theorization of how to organize thinking and ideas in a revolutionary manner based on the dialectical theorization of Marx.

Of particular importance to educators are the similarities between Lenin's framework and Lev Vygotsky's educational theory.[2] Wayne Au has argued that Vygotsky uses the terms "everyday" and "scientific" to mirror Lenin's differentiation of "spontaneous" and "conscious." In Vygotsky's paradigm, "everyday concepts" refer to Marx's original assertion that we are always "conscious" persons who move through the world, think, act, make decisions and choices, learn, and so on. "Scientific concepts," however, are qualitatively different in that they do not relate to a conscious awareness of reality as immediately given but to "an act of consciousness whose object is the activity of consciousness itself" (Vygotsky in Au, 2007b: 280). To be conscious is "to be actively conscious of your consciousness in a systemic way" (ibid.). Au argues that Vygotsky understood these concepts (scientific and everyday) to be dialectically related, or a "unified process of concept formation" (ibid.: 282). In this dialectical formulation Vygotsky found psychology to be inseparable from sociology, meaning that individual consciousness, the psyche, could not be understood apart from social relations and social forms of consciousness (Jones, 2009).

While Vygotsky is often reduced in learning theory to discussions of zones, scaffolds, and activity, he continues in the Marxist tradition of theorizing praxis. Marx's original theory of praxis, which is unfolded in his discussion of consciousness, is dependent on his empirical demonstration that "the principle of change in our social world was based on the movement and development of dialectical contradictions" (Allman and Wallis, 1990: 14). Embodied in the notion of praxis we find the theorization of consciousness as well as the dialectical formation of the relation between "spontaneous" or "everyday" forms of consciousness and "scientific" or "conscious" consciousness. Arguably one of the most sophisticated formulations of praxis in the Marxist tradition is that of Mao Zedong (Mao, 2007). Again, Mao rejects all dualism on the plane of ontology, meaning that for Mao consciousness is matter as well, a particular social product of the characteristics of the human mind, while epistemology requires a forced dualism so that humans may be able to understand their own processes of consciousness or how they come to know the contours of their material life (Knight, 1990). To put this another way, in everyday life, consciousness and matter are in struggle with one another, a dialectical relation. We move, both consciously and unconsciously, through the world, constantly mediating experience with meaning. However, in order to understand and make sense of daily life, to reflect on what we know and how we know it, we must conceptualize our consciousness independently of its intimate relation to material reality, even as it is constantly formed in this relation. This is a meta-theoretical position; while we all exist in the realm of "spontaneous" consciousness, we can also understand ourselves in such a sophisticated way that we can operate above the level of everyday understandings and appearances. This is the formation of the two kinds of praxis to which Allman refers (Allman, 1999, 2001, 2007).

Because of this dialectical formulation, "scientific" consciousness must emerge in relation to "spontaneous" forms. Lenin argued that spontaneous, rebellious activity was the ground from which a revolutionary consciousness would emerge (Holst, 1999). The emergence of such a transformation, however, was premised on the role of hegemony and the pedagogical activities of political parties. These conditions give rise to ongoing debates concerning the role of hegemony, so-called "organic intellectuals," vanguards, and the power relations implied therein. Our purposes here require that we focus on the dialectical formulation behind these questions: the implication that learning to think differently about life requires the recognition of spontaneous consciousness as consciousness. This is not the same thing as the pragmatic preference for all things "experiential" in which all knowledge that emerges from experience is treated as differing shades of "truth." Rather, experience is not fetishized, but becomes the object of reality that can be understood through the application of concepts. This is the approach to experience taken by Marx throughout his work. Imagine Marx in nineteenth-century London, living in a part of the city, present-day Soho, which had been notorious for its poverty, deprivation, filth, disease, crime, and pestilence for several hundred years, conditions so horrible that the community was blamed for the onset of the plague (Ackroyd, 2009). Somehow Marx goes from the everyday experience of this crisis to his scientific understanding of capitalism, just as Engels goes from the tedium of organizing a factory to a revolutionary communist position. This is the process under investigation.

An important component of Lenin's argument is that the movement from "spontaneous" to "conscious," the transformation of consciousness, happens through learning to think abstractly about concrete social conditions and relations. Lenin argued that processes of abstraction and generalization, based in historical materialist analysis and not idealism, are necessary for workers to see past the immediate struggle for rights, wages, and conditions (the "economist" argument) and into the totality of a social whole premised on violence and exploitation (Lenin, 1967). The ways in which we understand the categories of "abstraction" and "generalization" are extremely important in the divergences of the theorization of consciousness in the Marxist tradition. For example, Derek Sayer has devoted much attention to uncovering the ways in which these categories are misunderstood in "structuralist" Marxism and which result in the mechanistic separation of the ideal and the material, which reproduces the forms of abstraction Marx and Engels described in their critique of the Young Hegelians (Sayer, 1987). Lenin envisioned the role of abstraction as both theoretical and pedagogical, arguing "it is possible to 'begin' only by inducing people to think about all these things, by inducing them to summarize and generalize all of the diverse signs of ferment and active struggle" (Lenin, 1967: 231). This method of abstraction, generalization, and summation, however, had to be based in a dialectical understanding of history.

Au argues that Vygotsky built on this theorization of the emergence of "consciousness" through abstraction and generalization. For Vygotsky, "consciousness" was "conscious awareness," which he explained in this way:

> If conscious awareness means generalization, it is obvious that generalization, in turn, means nothing other than the formation of a higher concept in a system of generalization that includes the given concept as a particular case...Thus, the generalization of the concept leads to its localization within a definite system of relationships of generality...Thus

at one and the same time, generalization implies the conscious awareness and the systematization of concepts. (Vygotsky in Au, 2007b: 279)

Both Lenin and Vygotsky were working with a relationship between higher-order theoretical conceptualization and conscious mastery of a complex system of relations. Critical educators will recognize in this formulation the roots of Freire's "generative themes" and the process of moving from everyday experience to a larger meta-thematic organization of systemic relations (Freire, 1971). Freire describes the process as movement from the general to the particular and back out to the general. He argues, "When people lack a critical understanding of their reality, apprehending it in fragments which they do not perceive as interacting constituent elements of the whole, they cannot truly know the reality" (ibid.: 85).

The purpose of the theorization of consciousness, as Marx famously declares in the final *Theses on Feuerbach*, is not only to understand the world, but to change it (Marx, 1970b). However, Freire's argument that we cannot truly know our reality when we apprehend it in fragments is a critique that echoes across the Marxist and neo-Marxist theorizations of consciousness. Marxists are not the only critical scholars who have taken up this question; feminist and antiracist scholars have also devoted considerable time to building a body of knowledge around the question of consciousness. Their work illuminates a component of consciousness that is difficult, but not impossible, to see from the Marxist perspective.

Expanding Praxis through Marxist-Feminist Analysis

We have observed that there is a striking difference between the Marxist theorization of consciousness and the discussions of consciousness that circulate amongst feminist and critical race theorists. It is our hope to bring these conversations closer together. The most salient divergence is the emphasis in feminist and critical race theory on a felt duality in the consciousness of women and people of color in capitalist life. This duality has been described as "bifurcated," "outsider-within," and, famously, as "double consciousness" (Collins, 2000; Du Bois, 1897, 1903). Du Bois provided a visceral sense of this duality, formed through conflict and struggle, when he said:

It is a peculiar sensation, this double-consciousness, this sense of always looking at one's self through the eyes of others, of measuring one's soul by the tape of a world that looks on in amused contempt and pity. One ever feels his twoness—an American, a Negro; two souls, two thoughts, two unreconciled strivings; two warring ideals in one dark body, whose dogged strength alone keeps it from being torn asunder. (Du Bois, 1903: 3)

We want to argue that these alternative theorizations offer important insights to Marxist scholars that have been sidestepped in the historical development of the body of knowledge (Guy and Brookfield, 2009). Here we will primarily discuss feminist theory, but similar themes have been developed through a wide variety of antiracist and postcolonial scholarship (Fanon, 1952). The huge tension in Marxist-Feminist theorization is its two aims. On the one hand, we try to bring Marxism into feminist theorization. On the other, we endeavor to bring feminism into Marxism. Each has proved equally trying given the entrenched theoretical orientations of the fields. However, each also builds on a substantial engagement by feminists and antiracist scholars with Marxism because of the wealth of analytical tools made available by Marx, Engels, and their successors. Our purpose here is to extend those tools by borrowing from the strengths of feminist theory.

The theorization of consciousness has been a core component of feminist movements throughout the twentieth century. Consciousness-raising groups proliferated, particularly during the 1960s and 1970s, in response to the growing awareness by women of the systematic and widespread nature of gendered and sexualized oppression. Research on feminist consciousness expanded throughout the 1980s and seemed to find a home in cultural and psychological explanations of the phenomenon. The "phenomenon" under interrogation was how it is that women come to see themselves not just as individual women in interpersonal relations of domination or violence, but to understand these social conditions as a universal gender relation of patriarchy. Mojab has described this differentiation as "feminine" versus "feminist" consciousness and it expresses a deep similarity to Lenin's articulation of spontaneous and scientific forms of consciousness and Vygotsky's emphasis on movement from the individual to the social (Mojab, 2001). It is important to acknowledge that both academic and political work on feminist consciousness has largely focused on describing the psychosocial and emotional components of gendered oppression. To the extent that these experiences are explained in feminist theory, their derivation is largely attributed to the realm of culture.[3] This focus on culture may provide a historical linkage to the experience of exploitation or deprivation, but the arena of feminist politics is confined to language, ideas, representation, or discursive transformation. This orientation can be seen in a resistance amongst feminists to deploy or theorize the notion of "patriarchy," ironically in sharp contrast to the awareness of patriarchy as the historical impetus for feminist consciousness raising and its social movement orientations (Mojab, 2010).

Dorothy Smith argues that the inclination to see women's experience as primarily cultural performs the dangerous processes of abstraction described by Marx (Smith, 1988). Smith is correct when she argues that the focus must move from "culture" to "ideology." Moving from culture to ideology "directs us to examine who produces what for whom, where the social forms of consciousness come from" (ibid.: 54). Smith's argument is beyond the ideology critique. Rather, she is arguing that feminist theorization of experience and consciousness (or praxis) must begin with the *social* forms of consciousness. In other words, understanding consciousness in both subjective and objective forms directs our attention away from the *effects* of gendered oppression and toward the analysis of patriarchy as a universalizing social relation that "organizes asymmetrical, unequal divisions of labor, accumulation and access to economic resources that guarantee not only political privilege . . . of male over female, but, more important, the economic subjugation . . . of the 'other' gender as the very grounds of social arrangements" (Ebert, 1996).

One of the contributions of Marxist-Feminist theory is its ability to marshal the subjective experience of patriarchy as a way of seeing into larger social relations in order to understand where and how both subjective and objective forms of consciousness arise. This conversation is complicated by the implications of feminist epistemology. Feminists of many different theoretical orientations have toyed with the notion of epistemic privilege, or the idea that women, by virtue of their social location within racist, patriarchal, capitalist social relations, produce a form of knowledge that can only be generated from a particular subject position (Anzaldúa, 1987; Alcoff and Potter, 1993; Collins, 2000; Haraway, 1988; Harding, 2004). This assertion has been the cause of a tremendous amount of debate amongst feminists and its core epistemological assertion has constituted at least one reading of Lukács (Jameson, 1988). As Marxist-Feminists we reject the arguments for primacy that have arisen from the notion that there is something exclusively experiential about the ability to understand the realities of racism and sexism, particularly for the purposes of transforming these social relations. Instead, we gravitate toward Dorothy Smith's notion of standpoint, itself a hotly contested theoretical topic in feminism with various iterations circulating in the literature.

Feminist standpoint theory emerged in the 1970s as a response to the exclusion of women's experience from sociological theory and sparked a debate that has raged in feminist theory for more than 30 years (Harding, 2004; Hartsock, 1998; Howard and Allen, 1997). While there have been several permutations of standpoint theory, we work from the ideas articulated by Dorothy Smith in her critique of sociology and her development of institutional ethnography. Smith's perspective on standpoint theory emerged from an understanding of women's labor within the social relations of capitalism. Smith repeats Marx in her understanding that capitalist social relations produce the experiential separation of consciousness and matter. She argues that in modern capitalism this separation is spatially displaced, meaning that

> capitalism creates a wholly new terrain of social relations external to the local terrain and the particularities of personally mediated economic and social relations. It creates an extra-local medium of action consti-tuted by a market process in which a multiplicity of anonymous buyers and sellers interrelate and by an expanding arena of political activity. These extra-local, impersonal, universalized forms of action became the exclusive terrain of men, while women became correspondingly con-fined to a reduced local sphere of action organized by particularistic relationships. (Smith, 1988)

For Smith, both the "productive" and "reproductive" labor of women takes place within social relations that are not organized on a local, individualized basis. Rather, these relations emerge from a much larger, extralocal social practice. The forms of consciousness dialec-tically related to these relations similarly emerge from somewhere outside the daily experience of women, which Smith identifies as the objectification of forms of consciousness through the capitalist division of labor. These forms of consciousness can only be produced through the epistemological method of ideology, the violent abstraction of con-sciousness and matter as well as social and material life (Smith, 2004). As such, what emerges in the daily experience of women is a felt, per-ceived, immediate dissonance between subjective and objective forms of consciousness.

Smith borrows from Hegel's master-slave parable to provide an example of this formulation. In this parable, Hegel demonstrates that the master and the slave see very different aspects of the world they live in. The master does not worry about how his bed gets made or his food is cooked, nor does he understand the nuances of these processes. The slave, however, has an entirely different perspective on these activ-ities. As Smith has argued, "there is a difference between forms of consciousness arising in the experience of ruling and those arising in the experience of doing the work that creates the conditions of ruling" (Smith, 1988: 80). This parable has often been used as evidence for the claim to epistemic privilege we have already rejected (Mann and Kelley, 1997). However, another conclusion to draw is in the argument made by Marx and reviewed by Lukács that there is something in the experience of the proletariat that produces the "conditions of possibility" to see deeply into the organization of social relations and the potential to differentiate between uncritical and critical forms of praxis (Lukács, 1971). Similarly, this qualitative separation provides the basis for a spontaneous consciousness that can be transformed into a scientific consciousness. Without a dialectical understanding of the philosophy of praxis, this notion of "conditions of possibility," based in experience, is impossible.

For Smith, the "conditions of possibility" are found in the assumption of a feminist standpoint. A feminist standpoint is not epistemic privilege. It is not the idea that only women can know patriarchy or only people of color can understand racism nor is it the argument that because of a particular subject position one already "naturally" possesses a scientific, conceptual understanding of oppression. Rather, it is the idea that knowledge production is a political project in which scholars take up a position in relation to objectified forms of consciousness or, rather, ideology. Standpoint is a political, ethical, and intellectual commitment to understand social relations from a materialist vantage point that undoes the violent abstraction of bourgeois thought. At the same time, it is not an argument for the "essential" nature of the experience of patriarchy, but a claim to the universalism of patriarchy as an organizing practice of social life. Smith argues,

> when we take up the standpoint of women, we take up a standpoint outside this frame (as an organization of social consciousness). To begin from such a standpoint does not imply a common viewpoint among women. What we have in common is the organization of social relations that has accomplished our exclusion. (Smith, 1988: 78)

Feminist standpoint returns us to the dialectical relation of ontology and epistemology and provides a way of grounding and explicating this relation. The contribution of Marxist-Feminism to the theorization of this relation is to further complicate our dialectical understanding of not only this relation (praxis), but the constituent components of praxis (consciousness and matter). Standpoint theory is a commitment to work from gendered experiences in the world and argues that feminism is a scientific form of consciousness in which the material world is entered through the actual realities of a social world organized by social relations of gender and race.

The result of working from a feminist standpoint is a significant alteration to the traditional Marxist conception of "materiality." We say "traditional," because from our perspective Marx's original dialectical formulations of materiality do not theoretically exclude the lives of women. For example, Marx made reference to the sexual division of labor as the first division of labor, based in slavery and reformed in capitalist life. He failed, however, to realize this insight in his treatment of reproductive labor. Nevertheless, we take seriously Mao's assertion that materiality includes everything in the world including consciousness. When this expansive notion of materiality is used, far beyond the reductionist emphasis on "labor," understood as purposeful and conscious human intervention in nature, or "production," then scholarship of striking importance emerges. For example, we now know that the experiences of women during "primitive accumulation" in Europe provide us with an important understanding of capitalism as a way of social life that is entirely dependent on the formulation of some forms of labor as "value-less," that is deeply reliant on the hyperexploitation of women to accomplish its aims (Federici, 2004).

Federici's work is just one example of a growing body of Marxist-Feminist literature that retheorizes material life as necessarily gendered and raced, doing away with any notions of "abstract" materiality. Marxist theorization without a feminist and antiracist consciousness performs the same violent abstraction it accuses ideologists of performing. While in ideology consciousness is abstracted from materiality, in Marxism without feminism, material life is theorized as abstracted from the social relations that constitute its very essence (Carpenter and Mojab, 2011). For example, Bannerji has analyzed race and gender as "connative clusters of social relations," which are concretized through the dialectical relation of objectified forms of consciousness and material acts (Bannerji, 2005). In her formulation, "race" and "gender" cannot be understood as cultural formations or discourses or subtexts of class. Rather, they exist as the very social relations through which material life is organized under capitalism and through which capitalism developed. This kind of analysis makes a feminist consciousness as necessary as class consciousness. In a theory premised on a dialectical movement between the abstract and the concrete, the violence of abstraction is easily reproduced when the gendered and racialized organization of the social relations of production is ignored. For example, a Marxist analysis of ideology, consciousness, and capitalist social relations will help us understand the necessity of negating the labor-capital contradiction. However, only an antiracist Marxist-Feminist analysis will allow us to understand the internal contradictions in the organization of labor and capital. Only in this way can we see that a negation of labor-capital will not necessarily negate the relations of patriarchy or racism. If we return to the notion that consciousness must be theorized on the terrain of an ontology based in dialectical contradictions, then we must realize that a feminist analysis forces us to confront the real, experiential complexity of those dialectical contradictions. Not only does feminist analysis animate the reality of those contradictions, it elucidates a complexity that otherwise cannot be seen and remains in the realm of abstraction.

To Conclude: Implications for Marxist-Feminist Pedagogy of Consciousness

Having discussed aspects of theoretical and philosophical thinking about consciousness, we will conclude with reflections on the pedagogical and political implications of a Marxist-Feminist theory of consciousness. The goal of Marxism is to end the misery of human beings through a transition from the present, which Marx called "prehistory," to "history," that is, a future without classes, and surely without divisions based on gender, race, and other social cleavages. If this future ever materializes, it will happen through a conscious negation of the present and the construction of the envisioned future. This consciousness is multifaceted with Marxist-Feminist understanding at its very foundation. Marxist-Feminist consciousness is decisive because capitalism and all social formations reproduce themselves in innumerable ways and individuals cannot, in the absence of a politicized understanding, comprehend and replace a social formation.

In a similar vein, the central goal of feminism is to overcome the misery of patriarchal gender relations, and it has likewise no option but to negate patriarchy and build an alternative to it. This, too, cannot be achieved without Marxist-Feminist consciousness. And at the same time, patriarchy is an integral part of a socioeconomic formation. Capitalism without patriarchy or patriarchy without capitalism is impossible, and together they constitute a social whole. Hence, feminism and Marxism cannot fall apart.

Hopefully what has become apparent throughout this discussion is that the theorization of consciousness for critical and radical educators cannot rest solely on notions of "counter-hegemony" or "oppositional knowledge." It is not only the content of knowledge that is important, but the methods we use to generate this understanding and access our social reality. The core of the pedagogy becomes asking students to think about not only *what* they think, but *how* they think. In this sense, the pedagogy we choose is a question of politics: do we promote a consciousness aimed at creating a new world or do we train citizens skilled in reproducing the status quo? Students have not chosen the world in which they are born. Do we push them to create the consciousness and practice that can make and unmake their own history? The answer, for any educator, is primarily political.

Notes

1. Some commentators have argued that Lenin's theory of socialist consciousness is not based on Marx. Others, however, insist on its intensely Marxist formulation. Harding, using textual support from Marx, has noted: "The whole history of the British working class was testimony enough (to him [Marx] and later to Lenin) to the fact that the spontaneous labour movement, unassisted by social democratic theory and organization, fell easy prey to bourgeois political manipulation."
2. There is much debate concerning the role of Marxism in Vygotsky's work. What is unavoidable, and persuasively argued by Au, is that there is a definite historical and theoretical linkage between the two, which, together, lay an important dimension of our contemporary thinking on the question of consciousness.
3. For a critique see Ebert and Zavarzadeh (2007).

References

Ackroyd, P. (2009) *London: A Biography* (London: Knopf Doubleday Publishing Group).

Aguilar, D. (2010) *From Triple Jeopardy to Intersectionality: Women's Studies Today* (Toronto: University of Toronto).

Alcoff, L. and E. Potter (eds.)(1993) *Feminist Epistemologies* (New York: Routledge).

Allman, P. (1999) *Revolutionary Social Transformation: Democratic Hopes, Political Possibilities and Critical Education. Critical Studies in Education and Culture Series* (Westport, CT: Bergin and Garvey).

Allman, P. (2001) *Critical Education against Global Capitalism: Karl Marx and Revolutionary Critical Education. Critical Studies in Education and Culture Series* (Westport, CT: Begin and Garvey).

Allman, P. (2007) *On Marx* (Rotterdam, The Netherlands: Sense Publishers).

Allman, P. and J. Wallis (1997) Commentary: Paulo Freire and the Future of the Radical Tradition. *Studies in the Education of Adults,* 29(2): 113–20.

Allman, P. and J. Wallis (1990) Praxis: Implications for "Really" Radical Education. *Studies in the Education of Adults,* 22(1): 14–30.

Anzaldúa, G. (1987) *Borderlands: The New Mestiza* (San Francisco: Spinsters/ Aunt Lute).

Arthur, C.J. (1991) Editor's Introduction. In C.J Arthur (ed.) *The German Ideology*, 4–34 (New York: International Publishers, 1991).

Au, W. (2007a) Epistemology of the Oppressed: The Dialectics of Paulo Freire's Theory of Knowledge. *Journal for Critical Education Policy Studies*, 5(2) www.jceps.com/index.php?pageID=article&articleID=100.

Au, W. (2007b) Vygotsky and Lenin on Learning: The Parallel Structures of Individual and Social Development. *Science & Society*, 71(3): 273–98.

Bannerji, H. (2005) Building from Marx: Reflections on Class and Race. *Social Justice*, 32(4): 144–60.

Callincos, A. (1999) *Social Theory: A Historical Introduction* (New York: NYU Press).

Carpenter, S. and S. Mojab (eds.) (2011) *Educating from Marx: Race, Gender, and Learning* (Basingstoke: Palgrave Macmillan).

Collins, P.H. (2000) *Black Feminist Thought. Vol. 2* (New York: Routledge).

Colley, H. (2002) A Rough Guide to the History of Mentoring from a Marxist Feminist Perspective. *Journal of Education for Teaching*, 28(3): 257–73.

Du Bois, W.E.B. (1897) The Strivings of the Negro People. *The Atlantic Monthly*.

Du Bois, W.E.B. (1903) *The Souls of Black Folk* (New York: Bantam).

Ebert, T.L. (1996) *Ludic Feminism and After: Postmodernism, Desire, and Labor in Late Capitalism* (Ann Arbor, MI: University of Michigan Press).

Ebert, T.L. and Zavarzadeh, M. (2007) *Class in Culture* (New York: Paradigm Publishers).

Fanon, F. (1952) *Black Skin, White Masks* (Trans. Richard Philcox) (New York: Grove Press).

Federici, S. (2004) *Caliban and the Witch: Women, the Body, and Primitive Accumulation* (Brooklyn, NY: Autonomedia).

Freire, P. (1971) *Pedagogy of the Oppressed* (New York: Seabury).

Gilroy, P. (1995) *The Black Atlantic: Modernity and Double Consciousness* (Cambridge: Harvard University Press).

Guy, T.C. and S. Brookfield. (2009) W.E.B. Du Bois' Basic American Negro Creed and the Associates in Negro Folk Education: A case of Repressive Tolerance in the Censorship of Radical Black Discourse on Adult Education. *Adult Education Quarterly*, 60(1): 65–76.

Hamper, B. (1992) *Rivethead: Tales from the Assembly Line* (New York: Warner Books).

Haraway, D. (1988) Situated Knowledges: The Science Question in Feminism and the Privilege of Partial Perspectives. *Feminist Studies*, 14(3): 575–99.

Harding, N. (1996) *Leninism* (Durham, NC: Duke University Press).

Harding, S.G. (ed.) (2004) *The Feminist Standpoint Theory Reader: Intellectual and Political Controversies* (New York: Routledge).

Hartsock, N.C.M. (1998) *The Feminist Standpoint Revisited and Other Essays* (Boulder, CO: Westview Press).

Holst, J.D. (1999) The Affinities of Lenin and Gramsci: Implications for Radical Adult Education Theory and Practice. *International Journal of Lifelong Education*, 18(5): 407–21.

Howard, J.A., and C. Allen (eds.) (1997) Special Issue: Standpoint Theory. *Signs*, 22(2).

Jameson, F. (1988) "History and Class Consciousness" as an "Unfinished Project." *Rethinking Marxism*, 1(1): 49–72.

Jones, P.E. (2009) Breaking away from Capital? Theorising Activity in the Shadow of Marx. *Outlines*, 1: 45–58.

Knight, N. (ed.) (1990) *Mao Zedong on Dialectical Materialism: Writing on Philosophy, 1937* (London: M.E. Sharpe).

Knight, N. (2005) *Marxist Philosophy in China: from Qu Qiubai to Mao Zedong, 1923–1945* (The Netherlands: Springer).

Lenin, V.I. (1967) What Is to Be Done? Burning Questions of Our Movement. In *Selected Works, Vol. 1*, 97–255 (New York: International Publishers).

Lukács, G. (1971) *History and Class Consciousness: Studies in Marxist Dialectics* (Trans. Rodney Livingstone) (Cambridge, MA: The MIT Press).

Mann, S.A. and L.R. Kelley (1997) Standing at the Crossroads of Modernist Thought: Collins, Smith, and the New Feminist Epistemologies. *Gender and Society*, 11(4): 391–408.

Mao, T-T. (2007) *On Practice and Contradiction*, Edited by Slavoj Žižek (London: Verso).

Marx, K. (1970a) *Contribution to the Critique of Political Economy* (Trans. S.W. Ryazanskaya) (Moscow: Progress Publishers).

Marx, K. (1970b) Theses on Feuerbach. In C.J. Arthur (ed.) *The German Ideology, 2nd Edition*, 121–3 (New York: International Publishers).

Marx, K. (1977) *Critique of Hegel's "Philosophy Of Right"* (Cambridge: Cambridge University Press).

Marx, K. (1988) *Economic and Philosophic Manuscripts of 1844 and the Communist Manifesto* (New York: Prometheus Books).

Marx, K. (1972) The Eighteenth Brumaire of Louis Bonaparte. In *The Marx-Engels Reader*, 594–617 (New York: Norton).

Marx, K. (2008) *The Poverty of Philosophy* (New York: Cosimo, Inc.).

Marx, K. and F. Engels (1932) The German Ideology: Part One. In *The German Ideology, 2nd Edition*, 35–95 (New York: International Publishers).

Marx, K. and F. Engels (2002) *The Holy Family* (Honolulu, HI: University Press of the Pacific).

McNally, D. (2001) *Bodies of Meaning: Studies on Language, Labor, and Liberation* (Albany, NY: SUNY Press).

McLaren, P. and N. Jaramillo (2010) Not Neo-Marxist, not Post-Marxist, not Marxian, not Autonomist Marxism: Reflections of a Revolutionary (Marxist) Critical Pedagogy. *Cultural Studies—Critical Methodologies*, 20(10): 1–12.

Mojab, S. (2001) Theorizing the Politics of "Islamic feminism." *Feminist Review*, 69: 124–46.

Mojab, S. (2010) *(Re)theorizing and (Re)learning Patriarchy* (State College, PA: Pennsylvania State University).

Rikowski, G. (1996) Left Alone: End Time for Marxist Educational Theory? *British Journal of Sociology of Education*, 17(4): 415–51.

Rikowski, G. (1997) Scorched Earth: Prelude to Rebuilding Marxist Educational Theory. *British Journal of Sociology of Education*, 18(4): 551–74.

Sayer, D. (1979) *Marx's Method* (Atlantic Highlands, NJ: Humanities Press).

Sayer, D. (1987) *The Violence of Abstraction: The Analytic Foundations of Historical Materialism* (New York: Basil Blackwell).

Smith, D.E. (1988) *The Everyday World as Problematic* (Toronto, Canada: University of Toronto Press).

Smith, D.E. (1990) *The Conceptual Practices of Power: A Feminist Sociology of Knowledge* (Boston, MA: Northeastern University Press).

Smith, D.E. (2004) Ideology, Science and Social Relations: A Reinterpretation of Marx's Epistemology. *European Journal of Social Theory*, 7(4): 445–62.

Thomas, P.D. (2009) *The Gramscian Moment* (Leiden, The Netherlands: Koninklijke Brill).

Warminski, A. (1995) Hegel/Marx: Consciousness and Life. *Yale French Studies*, 88: 118–41.

Wilde, O. (1994). The Soul of Man under Socialism. In *The Complete Works of Oscar Wilde*, 1174–97 (New York: HarperCollins).

Chapter 6

A Little Night Reading: Marx, Assessment, and the Professional Doctorate in Education

Victoria Perselli

Many contradictions are inherent in the act of facilitating doctoral students' research projects from an agenda of widening participation in higher education. Indeed, this statement is already laden with conflicting ideology and, as you may have noticed, devoid of agency. This is because the persona of the teacher in academe is frequently neutered: "sexless and voided, like a broken pole" (Perselli, in press) by the impositions and demands of a range of similarly disembodied authorities and sponsors, including those who still adhere to the omniscient third person and passive voice—the "norms" of scientific reporting.

My first task, then, when thinking about research design with students embarking on the professional doctorate in education, is to initiate a focus on the personal and experiential, drawing from the knowledge we each bring to this endeavor as practitioners in our own fields (education, health, the social sciences). This seems to me an appropriate ontological position for doing research *in* professional practice *in* education, but with due recognition that it is neither apolitical nor unproblematic for anyone concerned. My second task is to urge students to read and think deeply about research methodology. I want them to come to understand for themselves that the ontological is an OK starting point for identifying and pursuing the kind of small-scale research questions that could eventually become their doctoral project, and to gain awareness over time that this is an art and a craft at least as demanding as any third-person alternatives. My third task pertains to theory, which will eventually fulfill a range of functions simultaneously: to inform the shape and direction of research questions, tools, and data-gathering methods, to provide an explanatory framework and underpinning to the project, and, finally, to contribute toward that seemingly alchemistic process of "turning data into evidence," which experienced researchers do with such apparent ease and fluency.

In this chapter I will focus specifically on the theory element of educational research, albeit with a continuing left-field recognition of those other features of methodology, ontology, and epistemology mentioned above, since in reality they are inextricably mixed. Similarly, whilst my discussion here is primarily concerned with theory-in-the-literature I intend to hold firm to that sense of theory-in-practice as a presence between the lines of what I am writing and thinking, together with an understanding of research *design* (Thomas, 2009) as necessarily mobile and malleable in the professional practice context. Thus my written contribution aims to reflexively double back on practice, in that it constitutes a testing ground of what we (the doctoral teaching team to which I belong) might bring to the table in terms of "theory" in the doctoral curriculum. In all other ways I am in this instance attending specifically and unapologetically to my own learning needs.

My quest regarding theory is further located in a small-scale, partially funded action research project on doctoral assessment process and practices that I initiated earlier this year. It began with a consideration of the learning and teaching relationships that constitute the cohort groups and project supervisory teams on our doctorate in education program (Perselli and Read, 2010; Read and Perselli, 2010). I became particularly interested in the perceived and material expectations of participants on the program in terms of "assessment" and "supervision," and what implications this might have for curriculum development or change. By "participants" I am here distinguishing colleagues according to their contextual and dialectical relationships as students (learners), tutors (teachers), supervisors, external examiners (to the program, to individual theses). The Education Doctorate is now in its seventh year of operation, so a thorough review of the supervision/assessment dyad in this context is timely.

With regard to wider research community activity, this project informs and is influenced by two national and indeed international debates in higher education that correlate directly with "doctoral assessment" as an overarching theme. Both have been prominently featured in recent conference presentations and the "grey literatures." First, what constitutes "doctorateness"? (see Proceedings of the International Conference on Professional Doctorates, Middlesex University, 2009; Higher Education Institute/Escalate events and publications, 2008–10.) Second, what is the role of theory in research? (see BERA

Research Intelligence, 2009–10.) These questions intersect a range of political discourses that are all-pervasive in UK politics at the time of writing. Specific to the United Kingdom is the Research Excellence Framework (BERA/UCET 2010), (formerly Research Assessment Exercise). To this should be added neoliberalism in education more generally (Harvey, 2005, 2010a; Harris, 2007), with its various sub-sets of accountability, transparency, incrementalism, managerialism and, indeed, widening participation as an *ideology* (Marx and Engels, 1846, Marx, 1867 [1976]; Freire, 1970; Allman, 2001: 33–59, 94–95; Small, 2005: 71–87) within the massification of higher education systems nationally and internationally (Burke, forthcoming, 2011). From this perspective "assessment" as an instrument of technical rationality can be seen to be ubiquitous in higher education, since all entrances to its formal and institutional structures involve scrutiny and surveillance in the forms of making assessments and being assessed. Further discourse sets arising from this standpoint include those that pertain to the self-interests and well-being of individuals or groups: learner centricism, risk aversion, the "vulnerable" adult, the therapeutic society (Ecclestone and Hayes, 2008; Colley, 2003; Furedi, 2004), as well as a range of power/knowledge implications and effects of assessment as an act of placement in (or displacement from) hierarchies.

An interim finding of the project is that the student-tutor relationship in doctoral education is predominantly asymmetric (Irving and English, 2008; Manathunga, 2007; Petersen, 2007). Whilst in the course of the relationship participants may temporarily challenge and undermine this ordering, nevertheless, the staging posts that constitute formal assessment (approval of the research proposal, ethical permits, viva voce events, and eventual conferment of the doctorate) all render decision-taking power back to the academy and, by proxy at least, into the hands of supervisory, tutorial, and examination teams.

At this stage, therefore, I am working from the notion that a Freirian-Marxian reading of doctoral education may effectively intercept doctoral assessment interpreted as a technical-rationalist, means-end process. This notion applies here on the page as a feature of my own theoretical orientation, but also in the curriculum that constitutes the taught element of the programme, where I find myself relationally imbricated: as tutor, supervisor, and administrator ("Chair")—a reluctant "mantle of expertise" that conceals a multitude of intellectual sins and surprises.

I can go further in so far as, regarding the wider political sphere of "doctorateness" and "theory in research," it is unsurprising that the name of Freire, in particular, is frequently secured—like a crucifix to the devil—in a kind of counterbalancing move to neoliberalism, albeit often in vague and unspecific ways. Diane Reay (2004) describes a similar phenomenon with regard to Bourdieu, who, she says, is peppered through research texts "like intellectual hair-spray." Bringing these theorists further into the frame is therefore not particularly novel; it rather mirrors, I think, the uneasy psychological state of that wider teaching and research community. Furthermore, it is based on the premise that, yes, theory is necessary and important in educational research, and that the uses of theory in the literature contribute vitally toward the totality of that which constitutes "doctorateness."

But how to move from Marx in theory to Marx as praxis? (I will consider Freire separately, below). Is there a reading from Marx that can propose antitechnical rational forms of assessment? A reading that problematizes canonic interpretations of the doctoral curriculum, that is, bibliographies in our module guides consisting of prerequisite or "suggested" literatures, accompanied by the tag: *Read these they are good for you?*

A helpful starting point arises from my empirical data, specifically external examiners' responses on assessed coursework, when they raise the question: "What do students understand by theory?" Like Reay, they are concerned that novice researchers tend to put forward a range of disparate or even contradictory ideas in their written work and then look for theories to "sandbag" the point they are making. This does not bode well for the coherence of research design and execution that examiners look for in a mature doctoral submission—the "smooth story," which, like my mantle of expertise, above, conceals as much as it reveals. But the question—and this particular expectation of the assessment process—opens up a number of avenues of thought regarding how different forms of knowledge develop in the context of students' professional practice. To put it another way, would it be possible—or desirable—to present as boxed sets the theories of Marx, Foucault, Butler, Bourdieu…(you can fill in the blanks) with an inference of *Have some of these; you are going to need them later*: Freire's "banking system" of education (Freire, 1970: 52–67)? Or to cultivate Foucault's "docile bodies" that diligently read + decide + apply theory to their already highly sophisticated practices (Schön, 1983)? Yet a criterion-referenced, objectives/outcomes approach to doctoral pedagogy (Stenhouse, 1985: 75–82) would imply this, which notion intensifies the complexity of the issue, since a further alternative—the joyful, serendipitous eclecticism that comes from exploratory, autodidactic "reading for reading's sake"—is, for one thing, voraciously hungry on time.

I will now turn to two significant aspects of Marx's own methodology for illumination: his critical attention to historical and actual contextualization (Harvey, 2010b), and his conceptualization of lifeworlds as an integrated whole (Allman, 2001)—the humanist aspect of his various theses which in recent world history has been so catastrophically ignored. Ideas are not "pure" abstractions; theory arises out of surface and deep analysis of that which is describable and knowable in the here and now, yet it is always and everywhere socially mediated. Likewise, practitioner research does not take place either remotely (i.e., positivistically) or outside the material pressures and constraints of numerous competing—if not incommensurable—influences and ideas. This is a positive, in that practitioner research methodologies offer space for consideration of just these vicissitudes. Action research projects, for example, are intended to reveal aspects of the "messy" reality of lived experience that, becoming an integral part of the text, are then open to further analysis, and, significantly, reflexivity: the inside-outness that centralizes the thinking and actions of the researcher ("self-giving" in Freire, 1970: 113). However, this in turn can induce *relational* insecurities and pressures that may have a cumulative effect, propelling the supervisor toward early closure and neat (happy) endings, prompting reductive: "Do you think I am good enough?" "Just tell me what to do" reactions on the part of the learner researcher; not least if/when the doctoral endeavor has been overinternalized as an *assessment activity*—a point I will return to later.

In practical terms, our regulatory frameworks (the doctorate is a collaborative program across two universities) stipulate that candidates must complete their thesis within a prescribed timeframe and word limit; they also need to be in practice in order to conduct their research. Many of our students are therefore categorically midcareer professionals whose workplace duties and personal commitments prohibit the possibility of full-time study—if that were a preferred alternative. Some are lecturers and managers in academe, whilst others occupy a range of professional settings and have no intention to become "career academics" or professional researchers. Their relationships with *theory* are as sporadic or ad hoc as mine have been; our various experiences of time-space compression locating us collectively and awkwardly straddling a postmodern *proletariat/bourgeoisie* not exactly unforeseen by Marx (Balibar, 1995). Curricular and bibliographic choices must be made; the kind of open agenda, the vagaries and flanuerish meanderings of my own Ph.D. experience just ten years ago seem a million miles away from this piece of writing here today. Besides which, and all these elements notwithstanding, the duration of a doctoral program is a very small unit of time in which to internalize "theory" to the extent that it is both transformatory and developmental in the Marxian/Freirian sense of actively changing the way we live our lives.

An analytical moment arises from these contextual features of the doctorate in education, centered on this issue of "time for reading," a bubbling undercurrent of anxiety for most participants in the doctoral program, which I will now unpack a little further. In this analysis I am working from an assertion, for practical purposes, that "reading" in this instance sits categorically within the field of "education," as opposed to the more general realm of culture or art—that is, "for art's sake," on which Marx had other views (Small, 2005: 63–4). In doing so I also take reading to be an essential part of "what we do" in our paid employment as educators, teachers and researchers, rather than what we choose to do (in our leisure time) that has no obligatory connection with this work.

Marx was not particularly sympathetic to the notion of "work" as "play." He believed, for instance, that children should participate in a proportionate amount of adult work—"necessary labour"—during their school years, and that through doing so (as opposed to being instructed thus didactically (Small, 2005: 126; Marx and Engels, 1975, Volume 21: 399), they would come to understand the importance of labor to the communal infrastructure. This for Marx was both an overarching principle of justice and a statement of duties and rights (Small, 2005: 124) as much as a practical necessity of the classless society, his argument being that if adults ought to work to eat, the same rule must apply to children (Marx and Engels, 1975, Volume 20: 188). Marx was suspicious of utopian or philanthropic arguments relating to learning through play as proposed, for example, by the French utopian Fourier (Small, 2005: 130–3): "travail attractif." He saw these arguments as a subterfuge (my word) that concealed the subordinating intentions of the ruling class (Apple, 1990). Whilst Marx advocated famously both the reduction of the working day and the redistribution of labor, he also believed that it was vital to be in possession of a range of manual and mechanical skills. This enabled workers' flexibility and employability, for which polytechnic "training"—in the fullest sense of the word—should be available to all (Small, 2005: 106; Marx and Engels, 1975, Volume 35: 491). He criticized the romantic nineteenth-century ideal of the farmer or artisan, for example, who develops only one skill and is therefore more inclined to be displaced by new technology.

Later in time, Marxist and Marxian scholars have similarly critiqued "learner-centred" or "child-centred" progressivism on the basis that its "inordinate emphasis on the child and child interests" (Counts, 1932

[1969]: 8 in Small, 2005: 172) was "too orientated towards the liberal minded middle class." Kozol in *Free Schools* (1972: 45, in Small 2005: 173) puts it more bluntly: "Harlem does not need a new generation of basket-weavers." This happens to be a rather neat illustration of a conflict of philosophical standpoints between Marxists and Progressives that, now I understand it better, was played out in my own education in the West Country in the 1970s (Perselli, 2006b: 22–3). It is implicit in a piece I wrote about training for Initial Teacher Education—albeit without the opportunity (time/willpower/guidance?) to expand theoretically the ideas I was grappling with just then (Perselli, 2006a: 71–88), a *developmental* point worth remembering here.

What Marx was angling for was the communal reorganization of labor, together with its redistribution across society, such that *in itself* work becomes more enjoyable, with time freed up for actual leisure and self-determined activities: "free work" or "self-activity" in his terms. "Labour is 'free' when its aims are 'aims which the individual himself posits'" (Marx in Small, 2005: 133). As Robin Small explains:

> In saying this, Marx is attempting to reconsider the distinction between "external" and "internal" aims, and, if possible, to show that the two do not exclude each other. The idea of freedom and necessity too are to be reconciled in the notion of "free labour" or "attractive work." To be free is to posit one's own aims and to realize them through acting upon the work. As Marx puts it, the worker "not only effects a change of form in the material on which he works, but he also realises a purpose of his own that gives the law to his modus operandi, and to which he must subordinate his will" (CW35: 188). That subordination is important: it represents the element of necessity which is present in all labour; but when it is subordination to a purpose which is chosen by the individual, it is consistent with the voluntary character of the activity as a whole. (Small, 2005: 133)

Whether students engage in the professional doctorate for the purposes of extrinsic rewards or for personal, intellectual satisfaction—and whether or not there is merit in perceiving this as a binary—I cannot think of a better way of encapsulating in a few words the construct that might apply when thinking about how *time for reading* may be located in the doctoral endeavor. To contemplate the matrix of those aspects of our daily life that comprise necessary labor, free work, and actual leisure activity is to begin to see how an economy of work, study, play, and so on, could be configured that legitimates doctoral study as *necessary work* (i.e., as opposed to popular and historical perceptions of the doctorate as an élite or bourgeois "trivial pursuit," but which distinguishes it from that which is unfree, "forced," or "alienatory" (Marx and Engels, 1975, Volume 28: 530).

In the short run, doctoral study is very hard work and to a large extent *graft* in the truly Marxian sense of the word. Reading is labor; reading theory can be extremely difficult—but this is tempered with the satisfaction that comes from the deep meaning and enhanced understanding of the human condition that theory sometimes yields, all the more so when this is experienced as self-directed learning (Stenhouse, 1985: 117). Regarding the skills and knowledge that are acquired in (and brought to) the doctoral process, what I think is important to consider with my students is the sense that elements of subordination of will in labor are always present, but that this is not a negative, per se. By doing a doctorate, creative space becomes available for conscious choice and deliberation, but it is never a neutral, individualistic space (Freire, 1970: 162). For a project to become realizable, personal goal setting or "blue skies" dreaming develop socially, with attentive and sensitized consideration of our own and others' material conditions: the I/thou relationship (Freire, 1970: 148) enacted through *cooperation*. Furthermore, they develop with a conscious awareness that "generic" assessment criteria and judgments of worth external to the project itself will be applied; that is, the research takes place within a range of intellectual and political parameters and constraints. Aspects of this "subordination" in practitioner research could be, for example, the necessity to reign in the text that is too unwieldy for its readership, to refocus ideas that have become dispersed and thus detached from the practice or the participants. These are dialogic and communal (Walsh, 2008) activities, understood as much through doing and by exemplar as through discussion and reading.

None of these features of doctoral labor and the interim judgments that are called into play is necessarily oppressive. They mirror, after all, the usual technical and craft elements of conducting educational research: Marx's polytechnic training. What is more complex and problematic is the *undecidability* factor of "assessment" as a summative activity in the context of "educational research" as we experience it today. Of all the disciplines, if it is a discipline (Bilager, 2010: 22–3), education is the most political (in the broadest sense of the word) and thereby the most permeable in terms of its boundaries with other disciplines (Rowland, 2006). Education intersects directly with notions of society, state, and citizenship (Olssen, 2008), producing controversial perceptions and expectations of what can and cannot be achieved, whether in terms of social or individual betterment, or indeed Western notions of "freedom" (Sartre, 1995: 409–10 in Perselli, 2008: 230–1). The realities of this, when it comes to the research endeavor as lived experience, can be something of a shock for the novice researcher, whose ontological security may have been gained from a more "secure" disciplinary environment (Nah, in preparation). The location of self, philosophically and epistemologically; the design and execution of the project; the influence of the literatures and the environment; the eventual contribution to the knowledge base and its material relevance; the numerous decision-taking moments in the doctoral project and its attendant assessment and evaluation processes are paradigmatically challenging for everyone and are surely not a happy place for the risk averse. Yet neither, I think, is it a place where the teacher should feel compelled to act out emollient or placatory behaviors—apologias for the ethics and politics that constitute the nature of the beast. In terms of learning, teaching, and the curriculum, there are many things we can do to successfully mediate the creative space that opens up once (1) undecidability is reframed as an opportunity for the practitioner researcher to make informed contributions to the debate itself (on research criteria, standards of judgment, value and "worth" in educational research) and (2) the *pedagogic* interdependence/autonomy dialectic of the doctoral endeavor is reasserted as a deliberate and self-conscious resistance to expressions of psychological "learned helplessness," student-as-customer, tutor-as-supplier orientations, and the like (Marx in Freire, 1970: 32–3, 35).

However, at this point I want to reflect again—a secondary analysis, if you like—on the issue of "time for reading," and in so doing demonstrate further how Marxian theory may be usefully put to work. I have so far referred to "the student" in a dialectical and asymmetric relationship with "the teacher." I have characterized participants (everyone) in the doctoral program as coming from a range of backgrounds and prior experiences without reference to the socioeconomic factor, which now requires expansion.

Participants' historical and actual contexts include higher and further education lecturers and administrators, teachers in schools, educators occupying a range of professional and disciplinary roles in the health and social sciences, as well as those of us whose routes into higher education did not involve conventional first-degree study. This means that not everyone will relate with equivalent familiarity to the kinds of "regular" craft knowledge (methods and skills training; "official knowledge," Apple, 1993) that I have outlined above any more than there will be parity among participants in terms of the material employment and domestic and financial conditions in which the various forms of labor/ leisure time might be located (Bowl, 2003; Cole and Gunter, 2010). Regarding our students, specifically, whilst some have conducted formal research projects and already have a profile of academic publications, others have little if any opportunities to present at conferences or participate in research communities outside the ones we have established around the program. Whilst some students fund their own studies, others receive varying degrees of sponsorship from their employers—again with diverse contractual expectations on successful completion of the thesis, and the further implications of this. All of which could, again, be summarized under the technical-rational umbrella of "differentiated teaching and learning." Yet one feature that is emerging as a unified theme among participants on the doctoral program is the *sensation* of "never quite doing enough." This is the element that I would now like to focus on, which I propose as evidence of education as ideology, the doctoral degree as a *fetish object*.

In simple descriptive terms I am taking ideology to mean "false ideas about society" with due regard to Marx and to the various scholars of Marx who have explained this in full and evocative terms that are not possible here. I can only urge the reader to refer to the sources I am citing for deeper engagement. First, Robin Small, who offers a working definition that configures the impasse that I think we tumble into when considering my account of "time for reading" in terms of its surface features alone, followed by Paula Allman, who likewise conjoins these two major Marxian concepts, ideology and fetishism, in her exposition of Marxist theory.

According to Small (2005: 72),

> False ideas about society ["ideology"] often arise from the tendency of aspects of human existence to take on an independent form, so that they appear as facts or "things," rather than having their reality solely in the activities of human beings. Wherever there is a division of labour, the varied activities of different members of society become fixed patterns and individuals come to be seen as belonging to classes which stand in relations to one another. Marx asks:
>
> > How is it that personal interests always develop, against the will of individuals, into class interests, into common interests, which acquire independent existence in relation to the individual persons, and in their independence assume the form of *general* interests? . . . How is it that in this process of private interests acquiring independent existence as class interests the personal behaviour of the individual is bound to be objectified, estranged, and at the same time exists as a power independent of him and without him, created by intercourse, and is transformed into

social relations, into a series of powers which determine and subordinate the individual? (Marx and Engels, 1975, Volume 5: 245)

Small (ibid.) continues by demonstrating how, from Marx, what appear
to be (merely) social relations are derived from divisions of labor and
thus "acquire an independent existence over against the individuals"
(Marx, ibid.: 363).

> Thus social relations seem not to be [...] historical phenomena which
> have risen through human activity, are maintained in the same way and
> may well be transformed by human action; instead they bear a resem-
> blance to natural laws. This is a mystification, but apparently a necessary
> one in any society which has a division of labour, even the oldest and
> most common divisions by age or sex. There is another process here as
> well, one in which relations between people appear as relations between
> things. Marx calls this "fetishism," and in *Capital* he gives an outline
> of the way it works. It is not found in any society whatever, but only in
> those whose economy proceeds by the production of commodities: that
> is, of things intended not for immediate use but for exchange on the
> market. (Small, ibid.: 72–3)

> A commodity is therefore a mysterious thing, simply because in it the
> social character of men's labour appears to them as an objective char-
> acter stamped upon the product of that labour; because the creation of
> the producers to the sum total of their own labour is presented to them
> as a social relation, existing not between themselves, but between the
> products of their labour. (Marx, 1975, Volume 35: 82–3)

This is reinforced in Allman:

> The section in Volume 1 of Capital that traces the development of the
> commodity form ends with an explanation of the type of ideological
> thought that will result as a consequence of the full development of
> the commodity form under capitalism. I previously mentioned that
> we tend to think that the value of a commodity derives from its own
> intrinsic properties. Perhaps the best examples of this are gold and
> gems, which seem to radiate these properties. We forget that like all
> other commodities they share the common factor that they are pro-
> duced [...] and circulated for exchange by a certain amount of socially
> necessary labour time. Capitalist praxis and the ideological explana-
> tions that arise from it and serve to justify the system, encourages us
> to think about commodities in a distorted way. However, even worse,
> according to Marx, these ideological processes become located in our
> subjective responses. We come to desire, even lust after, commodities
> or possessions. Marx calls this the "commodity fetish" (Marx, 1976:

163–6), the subjective or emotional location of bourgeois ideology. (Allman, 2001: 49)

Under these terms, I now suggest, my conceptualization of the professional doctorate as necessary labor, as opposed to "a bourgeois trivial pursuit," is bound to fail on a number of counts, as are my recommendations for polytechnic interpretations of the doctoral endeavor, when characterized as uncomplicated sets of differentiated, learnable tasks. This is because the deep structures from which this argument emerges remain not just textually undisturbed, they have also mutated in a variety of ways—taking the past ten years, the space between obtaining my Ph.D. and teaching the professional doctorate today ("a million miles away"), as an analytical yardstick.

The biggest problem with capitalism, according to Marx, is its capability to mutate and change. In postmodernity, this adaptability manifests as neoliberalism, that is, the commodification of everything, the pursuit of profit for the benefit of a *burgeoning* economic and social élite, at the expense of all other human lives and of the natural environment (Harvey, 2005, 2010a). I came close to this when I referred to the doctoral endeavor having been "over-internalised as an *assessment activity*"—but as a surface descriptor of social relations and research methodology, presented to you as though this were "the crux of the matter," rather than as a manifestation of other human activities that have mutated and change, via unspoken processes of *class* hegemony into something reified and fixed (fetishized): an intensely hierarchical structure that produces not only the learner/teacher "relationship" but also the behaviors I can experience and describe through language: "learned helplessness," consumer supply-and-demand orientations of the kind to be found, for example, in anonymized evaluation sheets and the like, or in those moments where I catch myself conflating students' needs and interests with tasks to be completed and texts to be enacted upon: the "thingness" of the doctorate that delimits its human and creative potential (Allman, 2001: 55).

Methodologically, according to Small, I was looking at the phenomenon from the wrong angle. If I now structurally invert these observations I can begin to reconceptualize the "pain, conflict, failure, chance [. . .] the rage for closure" (MacLure, 2006: 224) that inhibits participants in educational research from realizing what Marx calls our "species being": our human capability for autonomous choosing; for noncompetitive, interdependent relations that cannot be accounted for as (merely) products of social relations or indeed hierarchy per se, but rather as the unsurprising consequences of the dehumanizing material conditions of neoliberalism *in* postmodernity (Atkinson and Cole, 2007).

That psychological pressure of *never doing quite enough*—reading, thinking, writing, dialogue, and discussion—is a nag in the back of the head, a desire and frustration that despoils the pleasures of intellectual engagement, because so often the time it takes to engage meaningfully is usurped by all the other "stuff to do" that keeps everyone so preoccupied. For those of us who embark on educational research through a concern with the life of the mind, or indeed whose job it is primarily to care about the well-being of others (the health care professionals on the Doctorate in Education program, for example), this is a form of deep alienation (Davies, 2005). Furthermore it comes about, not through the undecidablity dialogic of "educational research"—which has always existed—but as a direct effect and product of the slippery position of education in the neoliberal class hierarchy. This makes education a curious commodity, one that sometimes reaps rewards (recognition, promotion, improved economic status)—but maybe not. For the professionals engaged in the doctorate this is particularly so when contextualized within the *indeterminateness of the working day* (Rikowski, 2004) and the unjust distributions of mind labor during that "working day": indeterminate role boundaries, pressure to perform; the *ideology* of the doctorate when perceived as a "gold standard" that might secure you a "brighter" future, but which might be completely overlooked—depending entirely on which way the market *moves* (Harvey, 2010b: 17).

Methodologically, therefore, neoliberalism is particularly demanding. It manifests as a Foucauldian diffusion of power that requires a leap of faith from sensory experience, via the various tickets, tokens, tariffs, targets, and other measures that constitute the "data" of our working day, to try to discover what *is* its material reality, the origins of its own "thingness." A significant point along the way is that neoliberalism is antihumanistic, concerning itself not with how people feel or think but rather with how we *perform*. Neoliberalism presents as a chimera, not a conglomeration of human activities that, emanating from a nameable source, coagulate to produce emotions and behaviors that can be traced to that source and identified: "outed" as such. It is, nevertheless, highly positivistic in essence, having no truck with personal narrative or testimony ("useless correlations" in Blunkett, 2000: para 57). Thus the fallout from neoliberal *strategy* in education—"lifelong learning," "the student experience," "staff satisfaction," "student satisfaction," "quality assurance," "work-life balance" and its continuous assessment *busywork*, in sum—does not matter, provided this fallout can be expressed as "statistically insignificant." As long as it is not so disproportionate as to topple the strategy itself, but remains (merely) the miserable experiences of isolated, abnormal individuals, neoliberalism retains its status of the "invisible hand" (Harvey, 2010a: 51–3). Nobody cares *because there is nobody there.*

Except that is not quite true. Human beings collude in the neoliberalization of society at every step when we participate in these obsessive acts of measurement and comparison, the totalizing vantage point from which to check how self/other is performing, to see who is "in" and who is "out"; the little shaming rituals beloved of folk who never take time to read anything properly, that have now come to constitute bourgeois education ("widening participation"); which make revolutionary praxis—Allman from Marx—so relevant and vital in, and beyond, education today. Neoliberalism, you might think, has done this to itself, but it is human beings that perpetuate neoliberal strategy: we "do" it to each other.

By comparison, then, "undecidability" in practitioner research could be a blessing in disguise. "Undecidability" in terms of standards of judgment of value and worth in practitioner research concerns itself with the various lexicons (my term) of our actual professional practices and disciplinary areas, which cannot be separated from methodology or from theory. It concerns itself with the texture and substance of professional practice, seeking direct and detailed correlations with praxis and the ways in which praxis is itself continuously evolving. "Undecidability" has the potential, always, to be the communal and collaborative forum critically illustrative of species beingness, expressed as space-/time-specific issues shared among nameable actors. It cannot, despite all the harmonizing and totalizing efforts of the educational élite, mutate into a "thing."

Such a forum may take the form of philosophical/epistemological dialectic and debate, for example, race/"race" (Warmington, 2009), Marxism/Marxian (Balibar, 1995) difference in Marx/*différance* in Foucault or Derrida (Atkinson and Cole, 2007), mentoring (Colley, 2003). Sometimes it takes a more overt practice orientation: "How can I improve *my* practice *in this situation here*?"—the ontological position adopted by my Masters students, for example, from whom exploratory theory is a "good enough" expectation. In each instance "undecidability" thus conceptualized offers the potential to defy and even divest the mantle of expertise of the "omniscient" assessor, since it is the research protagonist who reveals herself as the expert knower (Martin, 2006)—a rebalancing act and dissolution of the student/supervisor dialectic, manifest through the research text and in the viva.

A Marxian interpretation of "good" educational research goes further than this, however, and, as I have understood from my very partial and imperfect reading of Marx, brings me to my interim conclusion to this discussion, that is, the inferences for the curriculum of the doctoral programme. Allman again states:

> Have we not concerned ourselves with struggles for greater access and equal opportunities so that everyone can acquire the educational commodities? Have we not also engaged in attempts to replace one valued knowledge commodity with another or in redefining, more broadly defining, the locations in which we can acquire the knowledge commodities we need? For example, we have argued for the inclusion of "black" history, women's history and Marx's economics [...] These are [...] worthy arguments, but they do not strike at the real heart of the problem, which is the bourgeois concept of and relation to knowledge/education. By saying this, I am not decrying knowledge, only a concept of it and a relation to it that encourages us first to dichotomise the act of acquiring already existing knowledge from the activity of producing new knowledge. It then encourages us to relegate the latter activity to a separate and exclusive existence called research, not education. (Allman, 2001: 55)

Following Allman therefore, an outcome and judgment call in the assessment of professional practice research might be that the education/research dialectic is itself dismantled via the very specificity ("lexicon," in my terns) of the substantive and material concerns of its protagonists. This is the antitaxonomic (MacLure, 2006) element of educational research in professional practice whereby "robust and rigorous research design" constitutes the interweaving of design, method, context, and content and emerges as *good teaching*, that is, the educative relations between author and reader, assessor and protagonist, that emanate from this representation of the life-world (*Lebenswelt*) as "a really good read."

   In the final section of this chapter I will turn briefly to Freire, to illustrate how the doctoral curriculum could be strengthened in relation to my analytic themes of "time for reading," "not doing enough," "indeterminateness," and "undecidability." In so doing I aim to nuance further my understanding of participants on the program, specifically with regard to the diversity of students as revealed in their coursework. I am also reasserting the vitality of *theory as knowledge* in doctoral and postdoctoral studies. That is, its ability to generate questions and analysis; to contextualize, historically as well as actually, ideas that others "in the know" already possess, that may well be of use sooner or later in extending our lexicons of professional practice: Marx's "richness of needs" (Marx, 1858: 325 in Allman, 2001: 41)—not neediness—rendered visible through representations of deep engagement in socially useful work, also known as *educational* research.

I will do this through illustration of a practical dilemma in my teaching. Two activities constitute a significant part of the *Design and Method* module that I teach in the second year of the Doctorate in Education program, preceding the construction of students' research proposals. The first is for students to provide a written response to short readings on a methodological theme, selected by me and issued in advance of the readings seminar. Students are encouraged to circulate their individual written contributions among group members and subsequently to talk them through in the session—an informal, oral version of what might eventually form a base for critically reviewing the literatures. The second is a roundtable session where students are invited to share a small data set or artifact from their practice and discuss, in simple vernacular terms, its present significance. The various problematics that students bring to the session via these concrete objects (photographs, stories, newspaper cuttings, policy documents, timetables, children's schoolwork, a joke, an anecdote, or critical incident) likewise become a useful vehicle toward the very difficult task, methodologically, of "turning data into evidence"—at least, that is the rationale behind the activity.

So here is what surprises me about these supposedly open-ended, content-free activities: first that some students don't do them at all. Second, that whilst some students are evidently comfortable with the roundtable sessions, others find this a source of perplexity and struggle. Therefore they do not develop over time the experiential bank of data/critical analyses that would inform their written assignment for the module, which is in effect a more formal extension of this process. Whilst my intention in this class is to provide space for discussion and development of what might seem to be a straightforward question, that is, "tell us something that interests you currently about your practice" (Stenhouse, 1985: 85), this is evidently not so. Furthermore it suggests that I may be making a range of assumptions that privilege the more confident or flamboyant students, whilst putting others uncomfortably "on the spot." In order to unpack what these assumptions might be I need to reflect on the prior experience that motivated me to construct the roundtable activity, where, evidently, "free" does not equate with "safe."

For ten years I was an active participant in the Self-Study of Teacher Education Practices Special Interest Group (SIG) within the American

Educational Research Association (AERA): The Self-Study of Teacher Education Practices Special Interest Group (SIG). My fondest memory from this time is of the warm-up activity we routinely engaged in on arrival at AERA: a forum in the round where each person would introduce themselves and describe the research activity they were currently pursuing—sometimes with supporting artifacts of practice. I was so impressed by these (predominantly American) teacher educators' ability to go directly into detailed and specific aspects of their work, and, more than this, their ability to listen with such focused attention. When I reflected on my own practice I seemed to struggle with not only the fogginess of my own thoughts but also how to articulate them in this light-touch, conversational way. It was only more recently, via distance in time and space, together with cumulative experiences in my academic development, that I came to understand the cultural differences that underpinned my experiences in North America. Namely, the depth of *theoretical* influences—of John Dewey, Freire, and, more overtly, Donald Schön—that inform this way of being (content-free, safe space, open agenda, and so on) among academics who are, nevertheless, notionally and primarily committed to practice, such that "dialoguing" functions as a verb.

Neoliberalism as we know it in the United Kingdom has no truck with the slow start of educative relations formulated and theoretically justified on *principles* of intuitive professional knowing, mutuality, and trust (Freire, 1970: 42). For my U.S. colleagues, this was an established—and therefore implicit—understanding, such that I had to excavate the literatures and eventually make connections for myself (OK, so here is what "reflective practice" looks like in *research* practice and here is its underpinning). This is also true, it seems to me, with formal research reporting in general, because unless specifically dedicated to the task, it is rare for the author to reveal, in direct, "teacherly" terms, their prior theoretical influences—the corollary to this being that most practitioners are not perceived as theorists, at least until after they are dead: the philosopher queens and kings. Instead, the reader must *do her own work* of uncovering the theory embedded in practice, and vice versa.

There is, therefore, no "alchemy" (Freire, 1970: 67, 149–50) behind the polished educational research report. But there is, for the neophyte, a series of shibboleths—conceptual passwords, unspoken yet immediately recognizable once the reader knows what she is looking for—by which researchers are being continuously and implicitly judged, the hallmark or gold standard of the educational élite (in this instance the AERA) that offers much by way of ontological security, but which also gives "theory" its bad name ("alienating intellectualism" in Freire,

1970: 67). This is not easily compensated in our professional lives where, in reality, reading—of the scholarly kind—is by no means "necessary labour," "an essential part of what we do" (above). For many middle-manager academics—suppliers of education to the masses—it becomes rather a holiday aspiration, a series of elusive rungs on the (research) ladder of upperclassness. Thus it comes to pass that Marx, an unforgivingly "theoretical" scholar, may be used for material gain...but only if you are prepared to indulge him very late at night.

This returns me finally to my dilemma of practice and a central conundrum regarding Marx. I now recognize that in my enthusiasm to import my U.S. colleagues' way of working, I have perhaps focused on *process* (Stenhouse, 1985: 85–90): "reflexivity," "reflection," "experience," "epistemology"—at the expense of *content* (Stenhouse, 1985; Allman 2001: 86, 96). I have not attended sufficiently to the factual, historical contexts that might offer my students the ontological security to participate in the roundtable sessions with real confidence. In the construction of the roundtable activity I had created, in true Freirian spirit, what I thought was a curricular space that would be owned by the students—as their doctoral projects must be (Martin, 2006). I energetically engaged them with methodological process, competently reflected in the choice of readings, on the assumption that this would lead to deeper bibliographic engagement...at some later date: "progression and development."

My ordering of events therefore—"thirdly there is theory," above—must now be revised, so students can come to understand for themselves, not just the principles behind the roundtable activity or the curriculum thus conceptualized, but Freire's own thinking on knowledge, including how difficult it can be, from the facilitator's perspective, to draw this out: "Why don't you explain the pictures first?" (Freire, 1970: 42, 113; Martin, 2006: 2). It is therefore the readings and my own introductory lectures on the program that need to change, not necessarily the roundtable activity itself, in order to provide this vital contextualization and explanation ("rationale"). But I do also need tentatively to encourage students to read Marx, and it is through the construction of this chapter that I can see how primary sources—Marx's own writing, which can be so difficult and demanding—may be mediated through the many excellent secondary guides and indeed research projects cited here. In my class we frequently find ourselves talking about—and celebrating—plasticity and ambivalence in language, in the postmodern. We do not often consider how scholars such as Marx ("ideology"), Bahktin ("dialogic"), Butler ("performative"), Spivak ("subalterity")...you can fill in the gaps...construct their very specific vocabularies so that we can describe and critique, historically and actually, what otherwise presents as ephemeral (MacLure, 2006: 224): capitalism, neoliberalism, postmodernism toward reconceptions of how to be at a time when many folk are too depressed, afraid, or exhausted to carry out this work (Freire, 1970: 154, 162).

Experience cannot feed off experience, the self off the self, with no additional nutrients. These "theoretical" vocabularies need now to become more explicitly the building blocks of the *Design and Method* module, and whilst it is not appropriate to impose my views on my students, I do need to come clean regarding how I think and feel about higher education at this significant moment in history.

The truth of the matter is I don't "buy into" (Davies, 2005) an "agenda" of "widening participation" in higher education. Neither do I have a "strategy" for doing so. However, this does not mean that I do not care about my students, or that I am indifferent to students' individual differences and feelings. On the contrary, I have a great aspiration that through deep engagement with what they have elected to study, my students will be enabled to expand their emotional and political engagement in their work, expressed as lexicons of practice—against the odds and in defiance of the *discourse of workload* (real and imaginary) that seems to be endangering pedagogy at the time of writing. These are personal criteria of value and worth in the professional doctorate. Another might be that the meaning *and pleasure* students find in carrying out this important work may find them, from time to time, continuing deep into the night when everyone else's lights are out.

References

Allman, P. (2001) *Revolutionary Social Transformation: Democratic Hopes, Political Possibilities and Critical Education* (Westport: Bergin and Garvey).

Apple, M. (1990) *Ideology and Curriculum* (London: Routledge).

Apple, M. (1993) *Official Knowledge* (London: Routledge).

Atkinson, E. and M. Cole (2007) Indecision, Social Justice and Social Change: A Dialogue on Marxism, Postmodernism and Education. In A. Green, G. Rikowski and H. Raduntz (eds.) *Renewing Dialogues in Marxism and Education: Volume 1—Openings* (Basingstoke: Palgrave Macmillan).

Balibar, E. (1995) *The Philosophy of Marx* (London: Verso).

BERA/UCET (2010) Review of the Impacts of RAE 2008 on Education Research in UK Higher Education Institutions. Available at http://www.bera.ac.uk (accessed November 25, 2010).

Bilager, M. (2010) Education: Academic Discipline or Field of Study? *Research Intelligence*, CX.

Blunkett, D. (2000) Influence or Irrelevance: Can Social Science Improve Government? *Research Intelligence*, LXXI.

Bowl, M. (2003) *Non-traditional Entrants to Higher Education: "They talk about people like me"* (Stoke-on-Trent: Trentham).

Burke, P.J. (forthcoming, 2011) *Widening Educational Participation. Challenging Discourses of Difference* (London: Routledge).

Cole, B.A. and H. Gunter (2010) *Changing Lives: Women, Inclusion and the PhD* (Stoke-on-Trent: Trentham).

Colley, H. (2003) *Mentoring for Social Inclusion* (London: Routledge).

Counts, G.S. (1932) [1969] *Dare the School Build a New Social Order?* (New York: Arno Press).

Davies, B. (2005) The (Im)possibility of Intellectual Work in Neoliberal Times. *Discourse: Studies in the Cultural Politics of Education*: XXVI (1): 1–14.

Ecclestone, K and D. Hayes (2008) *The Dangerous Rise of Therapeutic Education* (London: Routledge).

Freire, P. (1970) *Pedagogy of the Oppressed* (Harmondsworth: Penguin).

Furedi, F. (2004) *Therapy Culture: Cultivating Vulnerability in an Uncertain Age* (London: Routledge).

Harris, S. (2007) *The Governance of Education: How Neo-liberalism Is Transforming Policy and Practice* (London: Continuum Press).

Harvey, D. (2005) *A Brief History of Neoliberalism* (Oxford: OUP).

Harvey, D. (2010a) *The Enigma of Capital and the Crises of Capitalism* (London: Profile Books).

Harvey, D. (2010b) *A Companion to Marx's Capital* (London: Verso)

Irving, C.J. and L.M. English (2008) Partnering for Research: A Critical Discourse Analysis. *Studies in Continuing Education*, XXX (2): 107–18.

Kozol, J. (1972) *Free Schools* (Boston, MA: Houghton Mifflin Company).

Manathunga, C. (2007) Supervision as Mentoring: The Role of Power and Boundary Crossing. *Studies in Continuing Education*, XXIX (2): 207–21.

Martin, P.J. (2006) *Professional Doctorate Portfolios: Helping to Select and Present Best Practice* (York: Higher Education Academy).

Marx, K. and F. Engels (1975) *Collected Works* (London: Lawrence and Wishart).

Marx, K. and F. Engels (1846) *The German Ideology* (Moscow: Progress).

Marx, K. (1867) [1976]) *Capital, Vol. 1* (Harmondsworth: Penguin).

MacLure, M. (2006) "A Demented Form of the Familiar": Postmodernism and Educational Research. *Journal of Philosophy of Education*, XL (2): 224–39.

Nah, G. (in preparation) Living the Discourse of Teaching and Learning in Higher Education: The Lived Experience of Participants of the Postgraduate Certificate in Learning and Teaching in the Creative Arts (Doctoral Thesis, Kingston University).

Olssen, M. (2008) *Towards a Global "Thin" Community* (Boulder, CO: Paradigm Publishing).

Perselli, V. (2006a) Paradoxes of Praxis: Thinking about Aspects of Social Justice in the Context of School-University Liaison. In D. Tidwell and

L. Fitzgerald (eds.) *Self-study and Diversity,* 71–88 (Rotterdam: Sense Publishers).

Perselli, V. (2006b) Heavy Fuel: A Case Story. In K. O'Reilly Scanlon, C. Mitchell, and S. Weber (eds.) *Just Who Do We Think We Are? An International Study of Teachers and Teaching,* 22–33 (London and Philadelphia: Routledge Falmer).

Perselli, V. (2008) "Troubling the Angels" Revisited. *Cultural Studies, Critical Methodologies* VIII: 224-245

Perselli, V. (in press, 2011) Painting the Police Station Blue: the Almost Impossible Argument for Poetry in the Élite Educational Journals. *Power and Education,* 3 (1).

Perselli, V. and B. Read (2010) Meaning What We Say and Doing what We Say We Do: Assessment in the Doctoral Process. Paper presented to the Discourse, Power Resistance Conference, Greenwich Universtiy, March 2010.

Petersen, E.B. (2007) Negotiating Academicity: Postgraduate Research Supervision as Category Boundary Work. *Studies in Higher Education,* XXXII (4): 475–87.

Read, B. and V. Perselli (2010) Trust and Power: Elements of "Supervision" and "Assessment" when Working with Doctoral Students. Paper presented to the British Educational Research Association, Warwick, September 2010.

Reay, D. (2004) "It's All Becoming a Habitus": Beyond the Habitual Use of Pierre Bourdieu's Concept of Habitus in Educational Research. *British Journal of Sociology of Education* 25 (4): 431–44.

Rowland, S. (2006) *The Inquiring University: Compliance and Contestation in Higher Education* (Maidenhead: McGraw-Hill International).

Rikowski, R. (2004) *On the Impossibility of Determining the Length of the Working Day for Intellectual Labour.* Paper presented to the Marxism and Education: Renewing Dialogues IV Symposium, Institute of Education, London, May 5, 2004.

Schön, D. (1983) *The Reflective Practitioner: How Professionals Think in Action* (London: Temple Smith).

Small, R. (2005) *Marx and Education* (Aldershot: Ashgate Publishing Ltd.).

Stenhouse, L. (1985) *Research as a Basis for Teaching: Readings from the Work of Lawrence Stenhouse* (J Ruddock and D Hopkins, eds.) (Oxford: Heinemann).

Thomas, G. (2009) *How to Do your Research Project: a Guide for Students in Education and Applied Social Sciences* (London: SAGE).

Walsh, J. (2008) The Critical Role of Discourse in Education for Democracy. *Journal for Critical Education Policy Studies,* VI (2): 54–76.

Warmington, P. (2009) Taking Race out of Scare Quotes: Race-conscious Social Analysis in an Ostensibly Post-racial World. *Race, Ethnicity and Education,* XII (3): 281–96.

Part III

Marxism and Education: Advancing Theory

Chapter 7

From Relational Ontology to Transformative Activist Stance on Development and Learning: Expanding Vygotsky's (CHAT) Project[1]

Anna Stetsenko

Introduction

Research in psychology and education today is going through a paradoxical phase, perhaps to such an extent that the cliché "the best of times, the worst of times" cannot be avoided when trying to describe it. On the one hand, we are witnessing much ferment and enthusiasm as novel ideas, exciting discoveries, and innovative methodologies are emerging and flourish across a variety of approaches that explore the effects of culture and society on human development. These new and innovative approaches are often underwritten by a common commitment to social justice and equity (these approaches will be termed *sociocultural* herein for lack of a better unifying term). On the other hand, it is impossible not to notice a rising tide, indeed a tsunami, of starkly mechanistic views that reduce human development (more boldly now than at any other time in recent history) to processes in the brain rigidly constrained by genetic blueprints passed on to contemporary humans from the dawn of the evolution. The sad irony is that these latter views represent a strikingly united front in sharp ascendance—drawing together resurrected tenets of sociobiology, innatist linguistics, narrowly conceived neuroscience, orthodox modular cognitivism, with the test-and-control, knowledge transmission–based educational models following suit—while the alternative sociocultural approaches remain starkly disconnected, without much dialogue or coordination among them. Indeed, no consensus of a sort now propagated by the "new" reductionist synthesis is apparent in sociocultural approaches that are scattered across areas as diverse as critical pedagogy, social theory, adult learning, disability studies, critical race theory, constructivist education, science studies, human-computer interaction, feminist studies, literary criticism, cultural anthropology, and developmental psychology, among others.

The broad rationale for this chapter is the need for a better integration, or at least a coordination, of sociocultural perspectives across these areas in social sciences and education. This is necessary if a sociocultural perspective is to compete with the alternative neurologically reductionist (often with sociobiological undertones) approach that is now claiming a bold vision on human nature (a vision that purportedly resolves all its complexities with the help of notions such as genetic endowment, innate cognitive modules, procreation, and mind-as-brain metaphor). Such an integration requires that a common position, united at least at the meta-theoretical level, on the broad questions of human nature, development, and learning, be worked out. The goal of such an integration is by no means merely academic. Broad theories and visions of human nature and development are not inconsequential abstract constructions; on the contrary, they are always intimately related, in a bidirectional way, to ideologies and policies of research and practice and have immediate practical ramifications in real life, worldly contexts, and everyday matters (with the split itself between theory, ideology, and practice being a remnant of the old-fashioned positivist concept of knowledge). The reign of positivist views on human nature as predetermined, fixed, and largely contingent on brain mechanisms on the one hand and the failure of sociocultural theories to provide an alternative broad vision that could unhinge ideas of development and learning (and the plethora of associated concepts such as mind, knowledge, and intelligence) from ideology of control and testing that has underwritten them for far too long on the other is a serious obstacle that needs to be dealt with to achieve changes in present policies and practices.

This chapter offers steps toward overcoming the current fragmentation within sociocultural approaches in psychology, education, and a number of neighboring disciplines by revisiting (drawing on a number of perspectives) and expansively reconstructing a broad dialectical view on human nature and development underwritten by ideology of empowerment and social justice. The first step is to recognize the need for an integrated perspective in sociocultural approaches—or, to use a stronger expression, for a "grand" synthesis in its own right—to counter the powerful alternative trend that is grounded in essentialistically understood human nature. The second step is to reveal and ascertain the common foundation that is tacitly present in today's sociocultural theories of human development—namely, the theme of *relational ontology* of human development and, more specifically, that of human active engagement with the world as the process through which both learning and development take place (with Piaget, Dewey, and Vygotsky all standing in opposition to the narrowly mechanistic and reductionist views). On this broad foundation, the third step is to dialectically expand the notion of active engagement by supplanting it with the notion that *collaborative purposeful transformation of the world is the core of human nature and the principled grounding for learning and development.* In making this step, I revisit and reconceptualize Vygotsky's project that pioneered (but has not completed) this theoretical move. The strategy is to restore and build upon this project's deeply seated *transformative activist stance* (overlooked in many of today's interpretations of Vygotsky) pertaining to all aspects of human development—a stance that initially permeated this project as a result of it being forged during a time of unprecedented revolutionary changes that profoundly imbued it with ideas of activism, transformation, and social change.

According to this stance, the core of human nature and development has to do with people collaboratively transforming their world in view of their goals and purposes—a process through which people come to know themselves and their world and ultimately come to be human. Importantly, although transformative social practices are profoundly and ineluctably social—afforded by and themselves affording employment of cultural tools including language and the associated cumulative growth of human culture, history, and society—this conceptualization does not eschew the role of individual human beings as agents of and contributors to social practices. Therefore, this conception overcomes the narrowness of both (a) the individualist views of positivist and humanist traditions that posit the primacy of an individual as some supreme entity existing prior to social practices and (b) the social reductionism "upward" of unidirectional collectivist accounts that tend to exclude individual processes and human subjectivity. In this conception, human subjectivity is neither a separate mental gadget for information processing nor a largely unconscious by-product of neuronal activity; instead, it is a process implicated in, produced by, and derivative (or made up) of the worldly, practical, purposeful activities of people who together transform their world and are transformed by it and in which each individual human being has an important role to play. Moreover, because meaningful activities not only build on experiences and present conditions in their subjective dimensions but also embed visions for the future, these activities are—even in their most mundane forms—endeavors of a critical activist nature. This approach therefore dismantles the rift between facts and values rendering all human activities, including research and science at large, ineluctably ideological and political. The notion of transformative practice is inexorably linked to ideals of social justice and emancipation as pursuits of common humanity that substitute for group particularism and the politics of difference inevitably associated with the emphasis on participation in local communities of practice. Arguably, such an emphasis is highly consistent with the challenges now facing researchers and practitioners of education given the rapidly globalizing world where communities are interrelated and the tasks facing them worldwide.

Today's Landscape and the Need for an Integrated Approach

Today is a time of a critical ferment in psychology and education. Especially from the late 1970s through 1990s, a variety of new approaches emerged to challenge the essentialist, positivist conceptions that had for centuries prevailed in science to instead build upon alternative meta-level paradigms of, among others, phenomenology, poststructuralism, hermeneutics, American pragmatism, and (to a lesser extent) Marxism. The new theories developed under the banner of critical and cultural approaches offer novel ways to conceptualize and study culture, context, social interaction, and, perhaps above all, language and discourse. These new ideas and methodologies have been widely successful and in some fields (such as education) even came to win the battle for the first-methodology position (see Eisenhart, 2001). Some branches within psychology, such as Vygotsky's cultural-historical approach, have also been influenced and themselves became influential in advancing and shaping the new agenda for social sciences striving to shift away from the individualist and mentalist models.

However, these new directions of scholarship today remain starkly disconnected, with little integration and few, if any, attempts to offer an overarching theory of human development that would entail explanations of how people develop, learn, and come to know their world. Indeed, these approaches are divided by thick walls of ostensibly nonoverlapping and seemingly irreconcilable theoretical groundings, conceptual traditions, methodologies, chosen target audiences, and affiliations (as well as, last but not least, exclusivist stances taken by many who prefer to keep to their own turf rather than open up to dialogue with other perspectives). For example, some branches of critical and feminist theory claim Kurt Lewin as their major conceptual source while hardly ever referring to Vygotsky and, in an almost mirror reflection of this trend, most Vygotskian scholars disregard writings in critical and feminist theory (for a rare exception, see John-Steiner, 1999). This is particularly ironic given how much overlap there is between Lewin's and Vygotsky's theoretical premises and how close the two scholars were both professionally and personally during their lifetime. No less ironic, again in view of a profound commonality in respective grounding assumptions, is the lack of coordination between critical pedagogy inspired by Freire- and Vygotsky-based approaches in education. Freirian and Vygotskyan projects have so much in common that it is truly a mystery how their shared roots, ideas, and commitments could be left unexplored for so long. Other examples include the lack of a dialogue (a) between constructivist pedagogies rooted in Piaget and Dewey (with not much coordination between these two either) on the one hand and Vygotsky-inspired education on the other (although exceptions to this trend have emerged recently), (b) between contextualist psychology and ecological tradition championed by Bronfenbrenner and Vygotskian scholarship (although on Bronfenbrenner's roots in and kinship with Vygotsky, see Wertsch, 2005; also the present author's personal communication with Bronfenbrenner on multiple occasions), and (c) among approaches that capitalize on the distributed, situated, embodied, dialogical, and dynamical nature of development. It is due to a lack of theorizing that cuts across these areas that a dialogue among them has been stifled, disadvantaging all potential interlocutors and weakening their overall message and import in a wider context of societal debates about research and education.

The lack of integration among sociocultural approaches can be attributed to, in large part, the recently cultivated general suspicion of grand theories (especially by the postmodernist movement) that are thought to represent totalizing discourses that dangerously flatten differences in points of view and positions, impose rigid standards of truth, and undermine the politics of diversity (as indeed they often do). As a result, many scholars of culture today are interested in addressing complexity and fluidity of identity and subjectivity by focusing on their permeable boundaries and fleeting expressions—their grounding in dispersed networks and multilayered sites—and are less interested in explicitly conceptualizing human development and nature, including the broadest question of what it means to be human.

However, these "big" questions do not and will not go away. When they remain undertheorized, the door is left open for essentialist premises to sneak right back into even the utmost critical and cultural conceptions of human development and, above all, into the practices of organizing social life including practices of education. Because no void remains unfilled, this is exactly what happens again and again when, for example, arguments are made that subjectivity is the product of cultural constructions, negotiations, and dialogues; yet the notion of the biological "real" as a universal given, and the motif of nature as prior to social life is left intact. Powerful grand theories of what it means to be human and how development and learning are possible are ineluctably present at each and every step in theorizing all and any social issues, shaping even the most seemingly atheoretical endeavors too, and being perhaps especially pronounced in education. For example, the No Child Left Behind (NCLB) policy is, no doubt, a product of a vast array of socioeconomical and political processes rather than of a particular worldview on human development; however, a worldview of this level is powerfully implicated in the fashioning and implementing of this policy. That most resources need to be allocated to rigorous testing rather than put to use to improve teaching and learning reflects a belief in learning to be contingent on a universal progression that unfolds at its own pace, with the notion of a fixed and predetermined human nature lingering just behind the surface of this belief. By way of another example, when explanations are habitually provided in mass media and professional discourse for why some groups of students underperform by evoking the common sentiment that "some are just not born with *it*" ("it" being talent or any other type of a presumably "natural," inborn propensity), a grand theory of a universal human nature constrained by innate mechanisms is again at work, pervading our common understandings and language. Similarly, when a prominent democratic politician claims to be "cursed with a gene of responsibility," this is meant as a metaphorical figure of speech; however, this statement communicates the same unfortunate message about genes being at the core of who we are. Such sentiments and ways of thinking are evidenced also by how little commentary by sociocultural scholars there is on the "cheerful march" of evolutionary psychology and reductionist neuroscience, with this silence speaking volumes. Given the recent tidal wave of simplified reductionist notions about human nature and development, of grave implications for psychology and education, the goal of developing an alternative broad vision appears to be not only important but urgently needed. However, the broadly conceived dialectical conception of development and learning suggested in this chapter is not offered as some final, ahistorical, and timeless "truth" (for such "truth" does not exist). Instead, it is offered with a full understanding that all theories and concepts are culturally bound and historically specific social constructions that ultimately depend on and make sense only within particular social practices and ideologies underpinning them.

Importantly, for the purposes of this chapter, the prevailing emphasis on local communities and group particularism, combined with the politics of difference and identity choice on the one hand (or alternatively, a noncommitted stance of some postmodernist approaches that profess neutrality as the only viable position) and the suspicion of "grand stories" about human development on the other, is increasingly out of step with the rapid globalization processes that bring communities to be increasingly interrelated and turn local challenges into worldwide concerns.

Relational Ontology: Complementary Contributions by Dewey, Piaget, and Vygotsky

Although there is not much in the way of an explicitly stated general consensus today among scholars of a sociocultural orientation, one theme does come across as particularly salient and potentially unifying across a wide range of approaches. This theme has to do with challenging the central essentialist premise about phenomena in the social world being "thing-like" entities that exist separately from each other and the rest of the world (if not without some extraneous influence from other independently existing entities). In opposition to this view, many sociocultural theories are based on the notion that social and psychological phenomena are processes that exist in the *realm of relations and interactions*—that is, as embedded, situated, distributed, and coconstructed within contexts while also being intrinsically interwoven into these contexts. The most evident common achievement across sociocultural approaches of recent years has been the advancing and elaborating of this particular mode of thinking. Its core has to do with overcoming the Cartesian split between the object and the subject, the person and the world, the knower and the known—to offer instead a radically different *relational ontology* in which processes occur in the realm *between* individuals and their world.[2] In this broad meta-level approach, organisms and their environment are not seen as separate and self-contained (neither in their origination nor in their functioning) but are posited to have shared existence as aspects or facets of one and the same unified reality. Within this logic, for example, development and learning are not seen as products of solitary, self-contained individuals endowed with internal machinery of cognitive skills that only await the right conditions to unfold. Instead, they are seen as existing in the flux of individuals relating to their world, driven by relational processes and their unfolding logic, and therefore as not being constrained by rigidly imposed, preprogrammed scripts or rules.

Thus, the reductionist metaphor of separation (typical of the previous mechanistic worldview) is replaced with the metaphor of "in-between-uity," that is, of mutual coconstruction, coevolution, continuous dialogue, belonging, participation and the like, all underscoring relatedness and interconnectedness, blending and meshing—the "coming together" of individuals and their world that transcends their separation. With its broad message of the meta-level, this perspective has profound implications for practically all steps in conceptualizing and studying phenomena in the social world, including the self, identity, mind, knowledge, and intelligence, as well as human development at large.

Although still far from being the mainstay of thinking in psychology and education (with many new adherents often reinventing its basics), this relational ontology has become quite prominent across a number of approaches and research directions such as developmental psychology (e.g., Müller and Carpendale, 2000), cultural anthropology (e.g., Holland et al., 2001), social psychology (Harré, 2002), science studies (e.g., Latour, 1987), literary studies (especially in Bakhtin's tradition, for example, Hicks, 2000), studies of communication and cognition (e.g., Clark, 1997), educational ethnography (e.g., Lave and Wenger, 1991), and education (e.g., Barab and Roth, 2006).

One way to capitalize on and strengthen the impact of relational ontology (as well as to overcome stark disconnections among theories grounded in it) is to realize that the three major frameworks on human development of the twentieth century—those by Piaget, Dewey and Vygotsky—all embodied strong relational thinking that aimed precisely at overcoming the subject-object dualism by replacing it with an emphasis on development being in constant dialogue and relation with the world. For example, Piaget (1977/1995: 188) argued that "the substantialist language of whole and part ought to be replaced by a language based on relations between individuals or individuals in groups." Piaget favored an interactive point of view, according to which "there are neither individuals as such nor society as such. There are just interindividual relations" (Piaget, 1977/1995: 210). The relations between individuals are primary and "constantly modify individual consciousnesses themselves" (Piaget, 1977/1995: 136). As noted by Kitchener (1996: 245), "Piaget . . . can be called a kind of transactionalist. Ultimately real are the basic transactions between individuals, or between individual and environment."

Dewey too displayed a deeply and remarkably transactional mode of thinking, as is evident when he stated that all behavior, including most advanced knowing, should be treated as activities not of a person alone, but as processes of the full situation of organism-environment.

Dewey's central notion of experience was a specification of transaction, referring to the relations of a living organism and its environment. As Kestenbaum (1977: 1) remarked, "[f]or his entire career, Dewey in one way or another was brought back to this realization that subject and object, self and world, cannot be specified independently of each other. His conception of organic interaction, and later his conception of transaction, were attempts to capture the reciprocal implication of self and world in every experienced situation."

Vygotsky is less often associated with the premises of relational ontology, with recent interpretations of his works often focusing on the importance of social context and interaction in human development, suggesting a model in which outside influences are seen as forces that shape development and learning. However, much of Vygotsky's efforts can be read as an attempt to conceptualize human development in terms of an organism-environment nexus in which the two continuously determine each other so that neither one can be conceived independently. In fact, one of Vygotsky's core achievements was that he substituted for the fixed, preformist views on development the notion that development exists in flux and constant change, with fluid and ever-changing, open-ended dynamical processes linking organisms and their environments. For example, Vygotsky (1997: 100) challenged the then accepted view that development could be understood as a set of static, predetermined steps when he wrote:

> Least of all does child development resemble a stereotypic process shielded from external influences; here [in child development], *in a living adaptation to the outside milieu* is the development and change of the child accomplished. In this process, ever newer forms arise, rather than the elements in the already preordained chain being simply stereotypically reproduced. (Emphasis added)

Vygotsky's affirmation of relational ontology is also evident in his statement that "relations to the environment stand at the beginning and at the end" of development (Vygotsky, 2004b: 194). And in yet another place, he asserts that his approach eventually resolves the argument between nativism and empiricism by showing that "*everything* in personality is built on a species-generic, innate basis and, at the same time, *everything* in it is supraorganic, contingent, that is, social" (Vygotsky, 2004b:190; emphasis in the original). In formulating these views, Vygotsky directly, and even quite literally, intuits the recently advanced developmental system theory (DST) according to which any psychological process is "fully a product of biology *and* culture" (Lickliter and Honeycutt, 2003: 469; emphasis in the original) and what counts as "biological" falls entirely within the domain of what counts as "cultural" and vice versa (see Ingold, 2000).

From this brief analysis, it appears that Piaget, Dewey, and Vygotsky all converged on understanding development and human nature as being a dynamical and fluid process taking place not just inside organisms and not just in the outside world, but at the intersection of the two, undergoing constant change and never following one preprogrammed path. As such, their views reflected much of the dynamism of the early twentieth century, best described perhaps by Roman Jakobson (quoted in Knox, 1993:1) who, when reminiscing about that time, wrote, "Everywhere there appeared a new orientation towards organizing unities, structures, forms whereby not the multitude or sum of successive elements but the relationship between them determined the meaning of the whole."

Moreover, having understood human development as inherently relational, all three scholars also moved to the next level of analysis and struggled to answer the question as to how can the mind, self, identity, knowledge, and learning be reconceptualized anew within this profoundly relational worldview? In making this move, their goal was not only to debunk the "sovereignty of the individual"—indeed a faulty and untenable assumption—but also to reconceptualize (rather than eschew) psychological processes while *unhinging them* from the premises of a mechanistic and elementarist worldview. It is at this level that these scholars again exhibit remarkable similarity, while also—at yet another level of analysis—revealing profound difference in their positions.

From Relational Ontology to Emphasis on Human Action

Piagetian, Deweyan, and Vygotskian approaches represent the relational, dynamical, and contextualized modes of thinking about human development and learning. However, and no less importantly, all three theorists understand *human action* as being constitutive of the relation between persons and the world. The dynamics and developments of embodied human action, in its increasingly complex transformations, as taking place in the world and not just in the head, is considered in all three frameworks to be the origin of psychological phenomena. The latter appear to be instantiations, parts and parcels, of ongoing actions through which people relate to their world. What this specification entails is a radical break not only with elementarism and essentialism of the mechanical worldview but also with the *spectator stance* on development, which, although challenged, is not eliminated by relational ontology per se. According to the spectator stance, the world—though being profoundly relational—is also essentially passive, with phenomena and processes co-occurring and *being* together, with no agency posited at the fundamental level of existence. In other words, relation implicates the ontological centrality of co-being as something that comes about through "copresence," but where existence is fundamentally inert and passive. In contrast, all three frameworks discussed herein have managed to overcome the "spectator stance" through the realization that the only access people have to reality is through active engagement with and participation in it, rather than simply "being" in the world. For example, the mind for Piaget, Dewey, and Vygotsky is not a container that stores knowledge, nor a mirror reflection of reality; rather, the mind is a dynamic system formed and carried out in and *as* actions by individuals who, through these actions, realize their relations in and to the world. Active engagement with the world therefore represents the foundation and the core reality of development and learning, mind, and knowledge—where relationality as cobeing and coexistence is dialectically superseded by the more agentive stance of acting in or engaging the world. Note that the emphasis on acting does not and is not meant to eliminate the relationality of cobeing; in fact, action is always and irrevocably relational for it entails and encompasses the subject and the object, the knower and the known, always crossing and essentially eliminating the boundaries between them. Therefore, relationality is not eliminated, but instead entailed, in activity that now becomes the supreme ontological principle, bringing organisms into relations with the world and with each other.

All action-centered theories implicate development, including cognitive growth, as occurring through an increasing elaboration of actions and posit learning as an active endeavor rather than a passive transmission of information. Here Vygotsky, Dewey, and Piaget converge in that they all imply that individuals *learn by doing*—through acting in and on their world. Importantly, activities are neither ancillary nor complementary to development and learning; instead, they are *the very realm* that these processes belong to and are carried out in. Moreover, activities are the very "matter" development and learning are made of, with no ontological gap posited between people actively engaging their world on the one hand and their knowing and learning on the other. This view places these three scholars in opposition to traditional views on mind as a passive container where knowledge is stored and on learning as a mere acquisition of information.

There are differences in how explicitly these ideas were expressed by the three scholars, with Dewey tackling it perhaps most directly and consistently throughout his career (with the exception of his latest works where he, inspired by post-Einsteinian physics—works by Heisenberg, Bohr, and Maxwell—appealed to transaction being spread across humans and the world rather than to the realm of individuals acting in the world; see Garrison, 1995). Piaget advocated this idea with particular clarity when he described early stages of development and the emergence of practical intelligence as an elaboration of action structures, whereas when he described the later stages of ontogeny he focused on elaboration of cognitive schemas, more in keeping with the Kantian tradition (which had a strong influence on his views). Vygotsky also placed action at the center of development, as is evident in his "general law" of development, which stated that *psychological functions emerge out of social, collective activity* (Vygotsky, 2004a: 83) and never completely break away from this activity. Thus development is not the result of a broadly (and rather vaguely) understood transferral of mental processes from a social plane to an individual plane of consciousness (as is often implied in recent interpretations) but a result of activity transformations. This theme cuts across many of Vygotsky's works, although he struggled to articulate it clearly and sometimes even appeared to waver between a radical new framework and a more traditional mentalist view (see Stetsenko, 2004). This theme comes out particularly clearly if one considers a unified Vygotsky-Leontiev-Luria school of thought that merged cultural-historical theory with ideas of activity into one composite framework: cultural-historical activity theory (CHAT; for details, see Stetsenko, 2005).

The delineation of these similarities sets the stage for a better coordination between the many (now disconnected) perspectives on learning and development that are in fact united in their emphasis on the active character of learning and development, as well as in their opposition to maturationist, elementarist, and essentialist views. Individuals' active engagement with the world as the ultimate ontological grounding for development and learning is a theoretical locus where theories on the effects of culture, social interaction, embodiment, and context already converge; and it is a place from which even more dialogue and coordination could be achieved. For example, the Gibsonian model that treats perception as a phase of activity of the whole organism through practical bodily engagements in response to environmental contingencies (see Ingold, 2000) is highly compatible with and falls under the umbrella of relational ontology of acting. The same applies to the recently developed theories that focus on enactment (e.g., Thompson and Varela, 2001), dialogical communication (e.g., Hicks, 2000 and others continuing the Bakhtinian approach), some versions of social constructionism (e.g., Harré, 2002), self-in-practice (Holland et al., 2001), and embodied cognition and dynamic systems approaches (e.g., Clark, 1997). Given the variety of these approaches and the broad scope of issues they cover, their de facto unity at the level of this common core premise could serve as a meaningful ground for coordination and perhaps even the merging of these theories into one composite approach that would be a powerful antidote to the neurologically reductivist "united front" that remains largely unchallenged.

Today's approaches continue to build upon Dewey, Piaget, and Vygotsky's (as well as Gibson's, 1966) insight that the relational ontology of action/activity is the grounding for development and learning and have made much progress by providing many useful specifications and methodological innovations. However, these contemporary approaches also stumble over a number of obstacles left unresolved in the early work of Dewey, Piaget, and Vygotsky, especially in terms of the status of human subjectivity (mind, self, and identity) within the ontology predicated on the centrality of human engagement with the world.

First, many of today's approaches to development and learning as distributed, situated, contextualized, participatory, and culturally embedded skip discussion of these processes' biological underpinnings and in so doing miss the important point that it is already at the level of these most basic foundations that development is profoundly relational, that is, necessarily dynamic, fluid, open-ended, and continuously brought into being anew. This view (present in works by Piaget, Dewey, and Vygotsky) is supported by recent trends in evolutionary biology, which, in challenging the extreme "genomania" of evolutionary psychology (ironically, often championed by linguists and philosophers), posit that development represents a multitude of events that influence each other, set the stage for each other, and run off in improbable sequences with no "genetic program" rigidly dictating them. According to this perspective, such rigid understanding of genetic programs for development is not viable from a biological point of view; instead, to understand development one needs to focus on succession of organism-environment complexes that repeatedly reconstitute themselves through ongoing activity (e.g., Gottlieb, 2003).

Second, because most sociocultural approaches emerged in direct and stark opposition to mainstream views on individual processes as self-contained "internal" essences separate from activities out in the world, they tend to stay away from conceptualizing mind, subjectivity, internalization, or any other processes habitually associated with the individualist and mentalist mainstream frameworks. The tacit assumption appears to be that individual processes, such as mind and self, cannot be accounted for within the relational approach and that relinquishing them is the price to pay for staying true to its premises. Accordingly, some of these approaches stop in their analysis of human development and learning at stating their relational character and do not proceed to the next level where the really difficult questions including the status of mind, self, identity, and knowledge just begin to arise. As a result, a depersonified suprahuman realm of distributed semiotic processes (e.g., "discourse" or "biosphere") takes center stage, whereas human agency and self-determination appear to be fleeting and ephemeral epiphenomena (e.g., Gergen, 2001 and works in the Peircean tradition). In some of these accounts, humans and nonhumans are treated symmetrically (e.g., Latour, 1987), defined relationally as arguments or "functors" in the network, with action evenly distributed along a chain of humans and nonhumans and effected by the unfolding logic of semiosis or other self-organizing systemic processes. Although appealing in its strong motif of relationality, approaches of this kind leave little space for theorizing intentionality, accountability, agency, responsibility, and, ultimately, development and learning.

Third, a number of approaches tend to collapse the individual dimension onto the social realm of everyday practices while undertheorizing the former, as in participatory learning and discursive theories where individual subjectivity is explained as being equivalent to, or a replica and sometimes a correlate of, the social-level process such as discourse, collaborative activity, or participation in shared practices of communities (e.g., Harré, 2002). Such work, while making many important and helpful clarifications in line with a nondualist approach to studying social and psychological processes, does not provide developmental explanations for how individual processes such as the mind or self might arise from participatory and social engagement with the world. Yet other approaches, such as those of embodied, situated, and distributed cognition and dynamic systems theory, do operate more directly with the notions of mind (as well as cognition, knowledge, self, and agency) while, for example, stressing the role of enactment, embodied action, or tools and artifacts as important constituents of these processes; however, these approaches, for the most part, provide only meager descriptions of the individual mind, often ultimately resorting to brain-level (such as connectionist models of cognition, for example, Hutchins, 1995) or information-processing level explanations. Thus, they essentially either relinquish the mind to reductionist views dominating mainstream psychology or sometimes directly resort to this level of explanation themselves.

Purposeful Collaborative Transformation
as the Grounding for Development and Learning

The relational ontology of human action does not and cannot provide all the solutions to the issues of development and learning, especially given a number of limitations in how action itself has been conceptualized in the three frameworks discussed herein, with many assumptions left unchallenged in today's sociocultural approaches. Specifically, both Piaget and Dewey remained strongly wedded to Darwin's doctrine in which adaptation was taken to be the central principle of development. Both regarded mind as a form of engagement with the world where humans interact with their environment as *biological organisms*, prompted to act by imbalances in these interactions. In particular, mind appeared as a contextual necessity that operates in response to contingencies in the immediate environment, in the *here and now* of problematic situations that initiate the process of inquiry. In this conceptualization, humans are viewed as responsive rather than deliberative, with the mind understood as an organ of adaptation to given circumstances. For Piaget and Dewey, humans develop, learn, and achieve knowledge—all in the spirit of adapting to existing conditions, to the here and now of their world—in order to "fit in" better with this world. Mind and knowledge, therefore, are also profoundly saturated with the goals and processes of adaptation, rendering social and political issues that require stepping beyond adaptation impervious to research.

The truly original contribution of CHAT in fact begins there where the relational, transactionalist, situated cognition, constructivist, and dynamic systems theoretical approaches exhaust their explanatory potential. Though not completed by the CHAT founders and containing many ideas only implicitly, this contribution has to do with conceptualizing the very type of relations that link humans to their world and will be expansively articulated in the following section while adding a number of specifications and extensions.

Whereas both Dewey and Piaget (and many of their contemporary followers in the relational ontology approach) treated human beings as no different than other biological organisms—thus keeping up with the Darwinian notion that "nature makes no drastic leaps"—Vygotsky and his followers postulated precisely such a leap and turned to exploring its implications. In doing so, these scholars followed with the Marxist dialectical materialist view according to which "[the] base for human thinking is precisely *man changing nature* and not nature alone as such, and the mind developed according to how human being learned to change nature" (Engels quoted in Vygotsky, 1997: 56; italics in the original).

According to this view, the evolutionary origins of humans have to do with an emergence of a unique relation to the world realized not through adaptation but through the social practice of human labor—the sociocultural collaborative, transformative practice unfolding and expanding in history. Through this collaborative process (involving development and passing on, from generation to generation, the collective experiences reified in cultural tools, including language), people not only constantly transform and create their environment, they also create and constantly transform their very life, consequently changing themselves in fundamental ways while, in and through this process, becoming human and gaining self-knowledge and knowledge about the world. Therefore, human activity—material, practical, and always by necessity social, collaborative processes aimed at transforming the world—is taken in CHAT to be the basic form of human life (or relation to the world). Activity is at the origin and is formative of everything that is human in humans, including their psychological subjective processes and the knowledge produced by them.

This new transformative relation to the world, precisely as a *new form of life*, brings about the emergence of human beings, whereby it supersedes adaptation and natural selection, as well as the distinction between nature and culture, and establishes the centrality of human practice in its unity of history, society, and culture as a supreme ontological realm for development and learning. This conceptual turn is actually quite radical because the shift from adaptation to transformation is taken to signify the end of biological evolution and a transition to processes now taking place in the realm where forces of history, culture, and society reign. This turn by the CHAT scholars is of a truly dialectical sort because it posits that human development is both continuous with and radically different from the processes in the rest of the animate world. Human history and life entail a radical break with nature, while at the same time continuing it. Thus, with the transition to humans there is a drastic leap away from biological laws and regularities that govern the animal world. In this leap, nature negates itself, turning into a radically new reality—the reality of cultural history of human civilization that proceeds in the form of a continuous flow of collaborative practices of people aimed at transforming their world.

Human development, from this perspective, can be conceptualized as a *sociohistorical project and a collaborative achievement*—that is, a continuously evolving process that represents a "work-in-progress" by people as agents who together change their world and, in and *through* this process, come to know themselves, while ultimately *becoming* human. Consonant with this premise, human nature is not an immutable, pregiven evolutionary residue that rigidly defines development within the constraints of biological endowment and functioning. Instead, *human nature is a process of overcoming and transcending its own limitations through collaborative, continuous practices aimed at purposefully changing the world*. In other words, it is a process of *historical becoming* by humans not as merely creatures of nature but as agents of their own lives, agents whose nature is to purposefully transform their world. In taking this step, the conceptualization of human development moves beyond the dualistic designation of nature and culture and does so not by simply stating their bidirectional relation or hybridity.[3] Instead, collaborative human practice is posited as the unified new ontological realm that takes over and dialectically supersedes (or supplants) both nature and culture, absorbing and negating them within its own unique, and radically new, transformative ontology.

It is the simultaneity, or, in even stronger terms, the unity of human transformative practice on the one hand and the process of becoming (and being human) and of knowing oneself and the world on the other that is conveyed in this conception. Human beings come to be themselves and come to know their world and themselves *in the process and as the process* of collaboratively changing their world (while changing together with it)—in the midst of this process and as one of its facets—rather than outside of or merely in connection with it. This proposition is in line with the famous statement by Marx that "[t]he philosophers have only *interpreted* the world, in various ways; the point however, is to *change* it" (Marx, 1978: 145; emphasis in the original). However, this statement draws attention to and has been interpreted only in its epistemic dimension—as the maxim that humans know the world through changing it. The expansion suggested herein (in the spirit of Vygotsky's project) goes beyond the epistemological level by stating that while there is indeed *no gap* between changing one's world and knowing it (a point well understood by Piaget and Dewey), there is also *no gap* between changing one's world, knowing it, *and* being (or *becoming*) oneself; all three dimensions *simultaneously* emerge from this process. There is, in other words, no knowledge and no human being that exist prior to and can be separated from transformative engagements with the world including, importantly, other people. In this perspective, the very distinction among acting, knowing, and becoming (including developing one's identity) dissipates.

Participating in and contributing to sociocultural practices of collaboratively transforming the world appear then as processes of a *dialectical coauthoring of history* and a collaborative historical becoming through which people establish their collective humanness while making unique contributions to sociocultural practices (see Vianna and Stetsenko, 2006). Therefore, human individuals are simultaneously ineluctably social and individually unique. That is, positing such a continuous flow of collaborative transformative practices as the foundation of human life does not eschew the fact that each generation and each individual human continues past achievements while, at the same time, also contributing to these practices, transforming and altering them (sometimes radically and sometimes only on a small scale), under the challenges of unique sociohistorical conditions and in view of aspired goals and visions for the future.

Taking the transformative stance does not mean that human subjectivity needs to be abandoned. Rather than positing "the world without within" as Dewey did (and as many of his followers today do), or explaining subjectivity through cognitive reorganization as Piaget (and adherents of his theory) attempted, the CHAT founders laid grounds for a viable alternative that offers a way to escape both extremes. In my formulation, this alternative consists of seeing collaborative practice as the foundational reality *within* which, *out of* which, and *for* which human subjectivity—knowing and being, mind and self—emerge and develop; once emergent, however, this subjective dimension becomes instrumental at mature stages of development (of both society and individuals) so that it plays an indispensable role in organizing, shaping, and otherwise regulating social life and practice. That is, human subjectivity is understood to emerge out of, within, and through collaborative transformative practices, representing just one form (or mode), though highly specialized, in which these practices exist. This grounding allows for human subjectivity to be conceived without any mentalist connotations exemplified in the traditional view of subjectivity as being a separate, ephemeral, mental realm withdrawn from human practices. Instead, subjectivity (mind and knowledge, self and agency) is seen as a this-worldly (object-related, in the CHAT parlance) practical instantiation of a historically emerging human ability to collaboratively use cultural tools, including language—itself a this-worldly, practical process and a collaborative achievement of people. With language and other tools, people come to be able to construct the future field of action (in line with their goals) as an observable, given situation and become driven by goals and purposes. In this conception, the pathway is opened to conceptualize psychological ("mental") processes not as a separate reality on its own or a by-product of brain processes, but as one of the many forms in which human engagement with their world takes place. Thus, psychological processes become essentially unhinged from the mentalist and reductionist premises of traditional psychology.

Importantly, this approach not only states that the human mind is a form of transformative engagement with the world but also provides an account of how psychological processes gradually emerge (in evolution, history, and ontogeny) through the mechanisms of semiotic mediation (primarily, by means of speech), out of the material practice while never completely breaking away from it. Much of CHAT scholarship was devoted to exploring how psychological dimensions of sociocultural practical activity (=human subjectivity) can be understood relationally and dynamically, without succumbing to mentalist and individualist assumptions (for details, see Arievitch and Stetsenko, 2000).

Moreover, the process of transforming the world by humans is taken by the CHAT founders (in line with the Marxist conception) as *always directional*—meaningful and purposeful—that is, defined by goals and requiring an authentic subject position. Activity entailing an authentic subject position—the directionality of one's pursuits, the way one strives to be and envisions one's world to be—is put forward as the ultimate anchoring for development and learning. This notion potentially overcomes both the narrowness of relational ontology (in which human beings are essentially passive) and uncommitted action (with its mere instrumentality of reacting to environmental demands). Because they are transformative, even the most mundane human psychological processes (such as perception) are impossible without a goal, a vision for the future that colors today's practices and imbues them with directionality and values. Given that transformative engagements with the world are taken as *ontologically and epistemically supreme*, and because transformation can only be achieved from a certain position and with certain goals in view, the ethical/moral dimensions become central both ontologically and epistemologically, with the gap between these three dimensions of social practices being eliminated.

In this sense, Vygotsky's project invites a vision for a unified human science that brings together the question of acting, being/becoming, and knowing on the one hand and the question of values and commitment to transformation on the other. That is, it brings together the questions of what is, how it came to be, how it ought to be, and how all of this can be known—with each question foregrounding the other questions (i.e., being answerable only in light of the others, and with the question of "ought" taking the center stage). It is the stance that affirms that society, especially education, could be different, therefore demanding that we discern why things are as they are at a given point in history by looking at how they came to be, while also trying to consider how things could be otherwise and how they ought to be. In other words, the true hallmark of Vygotsky's project is that it was predicated on two seemingly disconnected threads—the ideological/ethical commitment to social change and the historical materialist commitment to studying phenomena in their historical unfolding.

Necessary to the expansion of Vygotsky's project, in my view, is the revelation of how intimately these two threads are related. Namely, they can be revealed as interrelated because seeing society as in need of a change and also amenable to change (both being necessary components of a commitment to social transformation) presupposes understanding that social institutions are malleable, historically contingent, and fluid and therefore require a historically based understanding. And vice versa, understanding that the world and human development are socially and historically contingent grounds the belief that change is possible and therefore that the world with its social institutions is amenable to intervention through a purposefully organized social transformation.

Therefore, human science of this sort eschews neither systematic exploration and search for regularities and relations in the world (i.e., a study of human development as a historical becoming)—with this exploration always being contingent on ideological, ethical positioning—nor questions of ideology, ethics, and values, with these questions being intimately related to understanding the process of human historical becoming in anthropogenesis, in the history of civilization, and in ontogeny (where the inevitable and unavoidable contingency of human being/becoming and knowing on goal-directed, ethically committed action is made apparent). It is because acting, being, and knowing (including knowing through research) are all seen, from a transformative activist stance, as rooted in, derivative of, and instrumental within purposeful social practices of a *collaborative historical becoming* that a simultaneously ontologically, epistemologically, and politically ethically grounded position is possible.

This position can be described as an *activist* (or transformative) stance on ontology and epistemology that brings with it a message about the all-out importance of the authentic subject position *and* commitment to a certain vision for specific sociocultural arrangements as the starting point of any activity (including activity of theorizing and research). In this emphasis, the similarity of this perspective with the standpoint epistemology (e.g., Harding, 2004) is brought to the fore, although the perspective suggested herein (a) goes beyond the epistemological and instead embraces the unity of epistemological and ontological—where knowing, being/becoming, and acting are taken to be contingent on the ethical and the political and (b) simultaneously conveys the importance of not only the position *from* which the arguments are made (as in standpoint epistemology), but also the position *toward* which activity is directed (hence the activism that stands for commitment and active striving toward particular goals for transforming the world).

On this expansive reading, Vygotsky's project appears as a key precursor to Freire's writings and other works in critical pedagogy. Namely, in critical pedagogy, just as in Vygotsky's works, the notion that people produce history and culture and are reciprocally produced by them is understood as a defining ontological feature of human development. Coextensive with this claim, the Freirian notion of vocation (ethical commitment, ideology) as a struggle for freedom is taken to ground humanization (i.e., both development and learning, as well as human ontological capacities and human nature itself). Not only are practical reason and knowledge integral to the actions that create culture and history (as was well understood by Dewey too) but so are the ethical and political dimensions (vocation and struggle for freedom), forming the very core of knowledge and action, the latter being in sharp contrast with Dewey's position of ideological neutrality (see Stetsenko and Arievitch, 2004).[4] However, Freire provided a much less detailed account of anthropogenesis and ontogenesis than did the CHAT writers (especially Leontiev) and left the notion of human nature undertheorized. As a result, today's interpretations of Freire's position still often equivocate between the notion of "primordial nature" (independent of a struggle for freedom) and the notion of vocation as the core of human development (for a recent example, see Glass, 2001, which provides an excellent exposition of Freire's theory).

The important implication of this comparison is the following. Whereas Dewey opted for a naturalism that relied on a developmentally and evolutionary guided approach but eschewed values and commitment from ontological and epistemological realms, and today's critical pedagogy in Freireian tradition advances humanist, values-based views but relatively disregards systematic exploration into anthropogenesis and ontogeny, the expanded Vygotskian project offers grounds to work out a position that allows for reconciling and effectively combining the two positions. In this project, the centrality of a value-laden ideological/ ethical commitment as a "natural" grounding for development (where human nature is understood as a *historical becoming*) in both ontology and epistemology is arrived at by way of a systematic historical, developmental investigation. However, the reverse is also true in that this "naturalistic" investigation is grounded in ideological commitment to the revolutionary project of changing society in an aspired direction of social justice and equality.

Finally, in Vygotsky's approach, the processes of teaching/learning clearly have to be and are placed center stage. This is so because these processes (as Vygotsky insisted all along) constitute precisely the pathway individuals follow to acquire the cultural tools that allow for participation in and contribution to specifically human (and historically and culturally contingent) practices and, thus, no less than the *pathway to becoming human*. In this view, education is not about acquiring knowledge for the sake of knowing, but an *active project of becoming human*, a process that drives development and makes it possible (very much in line with critical pedagogy's stance). Learning then appears as the pathway to creating one's identity by finding one's place among other people and, ultimately, finding a way to contribute to the continuous flow of sociocultural practices. That is, learning appears as a project of constantly striving to join in with historically evolving, transformative practices of humanity and, through this, of becoming oneself—a unique human being who represents a distinctive and irreplaceable instantiation of humanness and a unique contribution to it. This is a view that celebrates the unity of knowing, being/becoming, and doing (as well as the unity of learning and identity)—all merged on the grounds of a transformative stance and its central motif of contributing to and changing the world.

Note that this conceptualization gives full credit to the historicized, profoundly social and relational character of learning. In this, there is a clear overlap with the recently influential participatory learning and communities of practice theories. In a thrust similar to these theories, the perspective suggested herein also considers it imperative to develop an alternative to today's mainstream view that naturalizes learning as taking place within an isolated individual. However, unlike these theories, the suggested perspective puts more emphasis not on participation in practices but on contribution to them—a more active, self-conscious, and directional process—and not just to the practices of local communities but to the unfolding social practices of humanity as a whole.

By shifting the emphasis from participation to contribution, this conceptualization avoids an unnecessarily stark opposition between knowledge and transformation, deference to the past (history and tradition), and the need for critique of the past as the baseline from which to challenge and transform this past. Instead, knowing the past (and present) is seen as the prerequisite to and even an initial form of transforming it in a struggle for new social arrangements. It is equally important that the impetus to transform the world or any of its aspects (including scholarly concepts) is the condition sine qua non for understanding them. In this conceptualization then, there is a place both for transformatively engaging the world to contribute to building a new one and for continuing past practices (including transmitting knowledge, though never in a passive and value-free manner, that is, not as a disengaged reproduction of facts), on the condition that knowledge itself is also understood as noncontemplative and always practically relevant, activist, and transformative. Thus, the emphasis is placed on the dialectical linkage between understanding and critiquing/transforming as two layers of the same process through which people engage with their world.

There are a number of implications for educational theories and practices that follow from a transformative activist stance and table 7.1 summarily presents these implications, while placing the notion of contribution at the fore (in comparison with the acquisition and participation models).

Conclusions

In this chapter, a number of steps in the direction of a dialectical conception of development and learning have been outlined. This sketch, generally following the major premises of Vygotsky's project that initiated but did not complete the formation of a dialectical conception of development, is presented against the background of today's social scientific landscape, which is marked by an ascent and consolidation of reductivist views on the one hand and a glaring lack of coordination among sociocultural approaches on the other. The transformative stance on human development and learning—dialectically superseding ontology of relations and actions while not abolishing them—is suggested as a foundation to conceptualize these processes in a way that does not exclude the dimensions of human subjectivity and individual uniqueness. These individual (but never "desocialized") dimensions are revealed, from a transformative stance, as having to do with the processes of individuals uniquely contributing to sociocultural practices of humanity and, therefore, as profoundly social and transactional, yet entailing ideological notions of determination, deliberation, activism, and commitment.

The idea about people transforming their world is often mentioned by today's scholars working in the CHAT tradition.[5] However, its foundational meaning and profound implications are not sufficiently discussed and often even avoided due to, among several reasons, the unwarranted beliefs that it (a) entails strictly and narrowly economic interpretation of history and human development which is incomplete and unsatisfying, and (b) is associated with the perils of instrumental control over nature that can only result in its destruction. This latter belief is especially pronounced today as ecological crises reach epic proportions. However, the likely solution to this global challenge is not a retreat from transformative activity (which would mean

Table 7.1 Transformative stance perspective: implications for the notion of learning

	Acquisition	Participation	Contribution
Key definition of learning	Information processing; obtaining knowledge; individual process "in the head"	Participation, i.e., becoming a member of the community; the permanence of having gives way to the constant flux of doing	Contributing to collaborative practices of humanity: continuing, while simultaneously transforming them
Key words	Knowledge, concepts, meaning, fact, contents; acquisition, internalization, transmission, attainment, accumulation	Apprenticeship, situatedness, contextuality, cultural embeddedness, discourse, communication, social constructivism, cooperation	Contribution, transformation, history as collaborative practices, cultural tools, vision and directionality, activism and commitment
Stress on	The individual mind and what goes into it; test and control of acquisition outcomes	The evolving bonds between the individual and others; the dialectic nature of learning interaction: the whole and the parts affect and inform each other	Dialectics of continuity and transformation, tradition and innovation; knowledge for and as action; learning for change
Ideal	Individualized learning	Mutuality and community building	Contribution through self-development and community development
Role of teacher	Delivering, conveying, inculcating, clarifying	Facilitator, mentor; expert participant, preserver of practice/discourse	Activist open to collaboration and dialogue; agent of a collaborative change
Nature of knowing	Having, possessing facts and skills	Belonging, participating, communicating	Collaboratively transforming the past in view of present conditions and future goals
Time line	Carrying out past experiences into the present; future is irrelevant	Focus on the presently evolving patterns of participation; the past is irrelevant and no future	Interface of the past, the present, and the future; the past and present are known through positioning vis-à-vis the future
Agency	No agency for social change	Collaborative agency	Coevolving individual and collaborative agency
Who develops?	Individual learner	Community	Learners through humanity and humanity through learners
Where is the mind	In the head	In patterns of participation	In continuous flow of transformative action
Key goals of learning	Knowledge of facts and skills	Ability to communicate in the language of community and act according to its norms	Knowing the past in order to be able to transform it; emphasis on the vision for the future from which the past can be known

Note: Descriptions of acquisition and participation models are partly based on Sfard (1998) and Collis and Moonen (2001).

the end of human civilization) but a radical change in its purposes and goals including the shift away from narrowly economic interests, unfair international policies, mindless consumption, and pernicious instrumentalism. The presently achieved humongous technological power (including the power to destroy all life on this planet) must now be matched with the new politics of global-social responsibility that requires, among other things, a dialectical conception of human development and learning. Such a conception, continuing Vygotsky's revolutionary project and expanded by notions from cultural studies, dynamic systems theory, and especially critical pedagogy (with much work in this direction remaining to be done), can be used as a powerful tool for a synergistically coordinated development of communities through self-development and of self-development through community growth and transformation.

As suggested throughout this chapter, a dialectical conception of development and learning based on a transformative stance appears to be in sync with the growing demands that globalization imposes on education and other practices of social life. Local communities can no longer be thought of as separate entities with clear borders and boundaries. Instead, communities belong together and coevolve with all other communities on the global scale, sharing one common fate and history. This requires that a unifying dialectical conception of human development and learning is worked out to substitute for a mosaic of approaches geared toward group-based interests. The elaborating of such a conception (itself a continuing project in which efforts of many sociocultural scholars need to be merged) is by no means merely academically relevant; instead, it is but part and parcel of a committed pursuit for social justice—predicated on and ascertaining our common humanity—especially on the global scale, through the active transformation of existing social institutions, politics, and ways of life.

Notes

1. With kind permission from Springer Science+Business Media: *Cultural Studies of Science Education*, "From relational ontology to transformative activist stance on development and learning: expanding Vygotsky's (CHAT) project," Volume 3, Issue 2, 2008, p. 471–91, Anna Stetsenko

2. Compatible accounts of relational worldview can be found in Overton (1997) and of transactional worldview in Altman and Rogoff (1987), among others.

3. This view can be found in the popular version of the biosociocultural codeterminism according to which biology, society, and culture (nature and nurture) are somehow intertwined in their effects on human

development. This latter approach insists on blending biology and culture into a composite (often referred to as a hybrid-type) process—a progressive step if compared with the narrowly one-sided perspectives that pit biology against culture as two independent forces and then attempt to calculate their relative impact on humans (e.g., by suggesting that variations in such processes as intelligence are due to both genetic inheritance *and* environmental influences). However, even these progressive coconstructivist approaches do not undertake a sufficient revision of the old notions of nature and culture. Namely, nature continues to be regarded as a static pool of genetic inheritance internal to organisms, and culture continues to be regarded as an equally static pool of cultural artifacts external to organisms; as such, these approaches do not resolutely break with the two-factorial models that have been in circulation since the nineteenth century in that they do not take the notion of activity as a primary ontological realm.

4. Dewey's theory, though linked to and formative of a liberal view of participatory democracy, is not associated with a program of actions or a social activist project with a clear ideological and political direction. By grounding knowledge and action in the present, Dewey rejected the notion of "grand" social projects and instead took the position that philosophy and psychology can neither give the direction to events as they unfold nor judge the meaning of events afterward (see Diggins, 1994).

5. References to Marxist ideas, including those about people actively transforming their world, were almost a routine in Soviet psychology during the 1970s through late 1980s, too often serving as an obligatory preamble to research based in a de facto contrary logic and paradigm. In Western psychology, Newman and Holzman (1993) pioneered a revival of interest in Vygotsky's roots in Marx; their interpretation of transformative practice, however, differs from the one suggested here in that Newman and Holzman saw it as a method that excluded "foundations, theses, premises, generalizations or abstractions" (see Holzman, 2006: 111).

References

Altman, I. and B. Rogoff (1987) World Views in Psychology: Trait, Interactional, Organismic, and Transactional Perspectives. In D. Stokolis and I. Altman (eds.) *Handbook of Environmental Psychology*, 1–40 (New York: Wiley).

Arievitch, I.M. and A. Stetsenko (2000) The Quality of Cultural Tools and Cognitive Development: Gal'perin's Perspective and its Implications. *Human Development*, 43: 69–92.

Barab, S.A. and Roth, W.M. (2006). Curriculum-Based Ecosystems: Supporting Knowing from an Ecological Perspective. *Educational Researcher*, 35: 3–13.

Clark, A. (1997) *Being There: Putting Brain, Body and World Together Again* (Cambridge, MA: MIT Press).

Collis, B. and J. Moonen (2001). *Flexible Learning in a Digital World: Experiences and Expectations* (London: Kogan Page).

Diggins, J.P. (1994). *The Promise of Pragmatism: Modernism and the Crisis of Knowledge and Authority* (Chicago, IL: Chicago University Press).

Eisenhart, M. (2001). Educational Ethnography. Past, Present, and Future: Ideas to Think with. *Educational Researcher*, 30: 16–27.

Garrison, J. (1995) (ed.) *The New Scholarship on Dewey* (Dordrecht, The Netherlands: Kluwer Academic).

Gergen, K.J. (2001). Psychological Science in a Postmodern Context. American *Psychologist*, 56: 803–13.

Gibson, J.J. (1966) *The Senses Considered as Perceptual Systems* (Boston, MA: Houghton Mifflin).

Glass, R.D. (2001) On Paulo Freire's Philosophy of Praxis and the Foundation of Liberation Education. *Educational Researcher*, 30: 15–25.

Gottlieb, G. (2003) On Making Behavioral Genetics Truly Developmental. *Human Development*, 46, 337–55.

Harding, S. (2004) *The Feminist Standpoint Theory Reader: Intellectual and Political Controversies* (New York: Routledge).

Harré, R. (2002) Public Sources of the Personal Mind: Social Constructionism in Context. *Theory and Psychology*, 12: 611–23.

Hicks, D. (2000) Self and Other in Bakhtin's Early Philosophical Essays: Prelude to a Theory of Prose Consciousness. *Mind, Culture, and Activity*, 7: 227–42.

Holland, D., W. Lachicotte, Jr., D. Skinner, and C. Cain (2001) *Identity and Agency in Cultural Worlds* (Cambridge, MA: Harvard University Press).

Holzman, L. (2006) Activating Postmodernism. *Theory and Psychology*, 16: 109–23.

Hutchins, E. (1995) *Cognition in the Wild* (Cambridge, MA: MIT Press).

Ingold, T. (2000) *Perception of the Environment: Essays in Livelihood, Dwelling and Skill* (London: Routledge Press).

John-Steiner, V. (1999) Sociocultural and Feminist Theory: Mutuality and Relevance. In S. Chaiklin, M. Hedegaard, and U. J. Jensen (eds.) *Activity Theory and Social Practice*, 201–44 (Aarhus, Denmark: Aarhus University Press).

Kestenbaum, V. (1977) *The Phenomenological Sense of John Dewey* (Atlantic Highlands, NJ: Humanities Press).

Kitchener, R.F. (1996) The Nature of the Social for Piaget and Vygotsky. *Human Development*, 39: 243–9.

Knox, J.E. (1993) Introduction. In L.S. Vygotsky and A.R. Luria (eds.) *Studies on the History of Behavior: Ape, Primitive, and Child*, 1–35 (London: Lawrence Erlbaum).

Latour, B. (1987). *Science in Action: How to Follow Scientists and Engineers through Society* (Milton Keynes: Open University Press).

Lave, J. and E. Wenger (1991). *Situated Learning: Legitimate Peripheral Participation* (New York: Cambridge University Press).

Lickliter, R. and H. Honeycutt (2003) Developmental Dynamics: Toward a Biologically Plausible Evolutionary Psychology. *Psychological Bulletin*, 129: 819–35.

Marx, K. (1978) Theses on Feuerbach. In R.C. Tucker (ed.) *The Marx-Engels Reader (2nd Edition)*, 143–145 (New York: W.W. Norton).

Müller, U. and J.I.M. Carpendale (2000) The Role of Social Interaction in Piaget's Theory: Language for Social Cooperation and Social Cooperation for Language. *New Ideas in Psychology*, 18: 139–56.

Newman, F. and L. Holzman, (1993) Lev *Vygotsky: Revolutionary Scientist* (Florence: Taylor and Frances/Routledge).

Overton, W.F. (1997) Beyond Dichotomy: An Embodied Active Agent for Cultural Psychology. *Culture and Psychology*, 3: 315–34.

Piaget, J. (1977/1995) *Sociological Studies* (London: Routledge). (Original work published in 1977).

Sfard, A. (1998) On Two Metaphors for Learning and the Dangers of Choosing Just One. *Educational Researcher*, 27: 4–13.

Stetsenko, A. (2004) Introduction to Vygotsky's "Tool and Sign in Child Development." In R. Rieber and D. Robbins (eds.) *Essential Vygotsky*, 499–510 (New York: Kluwer Academic/Plenum).

Stetsenko, A. (2005) Activity as Object-Related: Resolving the Dichotomy of Individual and Collective Planes of Activity. *Mind, Culture, and Activity*, 12: 70–88.

Stetsenko, A. and I. M Arievitch (2004) Vygotskian Collaborative Project of Social Transformation: History, Politics, and Practice in Knowledge Construction. *The International Journal of Critical Psychology*, 12: 58–80.

Thompson, E. and F. J Varela (2001) Radical Embodiment: Neural Dynamics and Consciousness. *Trends in Cognitive Sciences*, 5: 418–25.

Vianna, E. and A. Stetsenko (2006) Embracing History through Transforming It: Contrasting Piagetian versus Vygotskian (Activity) Theories of Learning and Development to Expand Constructivism within a Dialectical View of History. *Theory and Psychology*, 16: 81–108.

Vygotsky, L.S. (1997) The History of the Development of Higher Mental Functions. In R. Rieber (ed.) *The Collected Works of L.S. Vygotsky (Vol. 4)*, 1–278 (New York: Plenum).

Vygotsky, L.S. (2004a) Thinking and Speech. In R. Rieber and D. Robinson (eds.) *Essential Vygotsky*, 33–148 (New York: Kluwer Academic/Plenum).

Vygotsky, L.S. (2004b) Fundamentals of Defectology. In R. Rieber and D. Robinson (eds.), *Essential Vygotsky*, 153–199 (New York: Kluwer Academic/Plenum).

Wertsch, J. (2005) Essay Review of "Making of Human Beings: Bioecological Perspectives on Human Development" by U. Bronfenbrenner. *British Journal of Developmental Psychology*, 23: 143–51.

Chapter 8

Activity, Activity Theory, and the Marxian Legacy

Peter E. Jones

Introduction[1]

How should Marxists approach the analysis, critique, and transformation of social practices and institutions (including education) within capitalist societies today? What theoretical tools do we need for this task and what should be our starting point? It is these fundamental theoretical and methodological issues that are the subject of this chapter.

My intention is to think through these problems via a critical examination of a version of "activity theory" developed over the last 25 years or so by Yrjö Engeström and colleagues (see, for example, Engeström, 1987; Engeström, 1990; Engeström, Miettinen, and Punamäki, 1999; Miettinen, 2000; Tuomi-Gröhn and Engeström, 2003; Toiviainen and Engeström, 2009). The "activity theory," or "cultural-historical activity theory" (Tuomi-Gröhn and Engeström, 2003: 28), of Engeström and colleagues is not the only version of "activity theory," a theoretical tradition stemming from the psychological work of A. N. Leont'ev (see, in particular, Leont'ev, 1978). Anna Stetsenko's approach, for example (see Stetsenko, 2005, this volume), has developed independently and along different, to some extent opposing, lines. However, the significance of Engeström's "activity theory" for my purposes is that it has claimed allegiance to Marxist methodological principles in proposing an original framework for the analysis and transformation of working practices and has applied that framework in its interventions in the areas of educational activity and learning.

It should be said that Engeström's "activity theory" is not without its critics. Indeed, criticisms have come from many quarters—theoretical, philosophical, economic, and political (e.g., Jones, 2009; Bakhurst,

2009; Warmington, 2008; Avis, 2007). In this chapter I will concentrate more squarely on methodology, taking advantage of the fact that contributors to "activity theory" have explained and defended their own procedures by appealing to a specifically Marxist methodological precept, namely, that of the "ascent from the abstract to the concrete," otherwise known within "activity theory" literature as the "germ-cell" methodology (Tuomi-Gröhn and Engeström, 2003: 29). I will argue that the use of this method in "activity theory" involves a fundamental misunderstanding of Marx's own methodological practice and will conclude with some observations on the implications of this methodological divergence for educational research and action.

Marx and Methodology

Marx's own methodological discussions and pronouncements, notably his Introduction to *Grundrisse* (Marx, 1973), as well as his actual methodological practices in *Capital* (Marx, 1976a), have long provided rich, if contested, materials for theoreticians in various disciplines and continue to be the subject of much careful dissection and debate in Marxist circles. In particular, the methodological principle that Marx himself appears to advocate under the heading "the method of political economy" (1973: 100), a principle that has become generally known as "the ascent from the abstract to the concrete," has proved to be of special significance in the understanding and evaluation of the whole theoretical side of Marx's political and economic work (see, for example, Pilling, 1980; Ilyenkov, 1982; Sayer, 1987; Smith, 1990; Smith, 1999).

Putting differences of interpretation to one side (see, for example, Smith, 1999: 129–134), the "ascent" method could be explained in a nutshell as follows. Marx argued that a historically specific social formation like the capitalist mode of production could not be understood by approaching it armed with general concepts and notions that applied to any and all social formations throughout history, whatever similarities or commonalities may in fact appear to hold between them on superficial examination. Instead, Marx argued, it was necessary to begin from the specific economic phenomenon from which the *distinctiveness* of capitalist production in relation to other formations was derived, to isolate this object from all the extraneous facts with which it was necessarily interwoven in everyday life and subject it to careful analysis. From there, the theoretician could systematically uncover the logic of development of the whole economic structure of capitalist society as a process of growth and differentiation from this simplest economic object or "cell."

Now, in Marx's terminology (rigorously analyzed by Ilyenkov, 1982), the economic structure of society in all its detail is "the concrete whole," that is, the really existing totality of capitalist social relations, the theoretical understanding of which is the goal or target of analysis. On the other hand, the simple economic fact, isolated forensically at the beginning of the analysis, is "the abstract." It is abstract not because it is an abstraction—an idea, concept, notion, or model of some kind (see Jones, 2009)—but precisely because it is taken abstractly, that is, taken in isolation from the myriad empirical interconnections with which it is necessarily embroiled in the "concrete whole."

For his analysis of capitalist production Marx identified the commodity as the simplest economic form—the basic "cell"—from which the analysis could progressively ascend. The commodity as starting point, then, is a real thing—"the simplest economic *concretum*," as Marx himself puts it (1976b, p. 215):

> In the first place, I do not proceed on the basis of "concepts"...What I proceed from is the simplest social form in which the product of labour in contemporary society manifests itself, and this is as "commodity." That is what I analyse, and first of all to be sure in the *form in which it appears*. (1976b: 214)

Thus, Marx's "ascent from the abstract" begins, however paradoxical this may seem, with "the commodity" (a *concretum*), and builds from it—*ascends*—to reconstruct the logic of the development and dynamic of the whole social system of capitalist production.

Amongst the discussions of Marxist methodological principles, a work by the late Soviet Marxist philosopher Evald Ilyenkov (Ilyenkov, 1982) distinguishes itself by an exceptionally cogent account of Marx's method alongside a forceful defense of it. Ilyenkov's treatment is of particular relevance here because of its influence on "activity theory" via the intermediary of Soviet approaches to psychology, particularly educational psychology, which espoused and applied Ilyenkov's work. Notably, V. V. Davydov (1990) developed an approach to teaching and learning activity that was informed by Ilyenkov's account of Marx's "ascent" method. In turn, Davydov's work with its explicit Ilyenkovian underpinnings was a strong influence on the reworking by Engeström and coworkers of Leont'ev's "psychological theory of activity" (Leont'ev, 1978) as "activity theory," or "developmental work research" (see Miettinen, 2000: 114). Although the approach has gone through several evolutionary phases, it has stuck to its methodological guns, notably its appeal to the "ascent" method.

The "Ascent" Method and the Analysis of Activity

Engeström (1990: 52) argues that the "dialectical method of thinking is best characterized as the method of 'ascending from the abstract to the concrete'" and refers to Davydov's work as "the most sophisticated attempt" at "thorough psychological analysis" (1990: 52) of this method. Engeström also refers approvingly to Ilyenkov (1982) in connection with the "germ-cell" method of analysis (Engeström, 1990: 53). Engeström notes that the "most famous instance of this kind of analysis is the identification of commodity as the germ-cell of the capitalist socio-economic formation" (1990: 53). He then goes on to demonstrate the immediate relevance of the "germ-cell" method to the understanding and transformation of educational practice through an account of a case study of adult education students following a course in instructional theory (1990: 53) (see below).

Miettinen (2000) also acknowledges Marx's influence as a methodologist:

> Marx traced the germ-cell of a capitalist society (commodity and value), and then drew the whole system of concepts and determinations to uncover the developmental dynamics of capitalism. The unit of analysis is the capitalist society as a whole.

He goes on to ask the very pertinent question: "how did this project [namely Marx's analysis of capital] succeed in constructing the conceptual tools of analysing the diverse concrete developmental contradictions of local activities in society?"

In exploring possible answers to this question, however, Miettinen does not look directly at Marx's own way of "constructing" such "conceptual tools." Nor does Miettinen follow the line of his own argument according to which Marx identified "the commodity and value" as the "germ-cell" of capitalist society. Instead, he looks to Ilyenkov's discussion of the ground-breaking work of the Soviet psychologist A. Meshcheryakov with deaf-blind students. Miettinen argues that Meshcheryakov "applied the basic ideas of cultural-historical activity theory to the development of those handicapped children" (Miettinen, 2000: 113). In this, Mescheryakov's "basic conception was *joint activity* between the child and adult" (Miettinen, 2000: 113) and "joint action, starting from the elementary acts of self care, can be regarded as a kind of 'cell' realized in the educational practice and its development" (2000: 113). Joint action of this kind, Miettinen argues, is "Meshcheryakov's simple unit of analysis" (2000: 113).

Thus, Miettinen argues that Meshcheryakov's approach to the care and education of deaf-blind children can be seen as another, and rather different, application of the "ascent" method, given that "society and the individual, as systems, have different time spans in their developmental dynamics" (2000: 114). This, he claims, "permits us to think that the analysis of the method of *Capital* is not, necessarily, the only source available in our endeavour to understand and develop the idea of the method of ascending from the abstract to the concrete" (2000: 114).

A further source for extending the method is, he argues, the study of "the development of local communities of practitioners" (2000: 114), a study for which the new discipline of "developmental work research" ("activity theory") is specifically designed. In this discipline, he goes on, "the unit of analysis is a concrete work activity, understood as an object oriented, collective activity system" (2000: 114). Miettinen again looks to educational practice for an illustration of the approach. He takes the example of "teachers' work in a vocational school" (in this case Helsinki Business Polytechnics) as an "activity system" of this kind (see below).

Now, Miettinen is surely right to point out that our understanding of the "ascent" method as such can certainly be enhanced by attempting to apply it to different types of phenomena. But this is a different matter from thinking that an appreciation of the psychological development of a deaf-blind child, or the development of particular approaches to school subjects (as in Davydov, 1990), is going to alter the way we approach the analysis of capitalist economic structure. It sounds very reasonable to take "the elementary acts of self care" as a starting point for understanding child development, but if the object of our analysis is capital then we'd better start somewhere else.

Engeström and Miettinen (1999) explain the rationale for their new "unit of analysis" in different terms. Here they justify their approach from the complexities of contemporary work activity and the relations and interactions between working practices, science and technology, and other processes. They suggest,

> To be able to analyze such complex interactions and relationships, a theoretical account of the constitutive elements of the system under investigation is needed. In other words, there is a demand for a new unit of analysis. Activity theory has a strong candidate for such a unit of analysis in the concept of *object-oriented, collective,* and *culturally mediated human activity,* or *activity system.* (Engeström and Miettinen, 1999: 9)

How, then, will an "activity system" be analyzed? According to Engeström (1990: 79), "an activity system integrates the subject, the object and the instruments (material tools as well as signs and symbols) into a unified whole." In more detail, the "basic structure of a human activity system" includes "the subject" ("the individual or sub-group whose agency is chosen as the point of view in the analysis"), "the object" ("the "raw material" or "problem space" at which the activity is directed), "the tools" ("mediating instruments and signs"), "the community" ("multiple individuals and/or sub-groups who share the same object"), "the division of labor" ("both the horizontal division of tasks between the members of the community" and "the vertical division of power and status"), and "the rules" ("the explicit and implicit regulations, norms and conventions that constrain actions and interactions within the activity system") (Engeström, 1990: 79). Furthermore, each "activity system," Engeström argues, "is connected to other activity systems through all of its components" (1990: 84), offering us, it would seem, the prospect of mapping the whole social system in terms of a dynamic network of interacting activity systems embracing all the different spheres of work in society.

In sum, an "activity theory" analysis proceeds according to the following methodology: a "unit of analysis" is identified, such a unit being a "local activity" or "activity system," for example, adult education, traditional teaching activity, a working practice in health care, industry or banking; the activity system will then be broken down into elements (object, mediating artifacts, rules, subject, community, and so on); contradictions within the system (and between connecting activity systems) will then be identified in order to discover a potential developmental dynamic (and an opportunity for transformation) in accordance with a dialectically oriented "germ-cell" model.

Given, then, this turn to sources other than "the method of *Capital*" in the elaboration of the "ascent" method of "activity theory," the question is pointedly raised as to the precise relationship between Marx's method (with the commodity as "germ-cell") and the "activity theory" method with an "activity system" as "germ-cell" (or "unit of analysis"). So let us now turn to this question directly with a little help from Ilyenkov (1982).

"Activity Theory" and "Units of Analysis"

Toward the end of Ilyenkov's book, the author proclaims in characteristically forthright fashion: "Having accepted Marx's method, it is impossible not to accept all the conclusions of *Capital*" (1982: 288).

But now here is the curious thing. While Marx's *method* seems to have been adopted enthusiastically by "activity theory" scholars, Marx's *conclusions*—the *results* of his own application of the method—are more difficult to discern. On the one hand, Miettinen argues that Marx uncovered "the developmental dynamics of capitalism" on the basis of the commodity as "germ-cell" and that his "unit of analysis is the capitalist society as a whole" (2000: 112). On the other hand, when it comes to "analysing the diverse concrete developmental contradictions of local activities in society," the commodity germ-cell is bypassed with each local activity taken as a "unit of analysis" in its own right and treated as appropriate subject matter for independent modeling in "germ-cell" terms. Thus, while Miettinen seems to see that Marx's "germ-cell" (the commodity) is the germ-cell of "capitalist society as a whole," the methodology of "activity theory," in contrast, bestows the status of "germ-cell" on each local work activity taken separately and independently of "capitalist society as a whole" and *its* "germ-cell"! It is as if we agreed in principle that the motions of the earth and other planets relative to one another can be deduced from their orbits around a single central star, but insisted on studying the motion of each separate planet without taking any account of its relationship to the sun. Thus, those economic forms specific to capitalist production, including value, surplus value, and capital, whose dialectical development and differentiation from the commodity "germ-cell" are analyzed by Marx in *Capital*, do not, as we have seen above, figure in "the basic structure of a human activity system" (Engeström, 1990: 79) and, therefore, do not appear at all in the analytical models of work activities in "activity theory," something which has been noted by Warmington (2008) and Avis (2007).

The point, however, is that if Marx's analysis applies to "capitalist society as a whole," then the "germ-cell" with which he begins his analysis *must be the germ-cell for the totality of work activities specific to capitalist society!* We can't have it both ways. To be consistent with Marx's method, then, it would be necessary to show how such spheres of traditional teaching, adult education, vocational education, or health care emerge and develop from the social formation whose "germ-cell" is the commodity and to see the problems and contradictions within these spheres in that light. Whatever the value of the observations by Engeström and Miettinen on the work practices they examine, there is simply no way to concretely understand these different spheres, with their specific histories and contradictions, other than by an analysis that, proceeding in accordance with the method and the results that Marx outlined, places them within "the chain of mediating links through which both poles of value must pass in their transformation into each other" (Ilyenkov, 1982: 276, quoted in Engeström, 1990: 53).

What, then, is the "activity theory" unit of analysis a unit of analysis of? It would seem that the intention is to theorize the entire social system as a dynamically developing network of activity systems. In that case, "activity theory" is offering us a method for the analysis of capitalist work practices and their complex interconnections within capitalist society without the need for one particular piece of the jigsaw, namely capitalist production.

But perhaps we are simply splitting hairs. Why exactly does it matter what "unit of analysis" we begin from? Clearly, we cannot theorize the whole social totality in one go but must start from a part or element of the system and then build up from there. In that case, what is wrong with proceeding in the "activity theory" fashion and starting our analysis off from a study of the particular "activity systems" that ostensibly constitute the social world? Why could we not take each "activity system" in turn—here is an adult education course, here a medical practice, here a car factory, here a bus route, here a government department, here an investment deal, and so on—and then try to work out how they all fit together? In fact, why didn't Marx simply do it that way? Why did he start with the commodity rather than with, say, an inventory of different professions or types of work?

Ilyenkov's answer is that scientific thinking, in attempting to grasp the principles and dynamic movement of an organic system, cannot begin just anywhere. In connection, for example, with the phenomena connected with profit he argues,

> one may form an abstract generalised notion of them. But one cannot obtain a concrete concept of profit on this path, for a concrete conception of the place and role of profit in the motion of the system of capitalist relations assumes an understanding of their real proximate substance, surplus-value, that is, of a different economic phenomenon, and the latter in its turn presupposes cognition of the immanent laws of motion of the commodity-money sphere, an understanding of value as such, irrespective of profit or surplus-value...Profit may be understood through surplus-value only, through "something different," whereas surplus-value may and must be understood "by itself." (1982: 104–5)

It follows from this that

> while the theoretician has not merely a right but even an obligation to consider the commodity form in abstraction within the capitalist system, he has no logical right to consider just as abstractly any other form

of economic connection in the same capitalist organism, e.g., profit or rent. (1982: 104).

From this point of view, "the right to abstract consideration of a phenomenon," as Ilyenkov puts it, "is determined by the concrete role of this phenomenon in the whole under study, in a concrete system of interacting phenomena" (1982: 104). But precisely the opposite is happening in "activity theory": each sphere of everyday or professional activity (education, health care, and so on) is approached directly and separately on the assumption that it is an independently and coherently abstractable phenomenon—a "unit of analysis" no less. Each separate "activity system" will then be put into relation with other "activity systems" as the whole social body is built from its individual cells.

It may be objected that the activity of adult education, say, is a long way removed from the extraction of surplus value from living labor and that this distance gives us "the right" to consider these processes independently of one another. But this objection simply expresses the kind of abstract thinking that Ilyenkov, following Marx, was attempting to subject to rigorous critique. There is, certainly, a difference between the cell and the organism as a whole; Marx's method does not involve reducing each and every activity in society to the same "model" but in understanding how these activities are related on the basis of capitalist production. After all, political activity does not produce surplus value either, but one would be hard pressed to understand a single thing that governments are now doing throughout the world in response to the global financial meltdown without first of all understanding how capital works and how it is produced. In any case, the production of surplus value may take place just as well in the school or college as in the factory. The teacher, then, may be just as much a "productive worker" (producing surplus value) as the car worker or coal-miner (Marx, 1976a: 1044). But if teachers are not "productive workers" in this sense, then the place of their activity within *the social formation that is built around "productive work"* must still be discovered and analyzed.

From Ilyenkov's point of view, then, the theorist of social activity has *no right* to proceed by starting with each and every sphere of activity as a "unit of analysis." To do so is not to "ascend from the abstract to the concrete" in thought but to definitively remain in the sphere of the abstract and, therefore, a long way, indeed, from a scientific concept:

> The concept of a phenomenon exists, in general, only where this phenomenon is understood not *abstractly* (that is, *as a recurring phenomenon*)

but concretely, that is, in regard to *its position and role in a definite system of interacting phenomena*, in a system forming a certain coherent whole. (1982: 96, my emphasis)

In Ilyenkov's terms, the "unit of analysis" of "activity theory" ("the concept of object-oriented, collective, and culturally mediated human activity, or activity system") is not actually *a concept* but "an abstract general notion" (1982: 96). It cannot be a means of concrete apprehension and critique of the social relations of bourgeois society since it is obtained by a simple empirical generalization of the common features of all conventionally established and empirically observable activities under capitalism, indeed of all possible activities in all possible societies (on this see Bakhurst, 2009).

In fairness, it could be argued that Engeström has already anticipated and addressed the objections raised above. He argues, for instance,

Activity systems are characterized by inner contradictions. The primary inner contradictions reflect the basic contradiction characteristic to the socio-economic formation as a whole. In capitalism, the basic contradiction is the dual nature of commodities, the tension between the use value and the exchange value. In different activity systems, this fundamental tension appears in different forms, as the primary contradiction of that particular activity. This primary contradiction resides in each component of the activity system. (1990: 84)

This comment is certainly a significant concession to Marxist analysis, and one that clearly indicates that "activity theory" is not deliberately attempting to hide, disguise, or soften the contradictions within capitalism. And yet, Engeström's statement offers plenty of grounds for concern since there is a problem with his description of the "dual nature of commodities" as the "basic contradiction" in capitalism. The problem is this: while capitalist production involves making commodities, commodity production does not make capitalism. As Marx puts it, "The fact that it produces commodities does not distinguish it [capitalism] from other modes of production" (1909: 1025). Rather, capitalist production "is marked from the outset by two peculiar traits" (1909: 1025). The first has to do with the existence of wage labor, in which "the labourer himself acts in the role of a seller of commodities" (1909: 1025). From this, Marx concludes that "the relation between wage labour and capital determines the entire character of the mode of production" (1909: 1025). The second "peculiar trait" is "the production of surplus-value as the direct aim and determining incentive of production" (1909: 1026). The contradiction between use-value and value within the commodity, then, is not only *not* the main or determining contradiction within capitalist production but is not even a "peculiar trait" of this particular social system. The main contradiction, in Marx's view, is that between wage labor (i.e., the agents of productive activity) and capital (i.e., those who extract surplus value from these agents).

As Ilyenkov explains,

> Commodities, together with money, commercial profit, rent, etc. belong to "antediluvian" premises of capitalist development, to its "prehistoric" conditions. As concrete historical forms of being of capital, reflecting in their movement its specific history, they are *products of capital itself.* (Ilyenkov, 1982: 211, my emphasis)

Commodities, money, profit, surplus value, and so on, are *produced* within capitalist production, "produced" being the operative word here. "Activity theory" tells us that each activity system "reflects" the basic contradiction of capitalism but not how this basic contradiction is itself produced, or where—within which "activity systems"—it is produced. In effect, then, the "forms of being of capital," as Ilyenkov puts it, are simply the unanalyzed premises of the analytic division of the social formation into "activity systems."

The key methodological point that Ilyenkov is hammering home is that not just any analytical division of one's subject matter—however much that division may appear to be justified observationally, empirically, professionally, and so on—will produce an adequate theoretical abstraction. Having broken down the whole social system into its basic "units of analysis," "activity theory" then proceeds to connect them up again. But what the procedure cannot explain is why it is, and how it is, that when we put these separate "activity systems" together we get specifically *capitalist* production, the movement of capital, the production of surplus value. (And if we can't explain how we "get into" capitalist production, then we certainly won't be able to understand how we get out of it). The reason for this is simple: the social whole itself has not developed as an aggregate of "concrete work activities" and *does not actually function in this way*, despite everyday appearances. Its concrete and specific movement cannot therefore be derived by connecting up such "units." "Activity theory" proceeds, in Ilyenkov's terms, from a "unit of analysis" that "makes synthesis impossible" (1982: 227). This is a good example of what Marx called "the violence of abstraction" (Sayer, 1987).

A possible objection to Ilyenkov's argument might go as follows: in order to show the interconnection of different activities within the whole is it not necessary to start by showing that all these activities have something in common in terms of how they are organized? Isn't it in fact what all these "activity systems" have in common that is the basis for their interaction and interconnection into a wider social network?

Ilyenkov's response is that the "analysis of the category of interaction shows directly...that mere sameness, simple identity of two individual things is by no means an expression of the principle of their mutual connection" (1982: 89).

He explains,

> "Sameness" is always assumed, of course, as the premise or condition under which the link of interconnection is established. But the very essence of interconnection is not realised through sameness. Two gears are locked exactly because the tooth of the pinion is placed opposite a space between two teeth of the drive gear rather than opposite the same kind of tooth. (1982: 89)

Thus, "in general," as Ilyenkov puts it, "interaction proves to be strong if an object finds in another object a complement of itself, something that it is lacking as such" (1982: 89). From this point of view, therefore, taking each "concrete work activity" as an instance of the general, abstract category of "activity system" is not going to advance our theoretical understanding of the concrete interconnections and interaction between activities within the whole system. And this is precisely because the features that all "concrete work activities" without exception display do not, in fact, constitute the real basis of their interaction, or their emergence and development.

Activity and the Labor Process[2]

The final criticism of the methodology of "activity theory" concerns the source of the notion of "activity system" itself. According to Engeström, as we have seen, an "activity system integrates the subject, the object and the instruments...into a unified whole" (1990: 79), a whole that can be analyzed in more detail using the categories of "subject," "object," "tools," "community," "division of labor," and "rules" (1990: 79).

Naturally, one hears in this description of the system a clear echo of Marx's characterization of the labor process in *Capital*. In Marx's view, "the universal features of the labour process are independent of every specific social development" (1976a: 998). These "universal features," which Marx elsewhere refers to as "the simple elements of the labour process" (1976a: 284), are

> (1) purposeful activity, that is work itself, (2) the object on which that work is performed, and (3) the instruments of that work. (1976a: 284)

Engeström has slightly modified these features as Marx describes them and has thrown in a few more for good measure, but his "model of the basic structure of a human activity system" (1990: 79) is clearly based on Marx's description of the "universal features of the labour process." However, this apparent coincidence of approach conceals an essential difference in methodological orientation.

Simply put, Marx's characterization of the labor process is not a model or framework for the analysis of "concrete work activities" in capitalist society. He did not intend us to take particular forms of work as we find them under capitalism and directly fit the "simple elements of the labour process" to their various features. He did not intend this for the simple reason that what is "independent of every specific social development" (1976a: 998), that is, "common to all forms of society in which human beings live" (Marx, 1976a: 290), cannot serve as a means of identifying or analyzing the distinctive forms of work activity that are peculiar to, unique to, specific social formations:

> The taste of porridge does not tell us who grew the oats, and the process we have presented [that is, the labor process] does not reveal the conditions under which it takes place, whether it is happening under the slave-owner's brutal lash, or the anxious eye of the capitalist. (Marx, 1976a: 290)

In other words, the relationship between the labor process and the capitalist production process is not, for Marx, the same kind of relationship as the one between the general category of "activity system" and a particular instance of "concrete work activity" in "activity theory." When Marx says that the labor process is "*common* to all forms of society in which human beings live" he does not mean that the activities making up capitalist production as a whole are all exemplars of the labor process as an activity. On the contrary, Marx describes the specifically capitalist production process in terms of "the appropriation of the labour process by capital" (1976a: 998).

As Ilyenkov explains, Marx's usage of the term *common* is "characteristic of dialectical logic" (1982: 92). If we say that Paul and Mary have a *common* ancestor in Fred, this does not mean that Fred is the general type of which Paul and Mary are instances. In such cases the word *common* "has the meaning of bond which by no means coincides in its content with the identical features of different correlated objects, men, and so on" (1982: 92). Fred, the common ancestor of Paul and Mary, is a different person, who may well be still alive and interacting with his descendants:

> What is common to them [Paul and Mary] here is that particular object [Fred] which each of them has outside them, confronting them, that object through relation to which the relation between them is established. (1982: 92–3)

Marx is not saying, then, that slavery, feudalism, and capitalism are particular instances of the general type, namely, the labor process. He is saying that the labor process is *common* to all these social formations in the sense that *it runs through them all*; it is the bond that unites them in their historical evolution and in their specific differences. It is "the everlasting nature-imposed condition of human existence" (Marx, 1976a: 290) that is "appropriated," that is, ensnared, trapped, and subjugated within the different modes of production that Marx relegated to human prehistory. The labor process is *living labor*—"free, conscious activity" (1976a, p. 86); as such, it is the force that is never extinguished, and the force that constantly beats at the historically transient dehumanizing fetters that hem it in on all sides.

Thus, according to Marx's view, the labor process *is present within the capitalist production process* but *as only one aspect of the process*:

> Just as the commodity itself is a unity formed of use-value and value, so the process of production must be a unity, composed of the labour process and the process of creating value. (1976a: 293)

He explains further:

> We now see that the difference between labour, considered on the one hand as producing utilities, and on the other hand as creating value, a difference which we discovered by our analysis of a commodity, resolves itself into a difference between two aspects of the production process. The production process, considered as the unity of the labour process and the process of creating value, is the process of production of commodities; considered as the unity of the labour process and the process of valorization, it is the capitalist process of production, or the capitalist form of the production of commodities. (1976a: 304)

One must not confuse these processes, then, despite their forming a unity, since

> in the labour process looked at purely for itself the worker utilizes the means of production. In the labour process regarded also as a capitalist process of production, the means of production utilize the worker. (1976a: 1008)

It would therefore be quite wrong to describe "concrete work activities" within the capitalist process of production in terms of the "simple elements of the labour process." The theorist who subsumed the features of such "concrete work activities" under categories that pertain to "the labour process looked at purely for itself" would be guilty of "confusing the appropriation of the labour process by capital with the labour process itself" (Marx, 1976a: 998), however much they might draw attention to the contradictions and dilemmas within each activity system and to the role of fundamental economic contradictions within society. For the source of the antagonistic and destructive contradictions and problems within society is not to be found in tensions or conflicts within the labor process but, rather, in the capitalist production process, in "the appropriation of the labour process by capital."

So Marx's description of human activity is not meant to be used to describe capitalist production, but is put forward in order to show us the difference between acting freely, acting humanly, and acting as per the conditions and dictates of capital. Marx wants us to see precisely how the labor process has become entangled and imprisoned within the capitalist valorization process, so that we will appreciate the historically specific and, therefore, transient nature of the whole system. He wants to show that the whole kit and kaboodle of wage labor, commodity production, money, capital, and the market is not some natural or eternal way of doing things, whatever the solidity of appearances, but a crazy state of affairs that should be done away with. His characterization of the labor process is not a way of describing "concrete work activities" under capitalist conditions. On the contrary, *it is meant as a critique of those activities.* He is not offering us a general "theory of activity" but a criterion to be used for the criticism, in theory and in practice, of those social conditions within which the labor process is imprisoned.

It turns out, then, that the main theoretical problem with the "activity theory" unit of analysis lies in its failure to analytically distinguish the labor process from the valorization process. This failing is seen in its viewing "concrete work activities" as instantiations or exemplars of human labor, or the labor process. From this methodological orientation spring two consequences.

The first is that the valorization process itself, dressed up in terms proper only to the "universal features of the labour process," disappears from view altogether. Furthermore, if "the basic structure of human activity" is present in each and every "concrete work activity" within capitalist society equally then we seem to have lost our compass: there is just as much humanity, we seem to be saying, in healing the sick as in managing the corporate stock portfolio.

The second is the mirror image of the first. In taking each and every observable activity as an instance of "the basic structure of human activity" we run the risk of vulgarizing the Marxian conception of the labor process and thereby of demeaning the labor process itself. For if we put an equals sign between the labor process and every "concrete work activity," the result is that we begin to read the peculiar features of work under capitalist conditions back into the "universal features of the labor process" and, therefore, begin to see "concrete work activities" under capitalism straightforwardly as the process "common to all forms of society in which human beings live." By this procedure the labor process is immediately robbed of its revolutionary character and implications and the forms of "activity" under capitalist society are naturalized.

But Marx already anticipated this theoretical problem and explained its social and historical source:

> Labour seems a quite simple category. The conception of labour in this general form—as labour as such—is also immeasurably old. Nevertheless, when it is economically conceived in this simplicity, "labour" is as modern a category as are the relations which create this simple abstraction. (1973: 103)

As Marx explains in greater detail:

> It was an immense step forward for Adam Smith to throw out every limiting specification of wealth-creating activity—not only manufacturing, or commercial or agricultural labour, but one as well as the others, labour in general...Now, it might seem that all that had been achieved thereby was to discover the abstract expression for the simplest and most ancient relation in which human beings—in whatever form of society—play the role of producers. This is correct in one respect. Not in another. *Indifference towards any specific kind of labour presupposes a very developed totality of real kinds of labour, of which no single one is any longer predominant*...Indifference towards specific labours

corresponds to a form of society in which individuals can with ease transfer from one labour to another, and where the specific kind is a matter of chance for them, hence of indifference. Not only the category, labour, but labour in reality has here become the means of creating wealth in general, and has ceased to be organically linked with particular individuals in any specific form... *Here, then, for the first time, the point of departure of modern economics, namely the abstraction of the category "labour," "labour as such," labour pure and simple, becomes true in practice. The simplest abstraction, then, which modern economics places at the head of its discussions, and which expresses an immeasurably ancient relation valid in all forms of society, nevertheless achieves practical truth as an abstraction only as a category of the most modern society.* (1973: 104–5, my emphasis)

But Marx goes on:

Although it is true, therefore, that the categories of bourgeois economics possess a truth for all other forms of society, *this is to be taken only with a grain of salt. They can contain them in a developed, or stunted, or caricatured form etc., but always with an essential difference.* (1973: 106, my emphasis)

Marx seems to be suggesting that "labor" *as a category of bourgeois economics* may appear as if it is actually identical to the labor process, to that "immeasurably ancient relation valid in all forms of society." There is some truth in this equation of the two, Marx says. The general abstraction "labor," having the same relationship to any "concrete work activity" as the abstraction "animal" has to a cat, a dog, a tiger, and, so on, "becomes true in practice" in bourgeois society. The coal-miner is a wage-laborer, as are the car worker, the school teacher, the doctor, the professor, the soldier, the priest, the prime minister. At the same time, Marx cautions, this equating of labor with the labor process within "modern economics" must be taken "with a grain of salt," because there is "an essential difference" between them. The abstract generality of the category of labor within bourgeois society manifests the universality of the labor process only in a "stunted, or caricatured form." The modern category of labor displays an "indifference towards any specific kind of labour" *because of the form in which wealth is produced in bourgeois society.* In bourgeois society wealth is produced as value, whose substance is "abstract labor," a substance measured purely in quantities of socially necessary labor time. The modern category of labor, therefore, masks, in the form of its abstract generality, the narrow, historically specific, and transient basis on which it arises, namely, capitalist relations of production and, at the same time, steals the clothes of the labor process proper.

From this point of view, there are grounds for arguing that the "unit of analysis" of "activity theory" has actually more in common with the category of "labor" in bourgeois economics than with the conception of the labor process in Marx. Ironically, the paradoxical outcome of all this is that "activity theory," while endorsing and promoting Marx's "ascent" method, has moved in the opposite direction and found a "unit of analysis" that conflates and confuses the labor process with the valorization process, the very processes that Marx, through the whole of *Capital*, set out, systematically and methodically, to distinguish and on which his whole revolutionary vision rests.

Marx's Method and Education

What is the significance for educational research and practice in these abstruse methodological discussions? The general problem we have been looking at is the basic question of how we understand what is going on in society and how we work out what to do about it. At stake there too, therefore, are the issues of how we approach the task of understanding the specific social role and social function of educational institutions and educational practices within society today, what we might do to transform them, and how that transformation may contribute to the transformation of social relations more generally. It is in the light of these "big issues" that we must evaluate the use made of the "ascent" method within "activity theory" for the study of educational practices, to which I now turn.

In Engeström's case study of an adult education course, the "ascent" method was introduced directly to students who were given the task of producing a theoretical model of their own conceptualizations of adult education as a discipline (1990: 54). These models were then subjected to a process of critical comparison and analysis, the aim of the exercise being to disclose "some of the possibilities and problems involved in teaching dialectical thinking through model construction and model application" (1990: 67). Adult education is therefore the "unit of analysis" with "the central idea of their discipline" as germ-cell.

In Miettinen's application of the "ascent" method to traditional teaching activity in Helsinki Business Polytechnics he identifies the "'cell' or initial hypothesis, based on historical analysis," which in this case "depicted the basic contradiction of learning at school: decontextualized text turned into the object of activity" (2000: 123). Thus, teaching activity in a school is the "unit of analysis" and decontextualized text (the "object" of teaching activity) with its inherent contradictions is seen as the "germ-cell" of this activity. In discussing the implications of his analysis, Miettinen argues that "knowledge must somehow be connected to real life practices" (2000: 122).

There is no reason to doubt the value of this research. Engeström's original study gives an intriguing insight into the possibilities of the "ascent" method as a tool for critical reflection and self-reflection in the classroom, while Miettinen highlights the stultifying nature of traditional teaching practices, a key feature of "the encapsulation of school learning" (Engeström, 1991) and its separation from the world of work outside school. But both studies have limitations in relation to the "ascent" method. The "central idea" of adult education is not a *concretum* in Marx's sense (see above) and in that light the consequences of applying the method in this way are unclear. And while a critique of the focus on decontextualized texts within teaching is a positive thing, the bigger issue to do with the concrete social functions of "encapsulation," that is, the social conditions that constantly create this separation of the spheres of "education" and "work" (see Jones, in press), cannot be tackled by taking teaching activity (or work activity) as a "unit of analysis."

Ultimately, the significance of Marx's "ascent" method can only be appreciated in relation to the practical political aims that Marx set out and pursued. His analysis of capitalist production is not intended to be merely a scientifically superior depiction of contemporary economic relations but an exit sign to the whole system. In beginning with the commodity as a particular form of the product of labor, Marx shows us that the creative powers of humanity are exercised within capitalist production but are "appropriated" by another process in the interests of the few. The logic that takes us from commodity to money and from there to surplus value, capital, interest, fictitious capital, and all the baffling phenomena of today's hedge funds and derivatives is the logic of evolution of a system outside of human control; it is based on the forced exploitation of living labor and can survive only by containing the struggle of living labor against this forced exploitation. No institution, no activity, no individual stands outside this battle for the soul, the creative potential, of humanity as a whole. As Mészáros puts it:

> Marx strongly stressed the objective ontological continuity of the development of capital, embodied in *all* forms and institutions of social interchange, and not merely in the directly economic second order mediations of capitalism. (1970: 290)

The significance of Marx's method for education, therefore, is that it requires us to see the specific role that educational institutions, policies, and practices play and might play on this particular battlefield; it makes us try to understand and resist or mitigate the negative, dehumanizing effects of so-called "education" and to work out how the potential role of teachers and educational practices in the struggle for human freedom may best be promoted and realized. From this perspective, "education" as a professional sphere can hardly be seen as an "activity system" in its own right. This is not to belittle the positive contribution that "activity theory" has made to the critique of traditional teaching practices, to the reimagining of learning activity, and the transformation of relations between school and working environments. The disappearance of the "problem" of capitalist social relations from our theoretical vision, however, is another thing entirely.

Notes

1. The ideas in this chapter have been circulating for quite some time in conference papers and unpublished papers. I am grateful to a number of colleagues and friends for valuable feedback, in particular Chik Collins, Andrew Brown, and Andrey Maidansky. I should also like to thank Reijo Miettinen for his comments on my criticisms of his work. Needless to say, I take full responsibility for the chapter as it stands.
2. For a much more detailed statement of the argument of this section, see Jones (2009).

References

Avis, J. (2007) Engeström's Version of Activity Theory: A Conservative Praxis? *Journal of Education and Work*, 20 (3): 161–77.

Bakhurst, D. (2009) Reflections on Activity Theory. *Educational Review*, 61 (2): 197–210.

Davydov, V.V. (1990) *Types of Generalization in Instruction* (Reston: National Council of Teachers of Mathematics).

Engeström, Y. (1987) *Learning by Expanding: An Activity-Theoretical Approach to Developmental Research* (Helsinki: Orienta-Konsultit).

Engeström, Y. (1990) *Learning, Working and Imagining: Twelve Studies in Activity Theory* (Helsinki: Orienta-Konsultit).

Engeström, Y. (1991) Non Scolae Sed Vitae Discimus: Toward Overcoming the Encapsulation of School Learning. *Learning and Instruction* (1): 243–59.

Engeström, Y., Miettinen, R., & Punamäki, R.-L. (eds.) (1999) *Perspectives on Activity Theory* (Cambridge: Cambridge University Press).

Engeström, Y. and Miettinen, R. (1999). Introduction. In Y. Engeström, R. Miettinen, and R.-L. Punamäki (eds.) *Perspectives on Activity Theory* (Cambridge: Cambridge University Press).

Ilyenkov, E. V. (1982). *The Dialectics of the Abstract and the Concrete in Marx's "Capital"* (Moscow: Progress).

Jones, P. E. (2009) Breaking Away from "Capital"? Theorising Activity in the Shadow of Marx. *Outlines*, 1: 45–58.

Jones, P.E. (in press, 2011) Issues of Life and Death in Education. Commentary on Julian Williams. *Mind, Culture and Activity*.

Leont'ev, A.N. (1978) *Activity, Consciousness, and Personality* (Englewood Cliffs: Prentice Hall).

Marx, K. (1909). *Capital. A Critique of Political Economy.* Volume Three (Chicago, IL: Charles H Kerr & Co).

Marx, K. (1973) *Grundrisse* (Harmondsworth: Penguin Books).

Marx, K. (1976a). *Capital. A Critique of Political Economy.* Volume One. (Harmondsworth: Penguin Books).

Marx, K. (1976b). *Value: Studies by Marx* (London: New Park Publications).

Mészáros, I. (1970). *Marx's Theory of Alienation* (London: Merlin Press).

Miettinen, R. (2000). Ascending from the Abstract to the Concrete and Constructing a Working Hypothesis for New Practices. In V. Oittinen (ed.) *Evald Ilyenkov's Philosophy Revisited*, 111–29 (Helsinki: Kikimora Publications).

Pilling, G. (1980) *Marx's "Capital": Philosophy and Political Economy* (London: Routledge and Kegan Paul).

Sayer, D. (1987) *The Violence of Abstraction: The Analytic Foundations of Historical Materialism* (Oxford: Basil Blackwell).

Smith, C. (1999) *Marx at the Millennium* (London: Pluto Press).

Smith, T. (1990) *The Logic of Marx's Capital* (Albany, NY: State University of New York Press).

Stetsenko, A. (2005). Activity as Object-Related: Resolving the Dichotomy of Individual and Collective Planes of Activity. *Mind, Culture, and Activity*, 12 (1): 70–88.

Toiviainen, H. and Y. Engeström. (2009) Expansive Learning in and for Work. In H. Daniels, H. Lauder, and J. Porter (eds.) *Knowledge, Values and Educational Policy: A Critical Perspective*, 95–109 (London: Routledge).

Tuomi-Gröhn, T., and Y. Engeström. (2003) Conceptualizing Transfer: From Standard Notions to Developmental Perspectives. In Tuomi-Gröhn, T. and Y. Engeström (eds.) *Between School and Work: New Perspectives on Transfer and Boundary Crossing*, 19–38 (Amsterdam: Pergamon).

Warmington, P. (2008). From "Activity" to "Labour": Commodification, Labour Power and Contradiction in Engeström's Activity Theory. *Critical Social Studies—Outlines*, 2: 4–19.

Chapter 9

Critical Pedagogy as Revolutionary Practice

Peter McLaren

How would you define critical pedagogy? What is its essence and its purpose? What is the relation of critical pedagogy to a science of education?

That is a good question to begin this interview.[1] I know that critical pedagogy means different things to different people, so let me answer your question by sharing with you my own view of what critical pedagogy means to me—of the direction that I have been trying to take critical pedagogy in while living here in the belly of the beast, in the Northern Anglosphere, or in what my Mexican friends refer to as *gringolandia*. I locate the *differentia specifica* of critical pedagogy within a wider optic than classroom teaching, or popular education that takes place in community settings. I define it as the working out of a systematic dialectic of pedagogy that is organized around a philosophy of praxis. This praxis begins with an immanent critique of conventional pedagogy in order to see if its assumptions and claims are adequate to the type of praxis needed to both understand and challenge and eventually overcome capitalism's expansionistic dynamic. So we need both a philosophy of praxis that is coherent and forms of organization—horizontal and democratic—that best reflect our praxis. Now it is a praxis of being and becoming, of mental and manual labor, of thinking and doing, of reading and writing the word and the world (in the Freirean sense); in short, it is a practice of the self, a form of self-fashioning but not simply in the Foucauldian sense. I hope that becomes clearer in comments that will follow. So critical pedagogy, then, is both a reading practice where we read the word in the context of the world and a practical activity where we write ourselves as subjective forces into the text of history. But this does not mean that making history is only an effect of discourse, a form of metonymy, the performative dimension of language, a rhetorical operation, a tropological system. No, reality is more than textual self-difference. Praxis, as I am using the term, is directed at understanding the word and the world dialectically as an effect of class contradictions. As Teresa Ebert argues, the medium of meaning is language; but the meaning of meaning is not necessarily linguistic, it is social—and it is directly linked to the social relations of labor. So critical pedagogy then is a philosophy of practice lived in everyday life that attempts to uncover the congealed, abstract structures that constitute social life materially. It is a way of challenging the popular imaginary (which has no "outside" to the text) that normalizes the core cultural foundations of capitalism and the normative force of the state. In other words, it tells us that there is no alternative to capitalist social relations. So, then, critical pedagogy is a reading and an acting upon the social totality by turning abstract "things" into a material force, by helping abstract thought lead to praxis, to revolutionary praxis, to the bringing about of a social universe that is not based on the value form of labor, that is a socialist alternative to capitalism.

So here I am looking to critical pedagogy as a social process, a social product, and a social movement that is grounded in both a philosophy of praxis and democratic forms of organization. On the one hand, critical pedagogy deals with the becomingness of human beings, which is tautologically the defining feature of education, but it does so with a particular political project in mind—anticapitalist, anti-imperialist, antiracist, antisexist, and prodemocratic and emancipatory struggle. It works against what the Peruvian philosopher Anibal Quijano (1995[1988]) calls the "coloniality of power." Here critical pedagogy serves to make the familiar strange and the strange familiar (refiguring how we see the relationship between the self and the social so that we can see both as manufactured, as the social construction of multiple dimensions, and, at times, as the obverse of each other, and the suppressed underside of each other). In addition, it attempts to bring out the pedagogical dimensions of the political and the political dimensions of the pedagogical and to convert these activities to a larger, more sustained and focused project of building alternative and oppositional forms of sustainable environments, of learning environments, of revolutionary political environments, where capitalism can be superseded by socialism. Revolutionary critical pedagogy is not about engaging in specific modes of criticism but about the practice—and praxis—of critique.

This is not to gainsay the importance of modes of critique and distinguishing between systems of intelligibility, but when revolutionary critical educators invoke the category of critique, it means exercising critique in order to comprehend the process of reflection itself in a specific historical conjuncture while engaging in committed, protagonistic action. It involves the analysis and evaluation of the total context of the pedagogical encounter (the "act" of knowing) itself. In this case, the paradigms and frameworks of cognition and the affective dimensions of learning (or "structures of feeling") are interrogated by historically situating the living body of the thinker and her thought processes within the larger social totality of global capitalist relations. This historicizing self-reflection locates ideas, institutions, social systems in the transition from one historical stage of production to another, establishing the limits and potential of modes of thought in the wider project of liberating humanity from capitalist exploitation. Not only does critique liberate humanity from instrumentalist reification of the type unpacked by the Frankfurt school, but it also attempts to free humanity from racist, sexist, gender, and religious alienation based on alienated production relations through the protagonistic history making that accompanies reading the word and the world dialectically. So revolutionary critical pedagogy is about fostering the creation of a theory and philosophy of praxis by which they not only interrogate the limitations of occidental thought and the circumscriptions afforded by critical theory, critical race theory, Marxist humanist discourse, and other languages of critique, but are able to direct themselves and others toward alternative and oppositional ways of thinking about and acting in relation to and against modernity/coloniality and the epistemologies of empire. In other words, the "other knowledges" (those of indigenous peoples, women, and oppressed groups) attempt to disturb the hegemonic ontological categories that have saturated the imaginary of our age, imprisoning us in the normalcy of their ways of knowing, such that they have become impervious to critique. Consequently, revolutionary pedagogy is designed to blunt the limit horizon of our time by opening up different logics, rationalities, systems of classification and structures of power, and unleashing the epistemic force of the local histories of subaltern groups in order to enable us to reenunciate power, to expand the potential for coordinated growth and development, making us an enemy of forgetfulness and a protagonistic actor in revolutionary praxis from the point of view of the most invisible among us—*los olvidados,* who have been treated treacherously by the capitalist system.

Revolutionary critical pedagogy is a praxis, but it also operates within ways of knowing the word, conceptual systems, and so on. As with any system of intelligibility, it needs to be open to the strengths and limitations of different logics, rationalities, systems of classification, and structures of power. We can't fall prey to grandiose illusions and must always be open to criticism.

And finally, revolutionary critical pedagogy is not about the struggle for information so much as it is about the struggle for knowledge, a place where consciousness can discover itself, a place where knowledge gives way to a creative purposiveness—to a protagonistic agency. But it is even more than this—it is about the struggle to transform such knowledge into wisdom, by means of a dialectical reading of the word and the world, that is, in the reciprocally revealed relationship between consciousness and the world, and that which lies beyond the world, and in the unity of diversities in the individual and in the world that unites both the large and the small, the powerful and the powerless, in the dinergic unity of social life. And this can only be a *lived engagement*, as a habit-forming process that shapes harmonious relationships between the self and others, where possibility is collapsed into our muscle and brain matter so that we are able to struggle in the classrooms, on the streets, in our public squares and in our laboratories, seminar rooms, factories, community centers, offices and churches in our quest to join Freire along the craggy and rock-strewn paths traveled by "pilgrims of the obvious." Here we can discover the deep-rooted unity below the surface diversity of the world without imposing it. We discover it, together, in our shared human wholeness, as enemies of deception and lies and as friends of both the human and nonhuman worlds in a collective project to create a positively sustainable social order.

Critical pedagogy should neither remain Olympian in its self-assurance nor condescending in its skepticism. Rather, it must make its home in the provisional and promiscuous domain of praxis—in making the road by walking, without blueprints or prescriptions. As a language of the unacceptable, revolutionary critical pedagogy is a cultural artifact that needs to be protected from those who would condemn praxis as a distraction from high theory. Critical pedagogy is not only about creating the pedagogical context for teaching ourselves the stories of others, but it is about a new way of hearing what we say that enables us to listen in new ways, and hopefully learn to speak in ways that are open to others, while recognizing that the choices we have made for ourselves and for others are not real choices.

Am I being too ambitious? Perhaps. But I have always tried throughout life to move forward, and I am trying to build upon the shoulders of others, broad, powerful revolutionary shoulders such as those of Marx, Luxemburg, Paulo Freire, and the shoulders that I discovered late in life, those of Mariátegui.

You argue that there is no single critical pedagogy, but several critical pedagogies. What are the main differences between them? Why do you claim that critical pedagogy is revolutionary? And revolutionary in the educational sense or in the political and social sense?

Thank you for this question. Please understand that I make no claims to be writing with any great depth outside of the context of the United States and Canada. So, with that qualification, I shall try to elaborate an answer. I ascribe to revolutionary critical pedagogy, which holds that ideas need to be situated in history and experience as fallible generalizations that must be ideologically unveiled by means of the practice of historical materialist critique, a practice that attempts to generate critical knowledges of the social totality that we inhabit in this capitalist universe of ours. There is, for lack of better terms, left-liberal critical pedagogy, liberal critical pedagogy, conservative critical pedagogy, and variants of each of these. These are very rough terms, of course, and there are probably better terms. They certainly need to be refined but I don't have the space to do this here.

Critical pedagogy in the United States is overwhelmingly liberal, and converges, unintentionally in most instances, with neoliberal ideology, policy, and practice. In general, it views the state as the "social state" (here I shall borrow some terms from Tony Smith) where symbolic and moral philosophy is the systematic expression of the normative principles of the Keynesian welfare state. In other words, it is a version of the state that offers wage labor as the normative principle of modern society. Some conservative and even liberal educators take a neoliberal state as the norm, the entrepreneurial state, in which generalized commodity production requires a world market and they follow Hayek's principle that capital's law of value in the abstract must be followed.

Some left-liberal educators look to create a new model of the state that could be called an "activist state" (again, borrowing these terms from Tony Smith) that is based, in large part, on the work of Polanyi, and includes methods of aggressive state intervention into its industrial policy. International capital still predominates in this model, and there will be an inevitable government and global trade dependence on international capital. Of course, those who govern the activist state desire to place government restrictions on its rules and regulations for attracting global investment capital. So there is a concerted attempt to lessen the worst and most exploitative aspects of the state. Then again, you have some left-liberal educators who prefer the concept of the "cosmopolitan state." This model is largely derived from the work of Habermas, where forms of global market governance can prevail that are intranational rather than national; here there is a focus on the development of a global civil society.

Well, I don't ascribe to any of these models. I believe it is impossible to manage wage labor democratically on a global scale by placing severe restrictions on global financial and derivative markets. What about the question of property ownership of the mass means of production? Nathalia Jaramillo and I spoke a few weeks ago at *Industrias Metalúrgicas y Plásticas Argentina* (IMPA) where 172 workers make aluminum products, such as cans, foils, and wrappers. How would the cosmopolitan state help these workers? Yes, there would be a stress on greater democratic control of the economy by those who lack access to capital, but it would still support wage labor—and Marx has shown us that wage labor only "appears" to include an equal exchange. Workers sell their capacity to labor to an employer who is able to extract a higher value from the worker than the worker's means of surviving. How could a global state founded upon wage labor work? It is, in my mind, impossible to build a socialist state based on nationalized property because, as Peter Hudis has pointed out, capital can exist as a social form of mediation even in the absence of private ownership.

Well, of course, there are other models, such as market socialist models. Some of them incorporate a commodity market within a system of democratically self-managed and worker-run industries. I am not denigrating these more progressive models, some of them have good ideas and are much better than the neoliberal state model that now has international reach. But the question we need to ask is, How do you abolish value production, wage labor? We need to go beyond state intervention into the economy, since this is not socialism. State intervention into the economy doesn't prevent value-producing labor, alienated labor. In fact, capital is a social relation of abstract labor, and it is precisely capital as a social relation that must be transcended. Of course, this is the challenge for all of us. To go up against the ideological state apparatuses (that also have coercive practices such as nonpromotion and systems of privilege for those who follow the rules) and the repressive state apparatuses (that are also coercive in that they secure internal unity and social authority ideologically via patriotism and nationalism) is not an easy task. There are disjunctions and disarticulations within and between different social spaces of the superstructure and we must work within those, in spaces of the legal and ideological systems that can be transformed in the interests of social and economic justice. The struggle is multipronged. But the main point I have been making is that we need to create a social universe outside of capital's value form. Anything short of this will not bring about emancipation. Revolutionary critical pedagogy strives for the abolition of capital as a social relation. This is the major difference.

What type of person is to be formed through critical pedagogy? What kind of society should we aspire to?

This question is a major challenge for all of us. Especially with the control that the media exerts on our subjective formation as they wrap us up in the pedagogy of the spectacle. The state encourages forms of desublimation and freedom so as to distract attention from the oppressive and authoritarian dimensions of capitalist society. And we live in an era in which people are too willing to give over their sovereignty and liberty to tyrants in favor of engaging in the sensuality of the media spectacle and the commodification of everyday life. The media work through state-constructed monopolies whose business model is predicated on owning politicians through the operation of high-powered lobbyists. So it is difficult to work against this tide, but we must do the best that we can. I choose to do it through the work of revolutionary critical pedagogy. Critical revolutionary educators are interested in the movements of the world's totality and how this totality is uncovered by human beings, and how in our uncovering this totality we develop a particular ontological openness toward being. How can we discover ourselves as historical beings? The results of our actions in and on and through the world do not coincide with our intentions. Why is this? What accounts for the disharmony between the necessity and the freedom of our actions as human beings creating and being created by historical forces? These are questions that animate the work of revolutionary critical educators. Do we make history or are we objects of history? I do not believe we are summoned by some higher power to create historical outcomes but that, following Marx, we make history. Praxis in the form of production forces, forms of thought, language, and so on, exists as forms of historical continuity only because of the activity of human beings. But objectified and objectivized praxis that is fixed in human history seems over time to be more real than human reality itself and becomes the basis for historical mystification, of what Karel Kosik refers to as the basis of the possibility of inverting a subject into an object. Like Kosik, revolutionary critical educators are interested in fetishized praxis, and how to overcome it. Kosik stressed the importance of philosophy as the indispensable activity of humankind, with the dialectic as the revolutionary motor of liberating praxis. He is concerned about the object ruling over the subject, and capitalism as a dynamic system of total reification and alienation. Capitalism objectivizes the practical-spiritual activity of people but the historical struggle against capital entails not only an understanding of what this struggle is in itself but revolutionary practical action based on this understanding.

As Kosik and Che and others such as Mariátegui have taught us, we need to focus today on the development of a revolutionary subjectivity within the cohorts of teachers and cultural workers, and this also means that we need to develop a socialist way of life, an ethical disposition, as well as a philosophy of praxis, and forms of revolutionary organization that complement such a philosophy. Both Che and Mariátegui, for instance, rejected the sublimated morality of capitalism in creating the morality of the producers. They both believed in the importance of a socialist subjective agency. In the *Grundrisse*, Marx wrote about a new form of revolutionary subjectivity: "Not only do the objective conditions change in the act of reproduction, for example, the village becomes a town, the wilderness a cleared field, and so on, but the producers change, too, in that they bring out new qualities in themselves, develop themselves in production, transform themselves, develop new powers and ideas, new modes of intercourse, new needs and new language."

> Who are the most renowned representatives of critical pedagogy and what are their contributions? Would you consider José Martí, Makarenko, Lenin or Mao Tse Tung as contributors?

Well, yes, there are many renowned representatives of critical pedagogy. I have mentioned especially Paulo Freire and John Dewey, but there are others, such as Jean-Jacques Rousseau and Anton Makarenko, and of course Mao, and many others. And we cannot forget José Martí or Simón Rodríguez, the teacher of Simón Bolívar. I haven't written about them all, but certainly I am familiar with their contributions. Makarenko's system of education—his self-organizing "educational collective"—is actually built upon the entire life of students, the unity of the student's external and internal relations, and the importance of intra-collective relations in the formation of the collective as also the importance of labor in the life of the collective.

But I would like to stress the importance of José Carlos Mariátegui La Chira.[2] I am especially interested in Mariátegui because of his contributions to our understanding of the intersectionality of race and class in his Marxist analysis of capitalism (Mariátegui, 1971, 1981, 1996a, 1996b; Angotti, 1986; Chavarria, 1979). Marxist educators have been vigorously attacked by progressive educators in the United States for adhering to Marx's "economistic" and "Eurocentric" philosophy with its unilinear conception of social progress. However, there is good reason to refute many of these criticisms by returning not necessarily to the Marxists, but to the writings of Marx himself. Kevin Anderson's new book *Marx at the Margins: On Nationalism, Ethnicity, and Non-Western Societies* (Anderson, 2010) addresses some of Marx's published and to this date unpublished reflections on issues of race and non-Western social groups that will challenge the postmodernists who have chastised Marx so greatly over the last several decades. In addition to what Lawrence Krader published in the *Ethnological Notebooks* of Marx (Krader, 1972), there exist notes written by Marx between 1879 and 1882, the vast majority of which have never been published, and many containing direct reflections by Marx rather than simply summaries of other writers (of course those exist, too). According to Anderson (2007), Marx dramatically shifted from his unilinear concept of social progress revealed in works such as the *Communist Manifesto* (1848) and journalistic writings he did for the *New York Tribune* on India (1853) to reveal a form of anticolonialist thinking exemplified in later works done for the *Tribune* (1856–58) and in the *Grundrisse* (1857–58). Anderson reveals how Marx shifted to a multilinear theory of history where he acknowledged that Asian societies, for instance, developed along a different pathway than did Western European models of production. He began to concern himself with the dialectics of race and class during the American Civil War (1861–1865) when he supported the antislavery North. He wrote in *Capital* that "labor in a white skin cannot emancipate itself where in a black skin it is branded." Marx supported the Polish uprising of 1863, and he came to consider favorably the possibility of an agrarian revolution in Russia. He supported the Irish struggle and it is here that he expressly focused on ethnicity, race, and nationalism. His support for Irish national independence and his linking of this to race relations shows similarities to the position held by Mariátegui in the context of his support of the indigenous struggles of Peru and his interest in Indian communism or Andean Communism, and in prefeudal relations of production linked to the *ayllu*.

So, indeed, Marx wrote about non-Western and non-European societies in India, Indonesia (Java), Russia, Algeria, and Latin America and also wrote about Native Americans and Australian aboriginal peoples. He was interested in the North American Iroquois, the Aztecs of pre-Columbian Mexico, and the Celts of ancient Ireland. And he reflected upon the importance of clan and village culture across a range of precapitalist societies as well as upon the rise of social classes within tribal societies. He was, in other words, interested in the periphery as well as the center of the developing capitalist world. Mariátegui, it should be noted, challenged the "stagist" conception of economic production of the Second International. So both Marx and Mariátegui developed dialectical theories of social change that were not unilinear nor just focused on class relations (although, admittedly and importantly, class relations were primary). Both understood that the particularities of race, ethnicity, and nationality were determinants of the social totality.

As we struggle here in the belly of the beast against the cultural, educational, and economic czars of neoliberal imperialist capitalism, those of us working in critical pedagogy in North America need to learn more about the thinking of Mariátegui. Here was a radicalized liberal journalist who transformed himself into a nonsectarian and heterodox Marxist revolutionary philosopher and activist, a public intellectual who was deeply influenced by the non-Marxist currents of Risorgimento thinkers like Benedetto Croce, by the anarcho-syndicalist Sorel, and the Peruvian radical González Prada (although he understood and rejected their idealism without rejecting their sympathy and loyalty to the revolutionary working class). Mariátegui was one of the great anti-imperialist Marxists, struggling for the elimination of the *latifundo* (semifeudal estates that dominated the countryside). Denouncing Peru as a colony of imperialism and arguing that Peru's war of independence in no way smashed feudal relations in the countryside, Mariátegui developed a historical materialist analysis of classes in Peru. Throughout all of this he stressed the importance of the role of indigenous peoples, without losing sight of the role of the emerging proletariat, nor for that matter the importance of the international working class as a movement. While he underscored the importance of escaping and transforming the harsh, semifeudal agrarian society of his day, in which the urban, *criollo* proletariat enjoyed some limited economic and social privilege in relation to the indigenous peoples of the countryside, it is important to stress that Mariátegui wanted the indigenous regions of the Andes to continue in the context of the existing nations in Latin America, rather than through the development of an independent indigenous nation. In other words, he saw the emerging proletariat as the natural ally of the indigenous peasant. This was not a functionalist reading of Peruvian society but profoundly dialectical. While rejecting both *latifundista* capitalism and modern industrial capitalism (the latter would just turn indigenous groups from collectively minded toilers to individual entrepreneurs), he maintained that socialist development should be based on collective development (*ayllu* in Quechua and *calpulli* in Nahuatl). For Mariátegui, the "Indian question" was central to the question of nationalism, as he believed that the indigenous peoples were the source of social revolution in Peru, and he stressed the important role of women in indigenous societies. He was concerned with the organic application of Marxist theory to the struggle for national liberation in Peru in which indigenous struggle was paramount, but such a struggle also required the transformation of the state under the direction of the working class.

It is worth pointing out that for Mariátegui, educational reform needed to be grounded in a socialist vision of the future. Of course, there are many debates around the contribution of "El Amauta"—was he a populist, was he more concerned with peasant rebellion than with the struggle of the proletariat? I am not so much concerned with these questions. I am interested in Mariátegui's evolution as a Marxist thinker and his role in the Peruvian trade union and communist movement in so far as it led him to understand the historical formation of human consciousness, and what this has to say to educators both here in the United States and elsewhere. No, we are not likely to see *Mariáteguismo* here in the United States anytime soon, but we must, as critical educators, learn from his important contribution to liberatory struggle.

> Is there a relationship between critical pedagogy and the cultural-historical theory of Lev Vygotsky? If there is, in what way are they related?

Yes, there is a relationship between Vygotsky's work and critical pedagogy, but I would say indirectly through the development of CHAT, or what is called cultural-historical activity theory. Here, the work of Vygotsky is central in so far as he stresses the role of communication at the center of his theory of language and thought by arguing that "the thought is completed in the word." CHAT is an approach used in educational research and practice here in the United States as a means of developing higher psychological functions of students. I don't follow work in CHAT very carefully. It does not seem to have had a central role to play in critical pedagogy, but I am sure it is beneficial to learners.

> Some argue that the economic and social problems in countries like Peru have as one of their causes the economic policy of the United States. How is this problem understood from a critical pedagogy perspective?

Let's look at the problem in Peru and its relationship to the United States. The problem, as I see it, is not simply the United States, but neo-liberal capitalism in general—what has been called vagabond capitalism, fast capitalism, or finance capitalism. In the 1970s you had a strong push by the advanced capitalist countries to create more wealth for Western corporations, so they decided to influence—or force—so-called third world governments to halt import substitution industrialization (ISI), which saw the state regulate foreign trade and investment. The United States didn't want Latin America to continue their ISI programs based on protecting their local new industries through protective tariffs, import quotas, exchange rate controls, special preferred licensing for capital goods imports, subsidized loans to local new industries because this involved state regulation of foreign trade and investment. So they tried to impose their free market agenda on Latin American governments such as Peru, beginning in the 1980s. They did this by forcing these countries in the southern hemisphere to accept International Monetary Fund (IMF) and World Bank structural adjustment programs that mandated privatization, deregulation, and trade liberalization. But Latin American countries already had other debts related to financing earlier ISI efforts and this crisis was compounded by international interest rates rising significantly. As Hart-Landsberg and others have noted, so-called third world governments tried to achieve a trade surplus. But how was this possible when "free market" policies urged governments to boost imports? Governments were therefore forced to suppress domestic consumption in order to boost the surpluses needed to meet their debt obligations to the IMF and the World Bank. They were then forced to bring in the export-oriented transnational corporations to encourage growth and help with the debt payment. But from 1980 to 2005 there was much more import than export and trade deficits further restrained growth. Welcome to neoliberal capitalism! So Peru was hit with this problem, along with other Latin American countries.

How does this economic catastrophe speak to the vision of Mariátegui? Well, you now have wage labor in the Andean region—there is class differentiation and large-scale proletarianization. But there are still forms of communal solidarity, far different than in other spaces of capitalist development around the world. At a time when we are seeing a growth in the struggles of indigenous peoples throughout the Americas, we can see that capitalism must be denied as the ultimate social horizon. We are seeing a struggle against colonial systems of intelligibility, against epistemicide, organized around a decolonizing pedagogy. We need to be in solidarity with indigenous groups in Latin America as a new push toward a postcapitalist future. Mariátegui did not have a romantic or Platonic vision of indigenous groups, but rather grounded himself praxeologically in concrete solidarity with them and the historical and geopolitical specificity of their struggle. This is why the Bolivarian Alliance for the Peoples of Our America (*Alianza Bolivariana para los Pueblos de Nuestra América* or ALBA), an international cooperation organization based upon the idea of social, political, and economic integration between the countries of Latin America and the Caribbean, is so important, especially as an alternative regional development process to the failed Free Trade of the Americas (FTAA or ALCA in Spanish) proposed by the United States. Of course, we also need greater collaborative worker-community organizations and indigenous organizations working together as natural allies in the way Mariátegui envisioned. So more than ever, we need a critical pedagogy grounded in Mariátegui's ideas and those of Quijano (1995 [1988]).

> I think the United States is the country where you have most experi-
> ence in applying critical pedagogy. What are the achievements so far?
> We understand that in 2005 you participated with the government of
> Venezuela in the education reforms implemented by President Hugo
> Chávez and we assume that you are still participating. What role does
> critical pedagogy play in project XXI Century Socialism in Venezuela?

Well, this is a difficult question to answer. I have traveled extensively and with the insights and research expertise of Professor Nathalia Jaramillo of Purdue University, I have tried to bring an international lens to critical pedagogy. We have worked briefly in Venezuela in supporting the Bolivarian Revolution and the creation of the Bolivarian missions related to education, but unfortunately we have not had the opportunity to spend as much time in Venezuela as we would like. We greatly admire the work of the Bolivarian educators to develop their own versions of critical pedagogy in support of a socialism of the twenty-first century and we have lectured in Caracas and in other cities on our own work in critical pedagogy. And we have been fortunate enough to meet briefly with President Chávez. But in as much as critical pedagogy is the topic of many books and articles in North America, it is not something you actually see very often in the public schools. Sometimes you see it in alternative schools.

Many educators here in the United States claim that there are not enough industrial workers in the United States to claim that we have a working class here, and so there is no need for a socialist revolution. Well, this is quite a silly question. There might not be as many industrial workers as there once were in the United States, but there are many who still produce value the way industrial workers produce value. There are capitalist workers here—workers who are told what to do by their bosses, who serve the capitalist class. We have high-paid workers, and low-paid workers. Those with good salaries disguise the fact that they are workers. Ninety percent of the people in the United States are workers. Of course, many members of the ruling elite in the United States were never at the mercy of an employer who could terminate his or her job; there are many in this privileged sector who have never been humiliated by a boss, who never came home stooped in pain after a hard day of manual labor. They never were in a situation where they could not feed themselves or their families. But what about the working class and their struggles? The cold war basically frightened the American public from even uttering the word "socialism" in public, except to condemn it. Which is why it was heartening to see, on September 24, 2009, during a meeting with U.S. labor union leaders in New York, including leaders from the national and multinational electricity, food, commercial, automobile, public, and university sectors, as well as organizers of African American and Puerto Rican worker unions, that Venezuelan president Hugo Chávez invited the unionists to participate in the Bolivarian Alliance for the Americas (ALBA), and he also invited U.S. president Barack Obama to hold a "peace dialogue." This would be one way that the United States and Latin American social movements could work together more. But the U.S. media keeps demonizing Chávez, and the recently signed deal by the United States and Colombia to expand the presence of the U.S. military on seven Colombian bases—a move that President Chávez called "throwing gasoline on the fire"—does not bode well for future relations between the United States and Venezuela.

Clearly, in my mind, the development of the Union of South American Nations (UNASUR), the Bank of the South, and the Latin American television news station Telesur, in addition to the ALBA, has been an important regional accomplishment in Latin America. But the United States, even with Obama at the head of the administration, is still an imperialist power with imperialist designs and even if he wanted to Obama cannot fight the military industrial complex and survive.

I am impressed, I must say, by the new "Organic Education Law," which Venezuela's National Assembly passed unanimously. The fierce opponents of Chávez claim the Education Law is unconstitutional and antidemocratic, politicizes the classroom, threatens the family and religion, and will allow the state to take children away from their parents for indoctrination. Of course these condemnations are part of a well-orchestrated campaign, which I am sure is highly funded by Washington. This law is important in that the constitution requires it to uphold constitutional principles, which means that the state has the responsibility to ensure that all citizens have a high-quality education, free of charge, from childhood through the undergraduate university level. This concept of the "Educator State" (*Estado Docente*) is introduced in Article 5, which says the state must guarantee education "as a universal human right and a fundamental, inalienable, non-renounceable social duty, and a public service...governed by the principles of integrality, cooperation, solidarity, attentiveness, and co-responsibility."

One of the key principles, in my view, is the one that advocates "equality among all citizens without discrimination of any kind." In fact, this new law mandates "equality of conditions and opportunities," as well as "gender equity," "access to the educational system for people with disabilities or educational needs," and the extension of educational facilities to rural and poor areas. Spanish is listed as the official language of the education system, "except in the instances of intercultural bilingual indigenous education, in which the official and equal use of their [native] language and Spanish shall be guaranteed." In addition to promoting "the exchange of social and artistic knowledge, theories, practices, and experiences," the law sanctions "popular and ancestral knowledge, which strengthen the identity of our Latin American, Caribbean, indigenous, and Afro-descendant peoples."

Article 3 also stresses a recurrent theme: that of "participatory democracy." This is clearly important and you can hear this echo throughout the new Education Act. Article 15 is controversial in the eyes of the opponents of Chávez, because it says that one of the basic purposes of education is "to develop a new political culture based on protagonist participation and the strengthening of popular power, the democratization of knowledge, and the promotion of the school as a space for the formation of citizenship and community participation, for the reconstruction of the public spirit." Yet there are plenty of references to the importance of "learning to peacefully coexist," learning to learn and teach simultaneously, "valuing the common good," the necessity for education to be "integral" as opposed to highly specialized or multilinear, "respect for diversity," and the importance of life-long learning.

The legal definition of the educational community has been significantly broadened to include families, community organizations, and wage laborers in addition to the formal educational workers. This new educational community is described in the article as "a democratic space of social-communitarian, organized, participatory, cooperative, protagonist, and solidarity-oriented character," and maintains that "its participants will carry out the process of citizen education consistent with what is established in the Constitution of the Bolivarian Republic of Venezuela."

In terms of university education, some public universities will continue to be run by the state and others, known as autonomous universities, will be funded by the state but run independently. There will be automatic university admission for all high school graduates who satisfy basic grade and behavioral requirements and wish to obtain a university education. The aptitude test that is currently used would be replaced by a diagnostic test aimed at assessing the academic strengths and weaknesses, career interests, and socioeconomic conditions of the students, for the purpose of placing them in a corresponding university program. Approximately two dozen new universities across the national territory will be created, in order to help realize this goal.

The Education Act also deals with questions of labor rights, job security and benefits, and training in "liberatory work." Article 15 states that
the educational system must "develop the creative potential of each human
being for the full realization of his or her personality and citizenship,
based on the ethical value of liberatory work and active participation."
There is also a stress on human rights and free speech. The law also maintains that education should encourage an end to nuclear weapons in the
world, fight racism, and develop in the students an ecological consciousness to preserve biodiversity and social diversity. Now this is fantastic, and
fits the description that I have of revolutionary critical pedagogy.

The reaction to the law by the ruling classes in Venezuela is all too
familiar—it reminds me of the reaction of Republicans here in the
United States to the idea of a national health care system. They see it
as big government controlling the medical establishment. (They should
recognize that what already controls the medical establishment are the
pharmaceutical companies, the corporations, and other for-profit organizations!) If this law is passed, the conservative forces in Venezuela
believe that the country will be one step closer to becoming a totali-
tarian communist society. You can see their eyes roll to the backs of
their heads: Conspiracy! Conspiracy! The country will degenerate into
an authoritarian regime that is redolent of fascist regimes of the past!
Perhaps they will implant socialist microchips in the brains of every
student. The classroom, they argue, should not be politicized! They
reject the Education Act as a way of institutionalizing *populismo politi-
quero*. The schools will turn out automatons who will be mouthpieces
for Chávez and the cause of socialism. Children will be taken from their
homes and put into classes where they will have to chant in unison lines
supporting the Bolivarian cause. They fear the community councils will
train members in brainwashing techniques, forcing students to repeat
"Cuban values" and will set up panoptical webs to keep all the schools
under surveillance and to gain authoritarian control over local affairs.
Well, if I am exaggerating their reaction, it must be acknowledged that I
have captured a certain kernel of truth in their opposition to this bill.

If the opposition would look closely, and fairly, at this law they will
see that there is a section of the law titled "Prohibitions of Political
Party Propaganda in Educational Centers and Institutions" and Article
12 in this section clearly states the following: "Proselytism or political
party propaganda is not permitted in educational centers and institutions of the primary education system through any medium: oral,
print, electronic, radio, informative, telephone, or audiovisual."

In my view, this new Education Law, in effect, counters what the
education laws of former pro-capitalist governments have achieved: the

creation of passive, compliant, noncritical students who simply become instruments for the reproduction of the capitalist social order and the international division of labor.

Now that the new Organic Education Law has been passed in Venezuela, the most pressing and most formidable challenge will be to implement it. Changed laws make little difference if there does not exist sufficient enthusiasm to carry them through. No doubt there will be sabotage—some of it violent—by opponents of Chávez and the enemies of socialism, and don't be surprised if this opposition has funding sources in the United States. Of course, teacher education for social justice will also be important—if not paramount—because so many teachers have been trained in a system that valorizes techno-cratic rationality and possessive individualism, preaches the gospel of economic prosperity, and worships at the altar of capital accumulation for personal gain. There will be much to unlearn and much to learn. I hope that I will be involved in Venezuela for years to come, because I believe the socialist mission that the Bolivarian educators are involved in is crucial for the development of real democracy, not the democracy of empty forms that you so often find in the United States.

You ask me about the gains made in the United States. There are no gains, only losses. The choice of Arne Duncan as the Secretary of Education by President Obama is disastrous since he is basically going to follow many of the mandates—such as standardized testing, high-stakes testing, and accountability—of the Bush administration. It is a slightly softer version of Bush's No Child Left Behind Act.

In my view, every student is endowed with the capacity for reasoning critically about his or her life and should be apprised of the opportunity for understanding the complex and multilayered context in which that life is lived; every student is capable and deserving of developing a moral conscience that respects others as active, uniquely creative, and dignified subjects of history. Every student has a right to ask, what has my history, my experiences as an individual living in capitalist society made of me that I no longer want to be? How can I change my present, in order to live in the future with courage, commitment, and a critical disposition that can make the world a better place for all those who suffer and are oppressed? Those who run the educational system in the United States care noth-ing about the rights and capacities of students; the system works to keep students good patriots and capitalist workers, who believe their country supports and defends the cause of freedom and prosperity for all around the world. It is an education, in other words, in mystification.

When President Obama addressed the schoolchildren of the United States, the Republicans went crazy—much the same way that the opponents of Chávez would react to a speech by Chávez to students. Now if the Republicans believe that the moderate liberal, Barack Obama, is a socialist, as many do, how do you think they would react to a real socialist? During Arne Duncan's tenure as Superintendent of Chicago Public Schools, the dropout and literacy rate of the students worsened, the militarizing inner-city public school districts increased, the school system became more segregated, and schools were shut down that didn't meet the "standards" set by state officials. In addition, mass firing of teachers (sometimes, entire school staff) whose students didn't perform acceptably on standardized tests continued, and to replace these so-called failed schools Duncan advocated the creation of charter schools, which often perform worse than public schools. There is nothing on Duncan's agenda to improve the graduating rates of Black and Latino students, which stand at 50% and 53%, respectively.

So to answer your question more directly, critical pedagogy is something that teachers read about, and some very courageously try to implement, but it is hardly making any inroads in the public school system. Critical revolutionary pedagogy is an approach that socialist-minded teachers read and in fewer cases (because there are fewer teachers sympathetic to socialism) try to implement in their schools or in their communities. Many conservative parents want to see the school as a "neutral" terrain devoid of critical self-reflection and political advocacy. There is a lot of public pressure through the media not to discuss controversial issues in the public schools, such as the war in Iraq and Afghanistan, or criticisms of capitalism and imperialism. There are teacher education programs that use my work, or that of Freire, Giroux, and others in their classrooms, but these are the exception rather than the rule. Critical educators in the United States have written a lot of wonderful texts about critical pedagogy, but the challenge for us—and the teachers and cultural workers that we serve—is to fight for critical pedagogy in our schools, our communities, our workplaces, and in our daily struggles as agents of a postcapitalist future.

In 2006, during the Bush regime, a right-wing group offered to pay students 100 dollars to secretly audiotape my classes at UCLA (University of California, Los Angeles) and 50 dollars to produce notes from my lectures. They made the same offer to students if they would also spy on other leftist professors as well. Academic freedom is a battle that we are still fighting here in the United States and our opponents, who want no discussion of controversial political issues in the classroom, are very well-funded and receive millions of dollars to advertise to the American public that the universities are run by socialists and communists. So if we still are fighting these battles at the universities, it is even harder to initiate social justice and socialist agendas in the public schools. And we have powerful right-wing Christian evangelical groups who don't want evolution taught in the schools and who want the United States to be governed by biblical principles.

In Canada, I was fired from my first university professorship because of my use of critical pedagogy, and the climate is not much different today when it comes to trying to develop critical pedagogy as a vehicle for building a more just and humane world (what I refer to as a socialist world). The viceroys of capital still rule, and most of the public follows them. Such is the power of the corporate media to uphold the ruling ideas, which are the ideas of the ruling class. My goal is to continue to develop critical pedagogy, and to help in whatever way I can to advance the goals of social and economic justice and socialism.

We are learning about new ways of organizing, adopting a prefigurative politics that is distrustful of hierarchical structures and centralized organizations, that is horizontal rather than vertical, that avoids voluntarism (the notion that the success or failure of a movement is dependent on the will of the organizers rather than being determined by external forces and conditions), that embraces multi-issue groups that fight militarism, environmental destruction, patriarchy, racism, and imperialism, that supports organic movements that grow directly out of the struggles of the oppressed, that follows the Zapatista principles of changing the world without taking power, or the Chávistas' insistence on the importance of taking state power. In this new world of micropolitics, network organizing, coalition politics, we cannot forget that we need to fight harder, not less. The organizations won't carry us through to the end. Only we can do that.

Here we are all facing, in different ways, and to different degrees, the breakdown of neoliberal capitalism. What we could all benefit from is Mariátegui's analysis of class relations in the semicolonial world as a way of helping us consolidate new working-class movements such as the *Abahlali baseMjondolo*, the South African shackdwellers' movement, and other social movements in various countries such as the *Movimiento de Libertação dos Sem Terra* or the National Movement of Occupied Factories (MNER) in Argentina. Here we would benefit greatly from the Mariáteguista heritage. Mariátegui has taught us that socialism is not inevitable. The actions of the proletarian and peasant masses are crucial to emancipate the economies of Latin America and beyond, and of course this requires a regional anti-imperialist bloc strong enough to defeat the role of the United States and other so-called Western democracies in trying to bring Latin America to its knees. We need both Mariátegui's logos and his mythos, his scientific and his spiritual character, as Quijano so presciently reminds us. After all, Mariátegui's insights can lead us not to a sojourn into the past, but, as the founding moment of our exilic struggle out of the prehistory of the world, the capitalist world, into the historical present, the socialist present that we must claim.

Notes

1. A short extract from this interview appeared in Spanish in Caldas and De La Cruz (2009).
2. José Carlos Mariátegui (1894–1930), radical Peruvian thinker and political activist.

References

Anderson, K.B. (2007) Marx's Late Writings on Non-Western and Pre-capitalist Societies and Gender. *Rethinking Marxism* 14(4): 84–96.

Anderson, K.B. (2010) *Marx at the Margins: On Nationalism, Ethnicity and Non-Western Societies* (Chicago, IL: University of Chicago Press).

Angotti, T. (1986) The Contributions of José Carlos Mariátegui to Revolutionary Theory. *Latin American Perspectives of Left Politics*, Spring: 33–57.

Caldas, B. and A. De La Cruz (2009) La Pedagogía Crítica Como Praxis Revolucionaria: Entrevista con Peter McLaren. *Matinal, Revista de Investigación y Pedagogía*, 1(2): 13–17.

Chavarria, J. (1979) *José Carlos Mariátegui and the Rise of Modern Peru, 1890–1930* (Albuquerque: University of New Mexico Press).

Krader, L. (1972) *The Ethnological Notebooks of Karl Marx: (Studies of Morgan, Phear, Maine, Lubbock)* (Assen: Van Gorcum).

Mariátegui, J.C. (1971) *Seven Interpretative Essays on Peruvian Reality* (Trans. Marjori Urquidi) (Austin, TX: Texas University Press).

Mariátegui, J.C. (1981) *Defensa del Marxismo* (Lima: Amauta).

Mariátegui, J.C. (1996a) Art, Revolution, and Decadence. In M. Pearlman (ed.) *The Heroic and Creative Meaning of Socialism: Selected Essays of José Carlos Mariátegui*, 170–72 (Atlantic Highlands, NJ: Humanities Press International).

Mariátegui, J.C. (1996b) Introducing Amauta. In M. Pearlman (ed.) *The Heroic and Creative Meaning of Socialism: Selected Essays of José Carlos Mariátegui*, 74–6 (Atlantic Highlands, NJ: Humanities Press International).

Quijano, A. (1995[1988]) Modernity, Identity, and Utopia in Latin America (Trans. Michael Aronna). In J. Beverley, J. Oviedo, and M. Aronna (eds.) *The Postmodernism Debate in Latin America*, 201–16 (Durham, NC: Duke University Press).

Contributors

Paul Brook is a Senior Lecturer in service work and consumption at Manchester Metropolitan University Business School. He writes on service work, emotional labor, and labor process theory. Recent publications offering critical assessments of Hochschild's emotional labor theory have appeared in *Capital & Class* and *Work, Employment & Society*. His ongoing research is the development of a Marxist theorization of emotional and "whole person" labor power from within labor process theory.

Sara Carpenter is a PhD candidate in the Adult Education and Community Development program at the Ontario Institute for Studies in Education of the University of Toronto and a faculty member in the Community Worker program at George Brown College, Toronto, Canada. A former community organizer and educator, Sara's research and teaching focus on democracy promotion, citizenship learning, poverty, and imperialism. She is the co-editor (with Shahrzad Mojab) of *Educating from Marx: Race, Gender, and Learning* (Palgrave, 2011).

Chik Collins is a Senior Lecturer in Politics in the School of Social Sciences at the University of the West of Scotland. He is the author of *Language, Ideology and Social Consciousness: Developing a Sociohistorical Approach* (Ashgate, 1999) and of numerous book chapters and journal articles on language and social change, the cultural-historical tradition, urban policy, and community development. He has worked with a number of community organizations in the west of Scotland. More recently he has focused on the problem of health and mortality in Scotland, and its relationship to neoliberalism after 1980.

Helen Colley is Professor of Lifelong Learning in the Education and Social Research Institute at Manchester Metropolitan University and a Fellow of the National Institute of Careers Education and Counselling (NICEC). Her research focuses on inequalities of gender and class in postcompulsory and lifelong learning and, in particular, the construction of emotion in labor power. Her publications include *Mentoring for Social Inclusion* (2003, Routledge Falmer) and an edited collection, *Young People and Social Inclusion* (2007, Council of Europe).

Peter E. Jones is Principal Lecturer in Communication Studies at Sheffield Hallam University. A linguist by background, his research spans a broad range of issues in language, communication, and discourse theory. He also writes on Marxist philosophy and theory and its influence on psychology and semiotics. He is currently writing a book, *Language, Communication and Human Potential in Vygotsky's Tradition*, for Cambridge University Press.

Peter McLaren, formerly Professor at the Graduate School of Education and Information Studies, University of California, Los Angeles, is now Professor at the School of Critical Studies in Education, Faculty of Education, University of Auckland. He is one of the leading practitioners of Critical Pedagogy in the United States as well as one of its leading advocates worldwide. He was the inaugural recipient of the Paulo Freire Social Justice Award presented by Chapman University, California, April 2002. He also received the Amigo Honorifica de la Comunidad Universitaria de esta Institución by La Universidad Pedagogica Nacional, Unidad 141, Guadalajara, Mexico. Two of his books were winners of the American Education Studies Association Critics Choice Awards for outstanding books in education. He is the author and editor of more than 40 books and his writings have been translated into 20 languages.

Shahrzad Mojab, Professor, is an academic-activist teaching in the Department of Adult Education and Counselling Psychology, Ontario Institute for Studies in Education of the University of Toronto. She specializes in educational policy studies; Marxist-feminism, gender, state, and diaspora; women, war, and learning; and feminism and antiracism pedagogy. She is the editor of *Women, War, Violence, and Learning* (2010, Routledge) and the co-editor (with Sara Carpenter) of *Educating from Marx: Race, Gender and Learning* (Palgrave, 2011).

Victoria Perselli teaches research in professional practice in the School of Education at Kingston University, UK. Her current research interests include practitioner research methods, research paradigms, and pedagogy for critical leadership.

Anna Stetsenko is Full Professor in the Ph.D. Program in Developmental Psychology, with joint appointments in the Ph.D. Program in Urban Education and the Center for the Study of Women and Society, all at The Graduate Center of the City University of New York. Her research revolves around topics at the intersection of human development and education including mind, identity, personhood, and agency. In recent publications, she has developed an innovative dialectical approach of *Transformative Activist Stance* as the grounding for human development and learning in a changing world. This approach encompasses cutting-edge advances in dynamic systems theory, situated and embodied cognition, and cultural-historical activity theory frameworks. It has radical implications in helping to close a number of traditional gaps including theory versus practice, individual versus social, and objectivity versus ethics.

Terry Wrigley worked for many years as a secondary school teacher of English and various related roles, and was until recently a Senior Lecturer in Education at the University of Edinburgh. His teaching, research, and writing span and connect diverse fields of interest: school development, pedagogy, curriculum reform, social justice, and education for citizenship. He edits the journal *Improving Schools* and his many publications include three books: *The Power to Learn* (2000), *Schools of Hope* (2003), and *Another School is Possible* (2006). He is co-editor of the book *Changing Schools*, to be published in 2011.

Name Index

Note: Page numbers in **bold** refer to the main chapters of the contributors.

Subject Index